KIRK
ON THE ZAMBESI

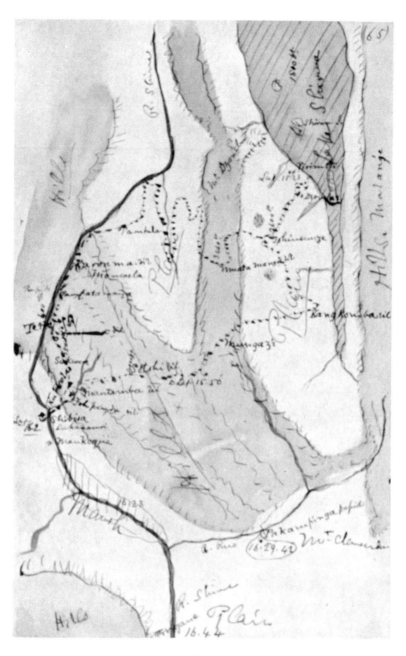

THE SHIRE HIGHLANDS

Sketch-map by DL, April 1859

KIRK
ON THE ZAMBESI

A CHAPTER OF AFRICAN
HISTORY

BY

R. COUPLAND

M.A., C.I.E.

FELLOW OF ALL SOULS COLLEGE
BEIT PROFESSOR OF COLONIAL HISTORY IN THE
UNIVERSITY OF OXFORD

NEGRO UNIVERSITIES PRESS
NEW YORK

Originally published in 1928
by The Clarendon Press, Oxford

Reprinted from a copy in the collections
of the Brooklyn Public Library

Reprinted 1970 by
Negro Universities Press
A DIVISION OF GREENWOOD PRESS, INC.
NEW YORK

SBN 8371-2916-8

PRINTED IN UNITED STATES OF AMERICA

PREFACE

THIS book is the outcome of an invitation to the author from Lt.-Col. J. W. C. Kirk to write an account of his father's life and work in Africa. The most important part of Sir John Kirk's career—his twenty years of official service at Zanzibar—will be described in a subsequent volume. His earlier experiences as a member of the Zambesi Expedition are here dealt with separately for various reasons. They have an interest of their own, if only because the personality of David Livingstone dominates the story. They stand apart from the rest of Kirk's life—a prologue to his African career. And, since the personal material provided by Kirk's daily journal of the Expedition is immeasurably richer than that which is available for any other period of his life, this prologue can be presented on a fuller scale and with more intimate detail than the main narrative.

It seemed desirable to set the little story in its historical background; to treat it, in fact, as a chapter of African history. One would like to think that Kirk himself would have preferred this method to that of those biographies or memoirs which never, so to speak, shift the limelight from the chief actor, leaving the audience to guess who the other players on the stage are and to imagine what the scenery is like.

The author is deeply indebted to Lt.-Col. Kirk and other members of the family for constant and sympathetic help; to the Director of the Royal Botanic Gardens, Kew, and the staff at the Herbarium for permitting and assisting the study of its invaluable records; and to the Regius Keeper of the Royal Botanic Garden, Edinburgh, for kindly supplying copies of certain letters.

A few words are needed about spelling. The use of the single instead of the double consonant in the spelling of East African place-names has now been generally adopted by British geographers; and it has been maintained in the following pages with one important exception. The native name for the great lake which Livingstone was the first white man to set eyes on was—so he tells us—Nyanza ia Nyinyesi (Lake of Stars), 'which the Portuguese, from hearsay, corrupted into Nyassa'. This corruption, so spelt, was adopted by Livingstone; but nowadays in Britain, though not in Germany, the orthodox form is 'Nyasa'. If the corruption is derived from 'Nyanza', it seems still more corrupt to represent *nz* by a single *s*. But the present writer neither wishes nor is qualified to argue about it. He can only confess that, when recording the discovery of the lake, he found it difficult to spell its name otherwise than its discoverer spelt it—and Kirk, too, of course. Can any one call the steamboat which Livingstone christened and cherished anything but the *Lady Nyassa*?

R. C.

WOOTTON HILL,
   September 1928.

CONTENTS

LIST OF ILLUSTRATIONS

MAP

I

AFRICA IN 1850

I

WHEN David Livingstone, in 1851, after making his way from
the outskirts of Cape Colony to the Zambesi, resolved to open
up a path from the centre of the continent to the sea, a new
chapter in the history of Africa began.

So far, it might almost be said, Africa Proper had had no
history. The northern fringe of the continent, it is true, had
been steeped in history from the beginning of recorded time.
It had seen the rise and fall of civilizations which in their day
were among the highest achievements of mankind—the grandeur of old Egypt, the sea-empire of Crete, the conflict with
Assyria, the Persian conquest, the coming of Alexander, the
Hellenistic kingdom of the Ptolemies and the bloom of cultured Alexandria, the wealth and cruelty of Carthage and her
death-struggle with Rome, the coming of Caesar, the camps
and cities of the Roman Empire spreading to the desert's
edge, the settlement of the Vandals on the ruins of the Roman
provinces, the Saracen invasion sweeping across from the
Red Sea to the Atlantic and thence over the Straits into the
heart of Western Europe, the long lethargy of Arab and
Turkish rule, and then the return of Europe, the coming of
Napoleon and Nelson, the establishment of British sea-power
in the Mediterranean. . . . A great history, but not a history
of the Africans. In prehistoric times the true Africans—the
black-skinned men, the Negroes—had made their home southwards in the very heart of Africa, cut clean off from that
northern fringe by one of the most effective frontiers in the
world—the Sahara desert flanked by the Atlas Mountains and
the swamps of the Upper Nile. Thus the peoples amongst
whom that northern history was made were not Negroes, but
Berbers and Semites; and the men who made the history
were not true Africans, nor, save at certain periods in Egypt,

Africans of any kind, but Asiatics and Europeans. That
northern fringe has never, so to speak, belonged to Africa.
It has always been an inseparable part of the Mediterranean
world, and its fate has been determined by its relations with
the peoples of the two continents which share with it the
Mediterranean seaboard.

The far South, similarly, had lain apart and aloof from
Africa Proper till very modern times. Its scanty population
consisted, indeed, of aboriginal Africans, but of a far less
sturdy and prolific type than the Negroes; and it was not till
the outset of the nineteenth century that the great Negroid
family of the Bantu, pouring out of the tropical belt in successive waves of conquest, began to penetrate and occupy
the country beyond the Limpopo and so linked the South
with the true life of Africa. But this great migration never
reached the southernmost point of the continent. Not far
beyond the line of the Vaal it ran up against the outposts of
an alien civilization. First the Dutch and then the British
had already settled and spread out in that southern corner
much as the Greeks and Romans long before in the northern
fringe. So the Bantu migrants never, as it were, annexed the
South. But they remained where they were—Bechuanas,
Swazis, Zulus, Basutos, and the kindred tribes of Kaffraria
—an advance-guard of the Central Africans; and their presence there in considerable and increasing numbers meant
that the South, though it had been in some degree cut off
from the Centre by European occupation, could never be so
completely severed from it as the North. Those Africans had
entered the South in far greater numbers than the Europeans;
they were, they still are, far the major part of its population.
Moreover, there was no great natural barrier, as in the North,
to obstruct interpenetration and intercourse between the
peoples of the South and Centre. On the contrary, from
Abyssinia to Cape Colony there stretched a vast undulating
inland plateau, lofty, dry, relatively cool, fertile in some
parts, richly mineralized in others, not merely providing a

broad bridge between the two sections of the continent, but uniting them within those highland limits into a single geographical area. For those reasons alone the further course of history in the South and in the Centre could not run far apart. One dominant feature of their life—indeed its cardinal problem—would be the same.

Meantime the main body of the Africans, the Negro peoples who remained in their tropical homeland between the Sahara and the Limpopo, had had, as has been said, no history. They had stayed, for untold centuries, sunk in barbarism. Such, it might almost seem, had been Nature's decree. Physical barriers secluded them from the currents of human progress in the North. They possessed no great navigable rivers, no spreading valleys, no alluvial plains, to provide the physical conditions for the growth of an indigenous civilization as in Egypt or Mesopotamia or Northern India or China. So they remained stagnant, neither going forward nor going back. Nowhere in the world, save perhaps in some miasmic swamps of South America or in some derelict Pacific islands, was human life so stagnant. The heart of Africa was scarcely beating.

It would be foolish to assume, of course, though some fools have assumed it, that the fact of this stagnation was in itself a proof of an inherent incapacity for progress in the Africans alone among the races of mankind. Backward they were and are—the most backward of the major races. But the life of every race was once little better than that of beasts. And the Africans, it is now well known, are not merely a fine people physically, very strong, fertile, enduring, but a people of many virtues, all the higher by contrast with the crude vices of their age-long barbarism; capable at need of courage, fidelity, industry, of transmuting their strong emotions and exaltations into art and music, of rising sometimes from the clinging slime of superstition to a spiritual life; capable, too, not only of patiently enduring the terrors and miseries of their environment or their imagination, but also, when the fates are kind, of an intense and simple happiness. They are, in fact, a child-race. It was not their fault that they did not grow up as fast as other races. Victims of their natural surroundings, unable by themselves to create the conditions of growth and progress, they lived on, century after century, awaiting the help of more fortunate and adult races from other continents, whose greater powers could alone avail to break the chains that held them rooted in the primitive past and to set them moving side by side with other men. And the first coming of that help, the beginning of that process of liberation, may be taken as the beginning of their history. What they will make of it remains to be seen when the process is complete.

2

It is not surprising that this dawn of a new destiny for Africa should have been long delayed. There was little inducement to the peoples of other continents to visit her shores, still less to penetrate into the interior. The coast on both sides was flat, marshy, and malarious. There were few good natural harbours. Nearly all the rivers were either blocked at the mouth by dangerous bars or not far up by rapids. Inland the country rose to that great central plateau of healthy highlands, nearer to the sea on the east side than on the west; but from either coast the journey to it was long, exhausting, and perilous; and what was to be gained by so much toil and risk? The life of the uplands was as primitive as that of the maritime belt. At one point only, at ruined Zimbabwe, was there any sign that anything which could be described as civilization had ever existed; and the walls and towers of Zimbabwe were probably the work of alien immigrants in some far-off age. From the same part of the country came rumours of great mineral wealth. The Empire of Monomotapa, like that of Prester John in the North, was another legendary Eldorado. But, though minerals were there, the Africans were quite incapable of exploiting them on any large scale; and a little gold-dust was all the adventurous trader actually acquired. A little gold-dust and plenty of ivory—for elephants abounded in parts of Central Africa —it was not enough to foster the development of a great trade with the outer world. When the sea-ways were opened, there were other more attractive, more hospitable, more remunerative continents available. The age of the great explorers was not much interested in Africa. Just as the merchants of Asia had found their best markets in Europe, so the merchants of Europe regarded Asia as their richest field of trade. It was in trying to reach Asia by new sea-routes, one westward, the other eastward, that Columbus ran into America and Diaz discovered the Cape of Good Hope.

Nor could it be supposed that, when the stronger peoples did come to Africa, they would come to help the Africans. Missionaries might be expected, in due course, in Africa, but not a missionary people. It is safe to say that no field or period of human life has not somewhere been adorned by individual altruism, but the morality of mankind is still far from having attained a capacity for altruism on a large political or social scale, on the part of one class or nation or race towards another. The only hope for the Africans, indeed, was that the new-comers, seeking their selfish ends in trade, might unconsciously bring with them some shafts of light from a higher civilization to lighten the African darkness; that the trade they built up might, in Africa as elsewhere, be legitimate and reputable and beneficial to both parties; and that, presently, it might profit them to show the Africans how to develop the latent riches of their country. Obvious risks would be run by the Africans in such an unequal partnership; but only so could they hope to obtain what they needed. Only so could a start be given to that process of economic development which was the first necessary condition of their liberation from the past and their advancement in the future. Unhappily the large-scale extraction of African minerals was impracticable and the profitable development of African agriculture very difficult until nineteenth-century science had transformed the methods and conditions of exploitation in the tropics and especially of health and transport. And meantime the stronger peoples had discovered that there was indeed one kind of trade with Africa which paid, and paid enormously, but it was neither legitimate nor reputable nor mutually beneficial. It was not a trade in ivory or gold or such-like, but in human beings.

It was Asiatics, not Europeans, who began the African Slave Trade. They were first in the field, and the institution of slavery was still so firm and flourishing throughout the Near and Middle East that the demand for slaves was never less than the supply. Thus when the Arabs, from the eighth century onwards, began to spread down the East coast of Africa, to settle and to colonize at favoured spots such as Mombasa, Zanzibar, and Sofala, and to overawe the natives in their neighbourhood with their far superior strength and skill, from that moment began also the rape of Africans from Africa. Stolen or bought, the stream of negroes—men, women, and children—began to flow north and east and south, to provide labourers for such parts of Arabia and Southern Persia as were not too dry for agriculture, to populate and cultivate the coastal islands which the Arabs had occupied, such as the Comoro Islands or Zanzibar, to serve the Arabized chiefs of Madagascar, and especially to swell the army of eunuchs that guarded the harems of Egypt and Mesopotamia. Steadily, ever deeper into the interior, the fierce Arab slave-traders made their way, kidnapping and killing. But Africa could never have suffered as much as she did, the Trade could never have grown to so vast a volume, if Europe had not joined Asia in the bestial work of depopulating another continent. Of the European peoples it was the Portuguese who began it, again because they were first in the field. In the fifteenth century, in that imperial age on which the lesser Portugal of modern times still prides itself, the Portuguese led the way in exploring the West coast of Africa: and in due course a cargo of negro slaves arrived at Lisbon. The

European market for them was not, could never have been, large. Forms of serfdom might linger on, but actual slavery was dead in the Christian West. The Portuguese, indeed, were rash enough to attempt its revival. They set their negroes to work on their soil with disastrous social and racial results. But with that one experiment European slave-holding, and with it the European Slave Trade, might have ceased but for a tragic coincidence. Quick after the discovery of West Africa came the discovery of America; and, since the indigenous supply of labour was quite unsuitable and insufficient for the new plantations that began to sprout and spread over North and South America and the West Indies, a new and growing society of European slave-holders came into being and a new and insatiable market for the European Slave Trade. Thenceforward, to a steadily increasing extent, America as well as Asia became the home or the prison of stolen Africans. Long before it came to an end, the European slave-traders were carrying negroes across the Atlantic at the rate of a hundred thousand a year. Nor should any Englishman refuse to face the fact that by the eighteenth century, while every maritime nation in Europe had a share in the Trade, the English share was the largest.[1]

Such, then, was the 'help' which the stronger peoples brought to Africa and were still bringing at the opening of the nineteenth century, not much more than a hundred years ago. Far better if they had left her alone in her stagnation. For bad as the state of the Africans was in the long ages of their seclusion, it was now worse. The new-comers did not alleviate, they aggravated the barbarism they found. They galvanized the sluggish life of the African tropics with a new energy, but it was a purely destructive energy. The population itself was being steadily drained away; and it was the best of the people, the men and women in the prime of life

---

[1] An account of the English Slave Trade and its abolition has been given by the author in *Wilberforce* (Oxford, 1923). See also Klingberg, *The Anti-Slavery Movement in England* (New Haven, U.S.A., 1926).

and the healthiest of the children, that were taken, and their
useless, unproductive elders left, often enough to starve. The
total of Africans enslaved can only be guessed at, but it must
have run into several millions. And probably at least as many
millions were killed or died as the direct result of the Trade.
It was not only the traders themselves that took life. Tribe
fought with tribe to capture slaves and sell them for alcohol
or powder. The more martial and restless tribes had doubtless preyed on their weaker neighbours before the Europeans
came; but the new incentive they brought with them created
a perpetual state of war over large areas of Africa. So barbarism became more barbarous. And, worst of all, perhaps,
the one chance of salvation, the hope of help and liberation
from outside, was now precluded. The West coast of Africa
had become a close preserve for slave-hunting. Scientific
explorers turned to less dangerous districts of the unknown
world. Reputable traders sought their honest gains elsewhere. The true Africa had been discovered only to be
wrapped in blacker darkness.

3

If England had taken the lead of the Christian West in
doing the greatest wrong one race has ever done another,
England took the lead also in putting an end to it. Before the close of the eighteenth century the new humanitarian movement had forced the great body of stay-at-home
Englishmen to recognize at last the realities of the crime
which, far away from the scene of its perpetration, unimagi-
native, and easily persuaded by material arguments, they
had so long tolerated as, at the worst, an inevitable, a 'necessary' evil. And once their conscience had been awakened, no
half measures, no mere regulation or alleviation of the methods
of the Trade, would content them. In 1807, mainly as the
result of Wilberforce's personality and perseverance, the
Trade was 'utterly abolished, prohibited, and declared to be
unlawful' by Act of Parliament. In 1811 it was made a

felony punishable by transportation, in 1824 a capital crime. In 1833 Slavery itself was abolished throughout the British colonies. Thus England was at least as thoroughgoing in destroying the slave-system as she had been in maintaining it. Nor was this the kind of philanthropy that costs nothing. The profits drawn by Englishmen directly or indirectly from the Slave Trade were enormous; it has been described as 'the most lucrative traffic the world has ever seen'. And to compensate the slave-owners for the loss of their human property, as equity required, the vast sum (for those days) of twenty million pounds was voted from British taxpayers' pockets. One wonders, after all, if large-scale altruism is really so far beyond the power of mankind; for, if indeed it were purely altruistic for a people to relieve its conscience, then the enactment of those historic statutes was something very like it. 'The unweary, unostentatious, and inglorious crusade of England against Slavery', wrote the judicious Lecky, 'may probably be regarded as among the three or four perfectly virtuous pages in the history of nations'.[1]

From the date of those Acts of Parliament began the deliverance of Africa from the destruction and degradation in which her first contact with Asia and Europe had involved her. But it was a slow process. The Acts abolishing and penalizing the British Slave Trade were enforced as strictly and effectively as they could be. British cruisers patrolled the West coast of Africa so vigilantly, their officers were inspired with such a zeal for their task, that it soon became very difficult indeed for British subjects in recognizably British ships to smuggle slaves over the Atlantic in defiance of the law. But that was not by any means the end of the Slave Trade. In the first place it was necessary that the other maritime States should be induced to follow the British lead and outlaw the Trade for their own subjects, and this

---

[1] Lecky, *History of European Morals* (1911 ed.), 153. Abolition Acts, 47 G. III, c. 6; 5 G. IV, cc. 17 and 113. Death penalty repealed as unnecessary, 7 W. IV and 1 V., c. 91.

end was only achieved after nearly twenty years and as the
result of unceasing activity on the part of the British Government. At the international settlement which followed the
Napoleonic Wars there was nothing which British public
opinion so vigorously or so unanimously demanded as a
general agreement of the Powers to abolish the Slave Trade;
and in the following decade there was no question of foreign
policy on which the pressure of British diplomacy was more
obstinate, importunate, and irritating. The last States to
give in—and then not without a bribe from British taxpayers
in the form of so-called compensation—were Spain and Portugal. But even then the Slave Trade still continued, for the
simple reason that, though all the States which had once
engaged in it had now outlawed it, Britain alone was genuinely
concerned to make the law obeyed. Smuggling was rife under
all flags but the British. So a second diplomatic campaign
was needed to procure general assent to a right of search,
reciprocal in form but inevitably one-sided in fact, for the
cruisers patrolling the coasts, and to a system of joint courts
for dealing with captured smugglers and their cargoes. In
time this second objective was also attained, but with one unfortunate exception. The United States had made the Trade
illegal for American subjects in the same year as Britain; but
the part taken by the American navy in the policing of the
Eastern Atlantic was intermittent and ineffective; and since
'the freedom of the seas' and the inviolability of the American flag thereon were the bitterest and most lasting factor in
Anglo-American discord, it was not till Lincoln was in power
and American Slavery itself was on the eve of abolition that
the right of search was granted. Till 1862 the slave-smugglers
could usually evade all interference from British cruisers by
hoisting the Stars and Stripes.

Thus, in 1850, the West African Slave Trade, though not
quite ended, was near its end. And to make the ending certain and permanent, to rob the hardiest smuggler of any
reward for his risk, the demand for slaves on the other side of

the Atlantic was now beginning to dry up. Slavery in the
United States was approaching the tragic crisis which destroyed it. In South America and the West Indies it only
lingered, soon to be extinguished, in Brazil and Cuba. For
the same reasons slave-smuggling in American and other
ships by a secondary track from the East coast round the
Cape of Good Hope was also petering out. Nor was the Arab
Slave Trade, so much older than the European and as
destructive to East Africa as the European to the West, so
completely immune from interference as before. Now Europe
had stopped wronging Africa, Europe or rather Britain was
bent on stopping Asia. Between 1822 and 1845 a series of
agreements were made between the British Government and
the Arab Sultan at Zanzibar which provided for the limita-
tion and finally the suppression of the export of slaves from
the Sultan's African dominions; and in 1848 and in 1849 the
Persian Government and the leading Arab chiefs on the Persian Gulf agreed on their part to prohibit the importation of
slaves by sea. But with the Arab Slave Trade, as with the
European, outlawry was by no means tantamount to abolition. British cruisers patrolled the Indian Ocean, intercepted
such as they could of the innumerable Arab *dhows* engaged
in smuggling slaves, and liberated their cargoes. But only
one or two ships could be spared for the work, and far the
greater part of that swarm of small craft escaped the net.
As long as the Arab Sultans allowed the Trade to operate in
their territories and to shelter in their ports—as long as
the huge and terrible slave-market continued to flourish at
Zanzibar—Africa could never be freed from the curse which
the outer world had laid on her.[1]

4

The abolition of the Slave Trade was not all that Africa
needed. It was indeed the negative condition of any progress

[1] An account of the Arab Slave Trade and its suppression will be
given by the author in *Kirk at Zanzibar*, now in preparation.

—the removal of an obstacle which precluded the very idea of progress. But, if that were all, the last state of Africa would be worse than the first. Her population decimated, her barbarism intensified, she would revert to her old stagnation. Her only hope still lay in contact with the outer world, in the chance that Europe would not regard the Slave Trade as her sole link with Africa and with its abolition break off all connexion, but rather that she should now start afresh, as it were, and seek in Africa the openings for civilized commerce and, perhaps, for colonial settlement which had hitherto been blocked by the Slave Trade. But was there any valid prospect of such a second start ? Were the peoples of Europe still interested in maintaining contact with the peoples of Africa ? To what extent had they entrenched themselves on African soil and how solidly ? Having done so much to harm, were they now doing anything to help ?

To judge by nothing more than length of occupation and extent of territory, one European people at any rate was very solidly entrenched in Africa. Before the beginning of the Slave Trade, the Portuguese, as has been seen, had skirted the coasts of the continent on their way to India. They had early secured landing-places or ports of call at intervals on the West coast or off it—in the Canary Islands; in Portuguese Guinea, just beyond the corner of the great westward bulge of Africa; in the isles of St. Thomé and Principe in the eastern waters of the Gulf of Guinea; and, half-way from thence to the Cape of Good Hope, at S. Paulo de Loanda and one or two other settlements which constituted with the adjacent territory the province of Angola. Then, rounding the Cape on his first historic voyage to Calicut (1498–9), Vasco da Gama, one of the greatest of the great explorers, after touching at Natal, had anchored for some weeks in the mouth of the Quilimane River, whence, though few knew it at that time, a boat could sail at flood-season into the Zambesi and up that wide waterway towards the heart of Africa. Da Gama had called also at the Arab ports of Mozambique and

Melinde before striking boldly eastwards across the Indian
Ocean. His successors, following in his track, did not merely
touch and pass. Along that East coast, as on the West, they
presently established trading-posts of their own—at Sofala
in 1505, at Quiloa (Kilwa) in the same year, at Mozambique
in 1507. The Arabs naturally resented this intrusion; but
in the fighting that resulted up and down the coast the
Portuguese soldiers and sailors in the age of d'Albuquerque
and d'Almeida were more than a match for any rivals. The
victory of Diu in 1509 made them masters of the Indian
Ocean, and for the better part of the sixteenth century the
whole East coast of Africa from Socotra to Delagoa Bay lay
within the orbit of the Portuguese Empire.

But its lot therein was relatively unimportant. The Portuguese Empire, one of the greatest political achievements in
history, stretched far round the world; and the spices of the
East Indies or the silver of Brazil were more attractive than
the gold-dust and the ivory of Africa. No vigorous or long-
sustained measures were taken, therefore, to develop the
East African settlements, and only one considerable effort
was made to penetrate and open up the interior. For many
years that rich and healthy *hinterland* remained in the un-
questioned occupation of a group of kindred Bantu tribes
who acknowledged the supremacy of a paramount chief,
known, amongst other honorific titles, as 'the Monomotapa'.
This name was wrongly given by the Portuguese to the 'Empire' he controlled, and he himself was called its 'Emperor'.
In fact, his status was similar to that of Lobengula in later
days, though his power was probably far less. The Mashonas
are held to be the nearest descendants of his people, and his
territory covered what are now the eastern districts of Rhodesia. Two goldfields lay within it, the more northerly of
which, the Manika, now the Umtali field, was known by
repute to the Portuguese; and in quest of it their traders
had soon pushed up the Zambesi valley. Fortified posts were
built on the river-side at Sena in 1531 and at Tete a few years

later; an export station was created at Quilimane in 1544; and a brisk trade in gold was established in this area through native middlemen. But in the second half of the sixteenth century the Court of Lisbon, anxious to replenish its sinking treasury, embarked on a more ambitious scheme. Francisco Barreto, one of its ablest servants and a fine soldier, who had been Governor-General of Portuguese India, was put in charge of the East African settlements: a great expedition was fitted up for him in the Tagus: and in 1572 he ascended the Zambesi with twenty-two ships and a thousand men. He exchanged friendly messages with the 'Emperor' and did him the service of defeating and scattering a powerful native tribe which had defied his authority. But that was all. In those days, centuries before European science had learned to cope with malaria, the fevers of the Zambesi flats were far more dangerous than all the spears of the Bantu. From the outset Barreto's army began to dwindle. Before long his men were dying like flies. Finally he died himself, broken-hearted, at Sena. His successor, Homem, reinforced from Europe, again pushed inland, and a trading-post was established as far up the Zambesi as Chicova, and on its tributary, the Mazoe, at Luanze, Bucoto, and Masapa. But it was up the Revue, north of Sofala, not up the Zambesi, that he ultimately reached the Manica goldfield. The results, however, were unsubstantial. Effective occupation and exploitation of the mines were impossible in those days so far from the sea. And though the Portuguese, early in the seventeenth century, obtained a 'concession' of all his mineral wealth from a weak Monomotapa, in return for a promise of aid against his enemies, the yield seems never to have been great. Already, moreover, when that measure of success was achieved, the heroic age of Portugal was closing. The little Atlantic kingdom had overspent its strength. Its dynasty of great men had failed. The springs of its power—energy, statesmanship, wealth—were drying up. Before the seventeenth century was half-way through its course, the great Empire was gone. Dutch,

French, British, had driven the Portuguese from all but one or two points in the East. That they did not drive them also from Africa was due mainly to the fact that it seemed scarcely worth while. As it was, the Arabs were now strong enough to recover their exclusive control of the northern half of the East coast; and the Portuguese perforce drew back their claim to dominion from Cape Guardafui to Cape Delgado. Still more humiliating, the fiercer Bantu tribes proved themselves capable of hemming the meagre garrisons within the walls of their forts and expelling the impoverished traders from their country. One by one, the posts in the interior were blotted out. The right to work the goldfield lapsed by default. Sena and Tete were at one time captured and pillaged. At these two points, and at these alone—except, perhaps, for a period, at Zumbo, higher up the Zambesi—could the Portuguese retain any foothold away from the coast. And if on the coast they still maintained themselves, it was primarily because the Bantu were too deeply disunited by their tribal feuds to unite and drive them out.

The tale to be told in this book requires for its understanding at least a brief survey of the subsequent fate of Portuguese East Africa. But for an historian of another nation it is not an agreeable task. For the period is one of almost unrelieved decay and degradation. The Portuguese province covered a vast area on the map. From Cape Delgado to Delagoa Bay it stretched for more than a thousand miles, considerably farther than the sister province of Angola on the West coast. In many parts of it the fertile soil was capable of bearing profitable crops. Coal lay beneath the Zambesi valley. The higher country inland was rich in precious metals. Here, it might well seem, was a rare chance for a colonizing Power. Here alone, surely, a Portuguese colonial system might have been built up which by itself would have formed no mean remnant of the sixteenth-century Empire. Real colonization, it is true, was then impossible. Up country the climate was as well suited for European settlement on a

big scale as many parts of America; but the occupation of
Rhodesia or Nyassaland, as they are occupied to-day, was
quite impracticable before the invention of nineteenth-century methods of transport and hygiene; and the maritime
lowlands have not been rendered, even by modern science, a
healthy country for white men to make their homes in. There
was nothing, on the other hand, to prevent the steady growth
and spread of civilized government and economic enterprise,
which, if rightly ordered, might have brought to Portugal the
commercial profits she increasingly needed and to the Africans of all that area their long-awaited chance of progress.
In the imperial age a beginning had at any rate been made
of economic development. From the East Indies and from
Brazil the Portuguese had brought and planted, for the first
time in East African soil, the seeds of fruits and corn and
vegetables from which great crops might have been raised—
oranges, lemons, maize, wheat, pineapples, beans, and lentils,
to mention only a few. That nothing substantial developed
from those invaluable imports was due to several causes. The
population of Portugal, in the first place, was diminishing in
numbers and in vigour; and such energy as it still possessed
for the adventure of emigration was not unnaturally directed
to Brazil in preference to Mozambique. Very little fresh
European blood found its way to that derelict coast. Portuguese women would not look at it. For those Portuguese
men who lingered on there, miscegenation was the inevitable
result. Before long the half-castes and quadroons easily outnumbered the pure whites. And the pure whites themselves,
except for some of the higher officials, sank steadily in the
social and moral scale. The garrisons, for instance, were
largely composed of soldiers who had been convicted of grave
offences and, incorrigible at home, were sent to Mozambique
almost as if it were a penitentiary. Such attempts as the
Lisbon Government occasionally made to increase and improve the colonial population came to nothing. Organized
immigration was only tried once, in 1677, when 'a few

artisans and agricultural labourers, with eight reclaimed women (*convertidas*) were sent out to Mozambique and the stations on the Zambesi'.[1] Another plan tried in the course of the eighteenth century was the *prazo* system. Tracts of land, sometimes of huge extent, were granted by the Crown to individual colonists at a small annual rental on condition that the eldest daughter of the first or second holder, to whom the title was to descend, should marry a Portuguese born in Europe. But the only outcome of this system, beyond the small revenue it brought to the Crown, was the transient efflorescence of a strange, picturesque group of slave-owning landlords, not without some of the easier virtues, but neither cultivated, nor industrious, nor self-disciplined, and altogether lacking in the vigour to resist the steady pressure of the Bantu. One by one the *prazos* were overrun. In 1854, when the system was at last abolished, nearly all the mansions were in ruins and the estates in native occupation. It may be said, in fine, that Portuguese East Africa was never a real colony, never even a place of temporary settlement for many Portuguese. In 1850 its capital island-city of Mozambique—irregularly built, with narrow streets, and very dirty, but with one or two good public buildings—contained a population of only about 7,000, of which a very small minority, including the officials and a garrison of 200, mostly convict, soldiers, were Portuguese. They were far outnumbered by the half-breeds and these again by the slaves. A few Arabs, a score or so of 'banyan' traders from Western India, and one or two commercial agents from European countries made up the total. The other coastal towns were proportionately meaner and their white population smaller. Inland there were very few white men at all. At Sena, for example, there were not more than twenty or thirty.[2]

[1] G. M. Theal, *The Portuguese in South Africa* (London, 1896), 249.
[2] See the description given in 1860 by the British consul at Mozambique, L. McCleod, in *Travels in Eastern Africa* (London, 1860).

This meagre, attenuated, unreplenished stock of Europeans
could not have achieved the effective economic development
of Portuguese East Africa; but, in any case, any such development was rendered practically impossible there as elsewhere in Africa by the growth of the Slave Trade. The East
coast might perhaps have suffered only from Arab slavers
and not European, if the Portuguese had not been cut out
of the West coast trade by the Dutch. As it was, about the
middle of the seventeenth century the evil work began in
Mozambique, and soon a stream of human merchandise was
flowing thence round the Cape and across to Brazil. Throughout Portuguese East Africa the tragedy of the West was thus
repeated. Slaves were no less easy to obtain. The more
militant native tribes found it just as profitable to engage
in periodical raids on the villages of their weaker neighbours
and to sell their victims to the ubiquitous Arab or half-caste
traders. And the curse continued longer in the East. Portugal indeed undertook in the treaty of 1836 to suppress it there
as elsewhere; but the number of British cruisers, the only
active agents of suppression, were fewer, the small Arab
dhows in Portuguese service were easy to hide in creeks and
corners, and, worst of all, the Portuguese officials, ill-paid
and corrupt, connived at the smuggling and shared in its
profits. The Govenor-General of Mozambique himself was
not always above suspicion, and his Junta or Council was
largly composed of notorious slave-dealers.[1] The provincial
Governors were often deeply involved. In 1848 the Governor
of Quilimane, the head-quarters of the traffic, absconded in a
ship which carried five hundred slaves to Rio de Janeiro.[2]
In 1850 his successor returned to Lisbon a far wealthier man
than he had left it; and the British Minister, at any rate,
had no doubt as to how it had been done. All the colonial
Governors, he told Lord Palmerston, did the same. 'Inade-
quately paid, they are enabled, almost without risk, to acquire

---

[1] *State Papers*, vol. 30, p. 910.
[2] Ibid., vol. 37, pp. 475, 508.

a considerable fortune in the course of a few years.'[1] It was reported in 1849 that slaves were being shipped from all the Portuguese ports except Mozambique, that in 1847 they had numbered at least six thousand, and that, with two 'honourable exceptions', the Portuguese officials did nothing to prevent it.[2] Nor, of course, could any of them plead ignorance. The traffic was not carried on in the dark. Sometimes the Portuguese flag was flown above the 'barracoons' in which the slaves were herded at the coast awaiting shipment.[3]

To these and many similar facts the attention of the Portuguese Government was directed by the British Foreign Office with tiresome persistence; and it must be fully admitted that Ministers at Lisbon, and specially Viscount Sá da Bandeira, Minister of Marine for several years, did their best to prevent their East African officials from exposing the Government they served to such constant and humiliating charges of broken treaty-faith. Orders were frequently dispatched insisting on the suppression of the Trade, demanding that the officials should do their duty, threatening penal action. In 1844 Viscount Sá confessed to the House of Peers that the evidence was such as 'to exclude all doubt of the culpability of the officers who govern those colonies either through connivance or remissness in the continuance of the Slave Trade', and he carried a motion for an investigation into the conduct of the Governors-General of Angola and Mozambique and the Governor of Quilimane amongst others.[4] By a protocol of 1847, moreover, the Portuguese Government agreed to permit British cruisers to operate against the Trade within the mouths of Portuguese rivers where no Portuguese authority was established.[5] And there were years in which the captains of those cruisers gratefully acknowledged the genuine co-operation of the Governor-General. But on the whole the Lisbon Ministers were well aware that they were fighting a

[1] *State Papers*, vol. 40, pp. 405, 489.
[2] Ibid., vol. 38, p. 504.   [3] Ibid., vol. 33, p. 397.
[4] Ibid., vol. 33, p. 409.   [5] Ibid., vol. 36, p. 586.

losing battle with what Palmerston bluntly described as 'the venality of their subordinate functionaries';[1] and as early as 1848 they recognized that the most effective step they could take to suppress the Slave Trade was to follow Britain's lead and do their part in suppressing Slavery. In that year a commission was appointed to consider its abolition in all Portuguese colonies;[2] and in course of time, as will appear, its labours bore good fruit.[3] Meanwhile, it was only the vigilance of the British patrol and, as has been explained, the dwindling of the demand for slaves that continuously or effectually checked the supply. The operation on the spot of good intentions at far-away Lisbon was neither continuous nor effectual.

It is impossible, therefore, to evade the ugly truth that the Portuguese occupation of East Africa, at any rate in its later stages, had profited neither Portugal nor Africa. It cost the home-country more than it paid it. It was destructive to the natives. And this is all the more pitiful because in the earlier, greater days of Empire the Portuguese had been the first to recognize at least one duty to the Africans and to pursue at least one path towards their enlightenment. The mission of Portuguese Jesuits established in Mozambique in 1560 was the first Christian mission in East Africa; and Gonzalo da Silveira—who led it, who boldly made his way to the *kraal* of the Monomotapa, who converted, as he believed, the chief himself and his elders to Christianity, and was then suspected, betrayed, and strangled—was the first of the many Christian martyrs in East Africa. The Dominicans followed the Jesuits. They planted missions on the coast and at Sena and Tete in the Zambesi valley. They, too, had their martyrs, Nicalao da Rosario, João da Trindade, and Luiz da Espirito Santo. But the missions, however heroic their faith and endurance, could not survive the general decline and decay. Early in the nineteenth century the last Dominican had disappeared. Here

---

[1] *State Papers*, vol. 35, p. 435.   [2] Ibid., vol. 37, p. 470.
[3] See p. 85 below.

and there over the country-side, a church, deserted or in ruins, was all that remained in 1850 of the only effort the Portuguese had made to help the Africans.

The same story must be told of scientific enterprise. Established on both coasts of Africa and at about the same latitude, the Portuguese had a notable opportunity of extending the geographical knowledge of Europe by exploring the unknown interior of the continent. Not only to find out what sort of country lay behind their coastal territories, but to seek a path from one to the other, from sea to sea—it was doubtless a difficult, a dangerous task, but surely one to fire the ambition of any man with a taste for discovery and adventure. Already in the imperial age the idea was in the air and something at least was attempted to substantiate it. But the savagery of the central tribes seems to have prevented missionaries or traders from penetrating farther west than, if as far as, longitude 29° east. Such geographical features, however, as were observed within these limits were duly noted, and the Portuguese maps of the period were the first maps which taught Europe anything of the heart of Africa. In the light of after events it is important to note that these early maps depicted a great lake or group of lakes somewhere northwards of the Zambesi. This notion of a central inland sea in which the great rivers of Africa such as the Nile and the Congo found their source was a common tradition among the tribes of the interior; and, as we know to-day, it was roughly true; but it is clear from the fanciful features with which the lakes were surrounded in their maps that those early Portuguese explorers never actually set eyes on them. And, of course, the claims of science fell even more into neglect than those of religion during the long period of decay. It was not till 1798 that a properly organized expedition set out to find a way across the continent. Led by Dr. Francisco de Lacerda e Almeida, a scientist, explorer, and administrator of the first rank, it advanced up the Zambesi to Tete, and thence northwards as far as chief Cazembe's *kraal*, at about longitude 29° near Lake Mweru, but there its gifted leader died of fever and exhaustion. A second expedition in 1831 got no farther west. The first men who actually succeeded in crossing Africa were neither Europeans nor Africans. In May 1806 two half-caste traders were entrusted by a Portuguese official in Angola with a letter addressed to the commandant of Tete. In February 1811 they delivered it, and then made their way back to Loanda. Some native traders, again, who had accompanied the expedition of 1831, continued westwards when the expedition withdrew, bearing a letter to the Governor of Angola, dated March 10, 1832, which they delivered on April 25, 1839. Three Arab traders also achieved a crossing, from Zanzibar to Benguela, reaching their goal in 1852. And then at last, between 1853 and 1856, a European, Antonio da Silva Porto, a Portuguese trader established in Angola, made his way from Benguela to the mouth of the Rovuma. He must have passed somewhere near Lake Nyassa, and one of his personal slaves was said to have seen it.

Thus the Portuguese had neither made anything of East Africa themselves nor opened it up for others. They knew practically nothing of the interior in 1850—far less than their ancestors had known three centuries before. Listless, unadventurous, improvident, they clung to their little townships by the sea, still claiming sovereignty over the up-country to a limit no one could define, but seemingly incapable of doing anything to make the fiction real. Better days might be approaching, but in 1850 Portuguese East Africa had learned to expect little from its name. Three thousand miles of coast still lay, as they had lain for two centuries, under a blight.[1]

[1] G. M. Theal, *The Portuguese in South Africa* (London, 1896); *History and Ethnology of Africa South of the Zambesi* (2nd ed., London, 1910). Dr. Theal's work was based on a study of the archives at Lisbon, and he published a selection of the documents in *Records of South-East Africa* (9 vols., London, 1898). Sir H. H. Johnston, *The*

5

The Portuguese were not the only European occupants of African soil in 1850. But the settlements of the other sea-going peoples of Europe were smaller and more disconnected than Angola or Mozambique. They were not the remains of an imperial domain, but only of the Slave Trade. Small and ugly groups of wooden buildings—not much more than a landing-stage, a warehouse, an agent's dwelling, with a little fort to protect the handful of residents—they had been dotted here and there along the sea, the sordid products of the sordid trade whose purposes alone they served, excretions of civilization dropped beside the oily mud-flats and the foetid mangrove-swamps. Yet over them, a century ago, flew the historic flags of Europe—the flags of Spain, Denmark, Holland, France, and England.

While the Slave Trade was still permitted by the laws of Europe, these wretched little settlements were active enough at certain seasons—when the slave-gangs came in from the jungle and the slave-ships from the sea—but the statutory abolition of the Trade paralysed what life they had. They were no longer part of a great, lucrative, and legal commercial organization. The busy smugglers could not make open use of them. The development of other and more reputable trade, even if the business men of Europe had thought it worth their while, was necessarily a slow affair until the natives could unlearn their terror of the white men. It seemed indeed so profitless to retain the posts at all that two of the smaller nations soon abandoned them. In 1850 the Danes had already gone and the Dutch were soon to go. The Spaniards stayed, but their holding was very small—only the island of Fernando Po and a scrap of mainland south of it.

Colonization of Africa (Cambridge, 1913), chap. iv. J. S. Keltie, *The Partition of Africa* (2nd ed., London, 1895), chaps. iv and vi. For later developments see R. C. F. Maugham, *Zambesia* (London, 1910); *Portuguese East Africa* (London, 1906).

The masters of Angola and Mozambique retained also their lesser property in Portuguese Guinea. But most of the old Slave Trade seaboard was left for France and Britain to make what they liked of it.

The foothold of the French was far smaller in 1850 than that of the British. Their settlements were in Senegal at the northern edge of the Mid-African belt, on the Ivory Coast and in Dahomey along the horizontal line of Upper Guinea, and at two points to the south between the Niger and the Congo. In fifty years' time these settlements, expanded into colonies, were to form the southern tongues, lapping the Atlantic, of a huge French African Empire, stretching from the Mediterranean over the Sahara and linking, politically at least, but politically alone, the true Africa to the northern fringe. But in 1850, twenty years before the war of 1870 deflected the currents of their policy, French interests or ambitions were more deeply engaged eastwards of Africa—not on the coast, where, as has been seen, only the Portuguese and Arabs were in occupation, but in the great unsettled island of Madagascar and its satellites, Réunion, Bourbon, and the Comoro Isles. Thus the connexion of France with Africa was too slender on the whole to have much effect for good or ill on African life. Frenchmen, it is true, like other Europeans and Americans, were employed in smuggling slaves across the Atlantic; but the members of that lawless gang may almost be regarded as denationalized.

At one point, however, definite harm was about to be done, quite openly, to some extent officially, by Frenchmen. Soon after 1850 a new method of providing labour for cultivating the plantations of the French tropical colonies was introduced in place of the old Slave Trade. In the East African area it was applied on the largest scale to Réunion, whence agents were sent to the mainland and the Arab islands to negotiate with the Arab or half-caste slave-traders for the purchase of negroes. These negroes, of course, were slaves, mostly obtained from the interior in the old way, and their masters sold them in the old way to the French for thirty or forty dollars apiece. But on each of the ships that were to carry them to Réunion there was a French official or agent of the Governor and an Arab interpreter. It was the business of the latter to explain to each slave that he was now a free man and to obtain an assurance from him that he was willing to go and work for five years in Réunion. It was the business of the former to accept that assurance. Under these auspicious conditions a brisk trade developed. Ships were sent out from France for the special purpose, and one merchant of Marseilles contracted to land 25,000 negroes in Réunion within two years. But still the planters did not obtain all the labour they wanted; still the system did not work as smoothly as it should. And this was chiefly because its legality was dubious. The French, of course, insisted that it was not a slave trade. They called it the Free Labour Emigration System. The negroes, they declared, became French colonists. And for a time at least the authorities in Portuguese East Africa were prepared to agree that the system did not conflict with Portugal's treaty pledges against the Slave Trade, and to allow or at least to connive at the operation of the system in Portuguese territory. But the Arab rulers of the islands and the coast northwards, mainly, no doubt, because their leader and suzerain, the Sultan at Zanzibar,[1] had a British consul at his ear, were less easy to convince. Three times at least between 1853 and 1858 official French pressure was brought to bear on the ruler of Zanzibar. The Governor of Réunion requested him in the name of the Emperor Napoleon III to authorize the export of *les travailleurs* from his dominions. Admiral la Guerre, on board a frigate of forty-four guns, threatened him with force. An unofficial French agent offered a heavy bribe. 'Do not listen', he said, 'to the English consul'. But none of those methods of persuasion was effective. The Arab did listen to the Englishman, who was always there

---

[1] Until 1856, Zanzibar was ruled by the Imam of Muscat: thereafter it became a separate 'Sultanate'.

and could also, no doubt, at need produce an admiral and a frigate. He could not, he protested, break the promise made as long ago as 1822 that nowhere in his dominions should slaves be sold to Christians or exported to Christian lands. Similar French efforts at Johanna and elsewhere had the same result. But illegality, of course, did not mean abolition. If the Slave Trade proper had defied the laws of Europe, the Free Labour Emigration System could defy the disapproval of an Arab sultan. It was only a little less easy to work it. The demand for labour in Réunion still so far exceeded the supply in 1858 that the price of slaves on the coast had doubled.

There is no evidence to show that the 'free emigrants' were ill-treated. Their short voyage to Réunion was under far more humane conditions than the notorious 'Middle Passage', and on the island their welfare was the special charge of an official Protector of Immigrants. Their wages were from one and a half to two dollars a month. They may well have been reasonably contented. But it was a cynical absurdity to describe them as willing 'colonists'. Most of them, probably, quite failed to realize that they were not still slaves. Few, if any, can have understood what their contracts meant. And in 1857 the British consul at Mozambique reported that the cases of return to the mainland, according to those contracts, after five years' service, were rare. The worst of the system, however, lay not in the fate of the slaves after they had been converted into 'free emigrants' but in their previous enslavement. As the British commissioners and naval officers wofully reported, the new traffic had resuscitated in the interior of East Africa all the evils of the Slave Trade proper. In 1856, when the old Trade round the Cape of Good Hope was fast dying out, the new Trade across the Mozambique Channel was very much alive. Nor did it seem possible to stop it. The British Government protested again and again. The Quakers presented a memorial to Napoleon III. But the answer was always the same short and simple answer—the Free Labour Emigration System was not a slave trade. To what lengths the French Government was prepared to go in maintaining this position will appear on a later page.[1]

6

There remain the British, who had outdone the French in their share of the Slave Trade and outdid them therefore in the extent of the commitments which the Slave Trade had bequeathed to them in Africa. The great majority of those scattered posts on the West coast were British in 1850. Apart from an outlying settlement in the north at the Gambia River, they were mostly situated on the Gold Coast, between the Ivory Coast and Dahomey, at the very centre of the old Slave Trade field. Interspersed at one time among them were those Danish and Dutch posts which had been or were soon to be absorbed, leaving all the Gold Coast in British hands. To the south a group of traders, headed by a pertinacious Scot, Macgregor Laird, had been busy since about 1830 in exploring the creeks of the Niger delta and making a beginning of the trade in palm-oil. But the whole of this area was overshadowed by the activities of the slave-smugglers who had found an ideal base of operations in the lagoon of Lagos. This pirates' nest became indeed so serious an obstacle to the effective operations of the patrolling cruisers that in 1861, after trying other methods in vain, the British Government went so far as to annex it outright. This step was ultimately to lead to the acquisition of Nigeria, but it was taken at the time without the slightest forethought or desire for imperial expansion. Neither Government nor public opinion in Britain had any territorial ambitions in West Africa. The activities of the traders on the 'Oil Rivers' were a purely private venture and inspired no public interest whatever. What interested the public and the Government was the suppression

[1] See p. 266 below. Full evidence as to the system will be found in the *State Papers* from 1856 onwards: see especially vols. 48 and 49.

of the Slave Trade. That was the reason why Britain had
been readier than other Powers to retain her derelict posts on
the coast and even to take over the Danish and the Dutch.
Created to serve the Slave Trade, they could now be used as
bases and points of call for the only navy that was seriously
engaged in its destruction.

Was that, then, the only British interest in West Africa or
East, the only objective? Was the British attitude to Africa
purely negative? When the Slave Trade was finally stamped
out, as soon it must be, would the British people go their
ways and leave the Africans, as far as they were concerned,
alone again in barbarism?

The great humanitarians of the preceding generation would
have vehemently denied it. The positive side of their crusade
was no less important in their eyes than its negative side.
For them the abolition of the Slave Trade was not enough.
It was not enough for Englishmen, after wronging Africa for
ages, merely to repent and sin no more. Conscience demanded
that something should be done to make amends. Having
done their best to worsen the barbarism of the Africans, they
must do their best now to civilize them. Thus the leaders of
the crusade had pleaded from its outset for civilization as
well as liberation, for the promotion of honest commerce and
missionary effort in place of the evil Trade. Nor did they
scruple to appeal to the acquisitive instincts of their countrymen as well as to their consciences. Utterly disinterested
themselves, the 'Saints' were yet not so unworldly as to
think that the connexion of Britain with Africa could be long
or largely maintained as an utterly disinterested duty. Indeed they would not have resented overmuch the jibe of a
later day that the motives of British enterprise in Africa were
'philanthropy and 5 per cent.'. Why should they? Outside
the text-books of the social revolution it is not asserted that
there *must* be something wrong in 5 per cent. None the less,
it seems surprising, at first sight, that Wilberforce and his
allies did not perceive that there *might* be something wrong

in it—that they did not foresee, or at least did not discuss, the new dangers to Africa which might arise from the new contacts they promoted. Even missionaries, until experience had revealed the complexities of their task, could do more harm than good. And the intervening years have shown that 'legitimate' commercial exploitation could be almost as injurious to the Africans as the Slave Trade. What was to ensure that European traders would discard the morals as well as the materials of the Slave Trade and do justice to their same ignorant and defenceless customers? What was to keep the lust of gain from stifling as before the instincts of humanity? What was to prevent the white men from making the Africans the victims rather than the partners of their trade, taking much and giving little, stealing the inanimate wealth of Africa by covert or open force as once they had stolen its manhood, appropriating finally, if and where it suited, the very land they lived on and reducing its occupants to virtual serfdom? Might not the new exploitation really differ from the old only in method or degree? Having begun by robbing Africa of the Africans, might not Europe end, as a recent critic has suggested, by robbing the Africans of Africa?

To-day, in a world a century older, these sinister possibilities seem obviously to have been inherent in the situation from the first. Yet it is not really strange that they should have been undetected or ignored by the Englishmen of the great age of emancipation. On that one issue, at any rate, they were rising to heights which public life had never reached before. Their hearts were being wrung by all the rigours of a newly-wakened conscience. As the crusade proceeded to its final triumph, it is not too much to say that the nation as a whole, as far as its attitude to the Slave Trade was concerned, experienced something like that Evangelical 'conversion' which was the frequent fate of individual Englishmen at that time. The nation felt the same sense of sin, the same remorse, the same desire for atonement, the same 'enthusiasm'. And in that mood the nation attained for once the individual's capacity for altruism. That, certainly, was a strange, a wonderful thing. But surely there was nothing strange in the conviction of those who had done most to bring it about that this great national change of heart was neither superficial nor transient. To Wilberforce and the rest it would have seemed incredible that their countrymen, once grace had come to them, once they had recognized the wrong they had done in Africa and wiped it out, could ever tolerate its repetition in some other form. In their belief—and it was not on the whole unjustified—they were planting in the public mind of Britain a conception of responsibility, of trust, towards the backward peoples of the world, so manifestly right, so plainly implicit in Christianity or indeed in any high creed or code of conduct, that, once it had taken root, however slow its growth or faint at times its influence, it could never die.

To the great humanitarians, therefore, the positive side of their policy seemed not merely the only way of helping Africa, but a safe way; and with no misgivings at all they expounded it and preached it from the start. 'Let us make reparation to Africa as far as we can' were the closing words of the great speech with which Wilberforce opened his long campaign in 1789, 'by establishing a trade upon true commercial principles'; and the last of the resolutions he then moved declared that the British merchants engaged in Africa might find a profitable substitute for slaves in the products of the soil required for British industries. Three years later, it was the same theme that gave the last touch of grandeur to what was probably the finest speech Pitt ever made—his almost passionate appeal to Englishmen to make atonement for their crime against the Africans by helping them to rise from barbarism, and his famous vision of the dawn of civilization breaking over the dark continent.[1]

The negative side, however, the abolition of the Trade, was obviously the first task; and it proved a far more difficult, a

[1] Coupland, *Wilberforce*, 130, 168–71.

far longer task than its promoters had foreseen. Each hardly, slowly won success only meant a further effort, a shifting of the objective, till at last it was clear that the Slave Trade would only really end when Slavery was ended. And since, on the one hand, the crusaders were necessarily preoccupied with these successive steps of their negative policy, and since, on the other hand, the mere continuance of the Trade was an almost insurmountable obstacle to the development of their positive policy, very little was achieved in the latter direction as the years went by. Something, however, was done, a beginning at least was made, in more ways than one. In the first place British explorers began to trespass on the old slave-preserves and penetrate into the interior. In 1795 the African Association, an offspring of the humanitarian movement, commissioned Mungo Park to investigate the course of the Niger. Ten years later he resumed his quest, this time under Government orders, and died in its pursuit. Five more expeditions were fitted out by Government, most of them unsuccessful, until at last, in 1830, the Niger had been tracked and mapped from the edge of the Sahara to the sea. The second achievement was more definitely philanthropic in origin and purpose. In 1787 a group of Abolitionists, headed by the veteran Granville Sharp, obtained a grant of territory from a native West African chief between the Gambia and the Gold Coast in order to make a home for some hundreds of freed slaves who had been stranded in England since the Somerset decision. Reinforced by others brought from Nova Scotia, who had been enfranchised after serving with the British forces in the American War, these freedmen constituted, with a handful of British officials, the colony of Sierra Leone. After thirty difficult years, during which it was maintained not unsuccessfully by a Chartered Company controlled by the philanthropists, the colony was taken over by the Crown and became not only the chief base for the British cruisers but also a dumping-ground for the slaves they released from captured smugglers. There, too, and in the adjacent country, the British missions began their West African campaign. The third positive achievement was not deliberately planned and organized. Like so much else in the history of the British Empire, it was the natural but unforeseen result of circumstances. In 1828 those old Slave Trade posts were handed over to the control of a committee chosen by Government from the body of British merchants engaged in the Gold Coast trade. The first Governor appointed by this committee was Captain George Maclean, a Scotsman of great vigour and ability and possessed of a rare gift for dealing with native peoples. His primary task was not directly philanthropic: it was the development of 'legitimate' trade. But no substantial trade could be developed as long as all that coast-land remained in barbarism and anarchy, its native population, as well it might be, bitterly suspicious of the white man, and exposed not only to the slave-smugglers but also to constant raids by the bellicose Ashanti who dominated the *hinterland*. In a few years' time Maclean transformed the situation. He concluded a tripartite treaty with the Ashanti and the coast natives guaranteeing peace and free trade between the sea and the interior; he prevented the slave-smugglers from operating on land; and he persuaded the local chiefs to submit their intertribal disputes and serious questions of crime and punishment to his jurisdiction. In fact, along a hundred and fifty miles of coast-land, with a parliamentary grant of not more than £4,000 and only a hundred native police at his command, Maclean established an informal British Protectorate, under which law and order were maintained in rough accordance with the principles of British justice. And when in 1843 the Crown resumed control and the Gold Coast Protectorate was formally instituted, Maclean's system was retained and Maclean himself appointed the first Judicial Assessor to administer justice among all such tribes as voluntarily accepted this measure of control.

All these achievements—the exploration of the Niger,

Sierra Leone, the missions, Maclean's administration—could be put to the credit of the positive side of the humanitarian movement. They were not all, it has been seen, the considered efforts of philanthropy, but they were all, in greater or less degree, philanthropic in effect, a help to the Africans or a means of help to come. Yet, all together, they were but an inconsiderable trifle in the scales against the harm inflicted by the Slave Trade. Nor were they the product of any such national purpose as had outlawed the Trade or demanded its outlawry by the rest of Europe. The British conscience, in fact, knew little and cared nothing about them. From the commercial standpoint, similarly, those West coast settlements were relatively unimportant. They could not be regarded as a serious and promising enterprise for developing the resources of Africa and supplying raw materials and a market for British industry. The traders on the Gold Coast or the Niger Delta were only a little *clique* in Liverpool and London who had always been connected with West Africa. The result of all their operations in 1834–5 was only a total of exports from Africa valued at about £450,000 and of imports from Britain valued at about £300,000. And against this meagre business could be set the annual sums which British taxpayers had to pay—and apparently would always have to pay—for the cost of the West coast governments.[1]

7

In fact, as has already been said, the only thing in Africa that really interested British public opinion was the destruction of the seemingly indestructible Slave Trade; and the positive policy would almost have faded out of men's minds if it had not presently been revived and reinstated, not in-

[1] A. B. Keith, *West Africa* (in Sir C. Lucas's *Historical Geography of the British Colonies*: Oxford, 1913). E. C. Martin, *The British West African Settlements, 1750–1821* (London, 1927). E. Stock, *History of the Church Missionary Society* (London, 1899), vol. i.

deed on its own merits, but as a method of achieving at last
that other, prior, negative end. While Wilberforce and Pitt
had pleaded for the civilization of Africa as a complement
or a sequel to the abolition of the Trade, Buxton, who had
succeeded Wilberforce as the leader of the humanitarian
cause, began in the late 'thirties to plead for civilization as
a preliminary, a means, the only effective means, to abolition.
In *The African Slave Trade and its Remedy*, which was published in 1840 and widely read, he demonstrated the inefficacy
of naval police-work, however zealous, to obliterate the Trade,
and argued, in detail and at length and in a sober, practical style, that it could only be done by civilizing the Trade's
victims. As soon as the Africans had been taught the possibilities of agricultural and mineral wealth which lay latent
in their own soil—and Buxton's elaborate description of it
was by no means exaggerated in the light of what is known
to-day—as soon as they realized the profit they could win
themselves from its exploitation, they would quickly suppress
the Trade on their own account by combining to stop the
supply of slaves. 'Strong external measures ought still to be
resorted to,' but they must be supplemented by a more
effective policy which could be defined in a single phrase—
'the deliverance of Africa by calling forth her own
resources'.

This new appeal was not unheeded. Public opinion was
deeply impressed by Buxton's overwhelming proof that the
Slave Trade was not being destroyed, in fact was actually
increasing; and it was therefore willing at last to be really
interested in the positive side of the old crusade. Men of
influence in society and politics at once came forward in
Buxton's support. A new Society for the Extinction of the
Slave Trade *and* for the Civilization of Africa was founded,
with Buxton in the chair, Stephen Lushington and Sir Peter
Inglis as deputy chairmen, and a noble list of peers and
bishops and members of Parliament (including T. B. Macaulay, whose father had been Governor of Sierra Leone) as the

provisional committee. The Society's first prospectus sketched an ambitious programme.

'One most important department [it declared] must entirely rest with her Majesty's Government—the formation of Treaties with the native rulers of Africa for the suppression of the Slave Trade. Such Treaties, however, will not be carried into execution, unless those wants which have hitherto been supplied from the profit arising from the sale of the natives should be satisfied through the means of legitimate commerce. It may appear expedient to the Government to obtain from the Chiefs the possession of some convenient districts which may be best adapted to carrying on trade with safety and success; and when this is effected, another and wholly distinct Society may perhaps be formed for the purpose of aiding in the cultivation of those districts and of promoting the growth of those valuable products for which the soil of those countries is peculiarly fitted.'

That paragraph alone was daring enough. It contained the first hint—and a broad one—that the positive policy required a more substantial basis than traders' wharfs and depots. It actually suggested territorial annexation! But that was not all. The Society was to promote every practicable means of civilizing Africa which were not already, like missionary work, in the charge of other competent bodies. The languages of West and Central Africa were to be studied and reduced to writing. Medical science was summoned to do battle with tropical disease for the benefit both of the natives and of the white men who went out to help them. Engineering, likewise, was to play its part: irrigation and drainage were to be undertaken: a chain of roads and canals was to be constructed. The natives were also to be taught the best methods of agriculture and the products most required in Britain, and tools and seeds were to be provided for them. And finally 'the manufacture of paper and the use of the printing press, if once established in Africa, will be amongst the most peaceful auxiliaries in the dispersion of ignorance and the destruction of barbarism'.[1]

[1] T. F. Buxton, *The African Slave Trade and its Remedy* (London, 1840). The prospectus will be found at the beginning of the book.

It is difficult in these days to read unmoved these aspirations of more than eighty years ago—so thoroughgoing, so sincere, so utterly untainted by any ignoble motive, reaching out along paths still only partly trodden towards a goal still unattained. But what chance was there, it may well be asked, of responsible British statesmen, of Lord Melbourne's Government, accepting the initial and by no means unsubstantial role allotted to them? The answer is rather surprising. Possibly through the earnest advocacy of Lord Glenelg, a child of the Clapham Sect, who was Buxton's natural ally in the Cabinet, but who must have been regarded by his colleagues as none too safe a guide in view of his recent dealings with Canada and South Africa—more probably owing to the shrewder judgement of his successor at the Colonial Office, Lord John Russell—more probably still because public opinion seemed to be catching fire again—for whatever reason, the Melbourne Government had no sooner studied Buxton's proposals than they promised to support them. The Cabinet, Glenelg told him, was unanimous. Melbourne himself had written strongly about it. 'The project of overturning the Slave Trade by civilization, Christianity, and the cultivation of the soil is no longer in my hands,' said Buxton on receipt of an encouraging letter from Russell; 'the Government have adopted the principle and taken the trust upon themselves.' And the first practical step in the execution of the task was soon decided on. An expedition was to be equipped and commissioned by Government to ascend the Niger, to make treaties with the chiefs on its banks, to examine the economic capacities of the adjacent country, and to prepare the way for commercial enterprise. 'A mere commencement', Buxton called it, 'on a most moderate scale. If it answer, we shall enlarge our operations.' But no pains were spared to make this *reconnaissance* a success. The technical questions involved were carefully studied by Captain Washington at the Admiralty, a lifelong enemy of the Slave Trade. Three iron steamships, *Albert*, *Wilberforce*, and *Soudan*, were allotted to the work, and a capable naval officer, Captain Trotter, appointed to command. A botanist, a mineralogist, a geologist, a zoologist, a draughtsman, and a practical gardener or seedsman were enrolled, and two missionaries—one of them, Samuel Crowther, a negro, and destined to be the first African bishop of the English Church—were added to the party in order that they might prospect the ground for mission work. That they were embarking on a dangerous adventure this little group of pioneers were well aware. The West coast of Africa was already notorious as 'the White Man's Grave'. Some of the London newspapers, indeed, attacked the scheme with acerbity as a wanton and useless sacrifice of life. But everything was done to reduce the risks. 'They will be carried through the mangroves and miasma of the delta by steam,' wrote Buxton; 'they will have the medical help of at least eight surgeons or physicians; above all, they will have the sound and cool judgement of Captain Trotter to restrain them from settling unless the circumstances of climate, soil, and disposition of the natives should be very favourable.' It was certainly not the wild, foolhardy enterprise its enemies suggested, nor was it so regarded in the highest quarters. Buxton was significantly invested with a baronetcy. And the Prince Consort himself not only attended and addressed a meeting of the African Civilization Society (as it came to be called), but personally inspected the three ships as they lay in the Thames. So, in the spring of 1841, with the British conscience on board, the Niger Expedition sailed.[1]

The sequel was a pitiful fiasco. The ships steamed quickly up the river, but within a fortnight from the start a malignant fever broke out and spread. First *Soudan*, then *Wilberforce*, were sent back to the sea, loaded with sick. Captain Trotter and his colleagues laboured hard to achieve at least some tangible results before the same fate overtook them. A treaty

[1] *Memoirs of Sir T. F. Buxton* (Everyman ed., London, 1927), chaps. xxv-xxvii. The Government saw Buxton's book before it was published. Glenelg resigned in February, 1839.

was concluded with the Attah of Eggarah. The cession of a site for a model farm near Mount Patteh was obtained from him and a little band of workers established on it. The scientists did what they could in the time to prospect the neighbourhood and their provisional reports as to the possibility of putting large areas under cotton and as to the readiness of the natives to trade and so forth were favourable. The farthest point reached was some 320 miles from the sea. But then, after only a few weeks in the interior, *Albert* was obliged to follow her consorts downstream, her crew so depleted that amateur members of the Expedition had to run her engines. Of 193 white men who had ascended the fatal river, 41 died, including Commander Bird Allen of *Soudan*.

The news made a profound impression at home. Those prescient newspapers raised a howl of execration against the philanthropic fanatics who, against all warning, had sent so many worthy Englishmen to a certain death. Lord John Russell characteristically insisted on 'claiming his share of the obloquy' and stoutly reaffirmed at a public meeting the soundness of the principles on which the ill-fated scheme had been based. Canon Samuel Wilberforce gave all the force of his eloquence and his name to a plea for continuing the campaign despite this initial set-back. Other eminent supporters displayed no less unflinchingly the courage of their convictions. But it was all of no avail. Public opinion had taken alarm. It was now as hostile as a year before it had been friendly. And Buxton himself bowed to the storm. At the beginning of 1843 he played his painful part in dissolving the African Civilization Society. Then, his spirit seemingly broken by the weight of disappointment, he faded out of public life. In 1845, his fifty-ninth year, he died.[1]

Five years later it might well have seemed that all hope of a positive policy in Africa had died with him. The missions, undeterred by the appalling death-roll, had continued their task in Sierra Leone and the Gold Coast, penetrating

[1] *Memoirs of Sir T. F. Buxton*, chaps. xviii–xxxi.

even to the heart of Ashanti. The traders were still at work in their old fields. But there had been practically no expansion eastwards, no enlargement of the area of contact, no new knowledge of the interior. Mid-Africa remained in darkness. On the other hand, the illicit Slave Trade, it is true, was beginning to diminish, if only, as has already been pointed out, because Slavery itself was dying. And, that being so, British opinion was drifting to the conclusion that the continued occupation of the West coast was fast becoming purposeless. Only fifteen years later, indeed, a strong Select Committee of the House of Commons, appointed to consider 'the state of the British establishments on the Western coast of Africa', reported with decisive brevity that the object of British policy should be an ultimate withdrawal from the whole of that part of the continent with the probable exception of Sierra Leone. In other words, when the Slave Trade had at long last been actually abolished, what more was there fòr Britain to do in Africa? Her permanent need of Europe's aid, the old idea of atonement, the vision of the dawn—it was all forgotten. The British conscience, too, it seemed, had been done to death in the mangroves and miasma of the Niger.

8

Among the audience at the meeting of the African Civilization Society at which Prince Albert presided in 1840 was a young Scotsman then in training for the career of a medical missionary: and in the following year, the black year of the Niger Expedition, David Livingstone entered on his first charge at Kuruman, an outlying station of the London Missionary Society in South Africa. Between two and three thousand miles separated Kuruman from the Niger; but, though no one knew it then, between them lay the highland bridge; and the tribes of Bechuanaland among whom Livingstone was working were part of the southern advance-guard of the great Mid-African race. Destiny was to weld those links together. For Livingstone was to pursue the same general aim as the Niger Expedition, succeeding in the end where it had failed. And the African race was to find in Livingstone a champion of their cause, a servant of their welfare, in influence and achievement second only to Wilberforce himself.

Of the qualities which enabled Livingstone to do what he did, the first, unquestionably, was his faith. Strong in its simplicity, it burned through all his life, irradiating, as the constant communing of his private journals testifies, the thoughts of every day, directing all his purposes, giving him the conquering conviction that for the work at his hand he was, in all humility, God's instrument. And with this faith, in some degree, perhaps, a product of it, went an almost superhuman courage. Brave men are often afraid; their bravery is in the overcoming of their fear; but Livingstone—it was remarked by every one who was with him on his travels—seemed not to know what fear was. And, though it would be idle to try to explain his unique personal influence over the African peoples with whom he came in contact, that fearlessness was doubtless one of its secrets. Without a thought of his own safety he could be quite at his ease with black men who had never seen a white—natural, simple, unself-conscious, talking quietly and slowly and not too much, never fussy, never excited. He had, moreover, it is clear, a peculiar gift for seeing what lay at the back of the native's mind. Irrational suspicions, mysterious motives, ridiculous arguments—he could understand and deal with them all. And just as he was invariably considerate of the physical well-being of any natives in his own charge, watching over their health in fever-stricken areas, tending them in sickness with a gentleness rare in men, so he could consider also the feelings and the prejudices of any strange tribe he met. If they obstructed his progress, he never roughly overrode them. He argued, and, if argument was useless, he waited—waited sometimes for weeks before he gained his point. But he never gave it up, he never turned back. Of all the qualities which

enabled him to succeed as an explorer nothing was more vital
than this tenacity. And the strength of will, the power of
endurance, with which he drove himself on to his goal, not
merely at intervals of brief, intense endurance, but month
after month and year after year, were beyond the range of
ordinary men. In the last months of his life, in the wilds of
Mid-Africa, utterly exhausted, suffering from a severe internal
haemorrhage, unable to walk or even to ride, he still had himself carried in a litter a little farther on and on each day.
'Nothing earthly', he wrote in his diary a few weeks before
the end, 'will make me give up my work in despair.'

It was partly, perhaps, this very strength of will that made
Livingstone less successful in his dealings with white men
than with black. Though the friendships he made were intimate and lasting, he was slow to make them. As often
happens with strong men and sometimes hampers their success, he lacked the capacity for co-operation. In a conflict of
wills he could not easily give and take. He was as impatient
with the follies of white men as he was patient with those of
black. There was no touch of arrogance in his self-confidence;
in the deepest sense he was a humble man; but his personality
was too original, too individual, for him to work smoothly in a
system, to be anything but restive in harness. And even with
his friends he could be very obstinate. One of the closest of
them, and his companion on his first long journey, William
Cotton Oswell, described this trait, a little crudely perhaps,
as 'Scottishness'. 'It was not', he says, 'the *sic volo, sic iubeo*
style of imperiousness, but a quiet determination to carry out
his own views in his own way, without feeling himself bound
to give a reason or an explanation further than that he intended doing so and so. This was an immense help to him,
for it made him supremely self-reliant.' No doubt; but it also
made him a difficult man to work with. Even Oswell, who
was also strong-minded, admits that 'we generally agreed to
differ', and that is scarcely the best kind of agreement. There
was a hardness, too, in Livingstone, not of feeling—he was

sensitive, affectionate, a man of strong emotion under the still surface—but of bearing. He lacked altogether the lighter social graces, the natural *cameraderie* which makes its possessor at home with all sorts of his fellow men. He was awkward, brusque, inarticulate, and, as if he realized those failings, self-conscious sometimes among white men as he never was among black. He was not without a sense of fun; he could enjoy a joke; but it is doubtful if he had much sense of humour. He was usually rather serious, often preoccupied with his own thoughts and dreams. He would be silent sometimes for hours and hours together. Drawing his strength from within himself, he could do without the praise or encouragement, even without the society, of others. Nature, in fact, had made him, as far at least as his own race was concerned, a lonely man. And it was his not uncongenial fate to live the greater part of his adult life with no white man to companion him and to die at last with no white man at his side.

It was not to be expected that the peculiar personality of this strange, great man would be merged, so to speak, into the common stock of mission-work in South Africa. A missionary's career, however strenuous, is often uneventful, sometimes almost monotonous. He may feel it to be his duty to live a lifetime in one district of a pagan land, making its people his own, patiently labouring, year after year, to lead them on stage by slow stage to enlightenment. But there was something in Livingstone that made it almost impossible for him to live that kind of life. He had not been long in South Africa before a hint of it appeared. 'My life', he wrote in one of his earliest letters home, 'may be spent as profitably as a pioneer as in any other way.' If he had emigrated as an ordinary colonist, he would undoubtedly have taken his place amongst the frontiersmen in the wilderness, not among the farmers in the settled areas behind the line; and likewise, as a missionary, he found himself not so much interested in the intensive cultivation of ground already occupied as in extending the field of occupation, working for the future rather than the present, cutting new paths for the advance of Christianity into an unknown world, and giving its peoples as he passed—for he preached wherever he explored—a foretaste of the light to come. His first task, therefore, was to his liking. He had been sent to Kuruman, head-quarters of the great Robert Moffat, with instructions to prospect for a new station farther north. Before a year was out he had made a journey of 700 miles, partly in an ox-waggon, partly on foot, round the fringes of the Kalahari Desert. After a second journey in 1842, he selected a site at Mabotsa, 200 miles north of Kuruman, and the formation of a new settlement there was duly sanctioned by the L.M.S. Livingstone hailed 'with inexpressible delight . . . the decision of the Directors that we go forward to the dark interior. May the Lord enable me to consecrate my whole being to the glorious work!' But Mabotsa could not hold him long. He was restless, straining on the leash, often itching, one suspects, to follow his call unchecked by far-away Directors, fitting uncomfortably into any organized system, his individuality already at times in conflict with that of his colleagues. Nor did his marriage, in 1843, induce a tamer, more quiescent, homelier mood; Moffat's daughter was the last of women to hold her husband back. So the scene shifts quickly in those early years—and always in one direction. In 1846 the pioneer was at Chonaune, forty miles north of Mabotsa; in 1847, forty miles farther north, at Kolobeng. And by now the supreme idea of his life had already fastened on his imagination. Still to the north, in front of him, stretched for thousands of untrodden miles the great central mass of Africa. To find a way into it, as no white man, no Christian, had yet done; to see for the first time what it was like and what white men and Christianity could do to help its helpless, isolated peoples; to find a way through it, yes, right through it—was there anywhere on earth a greater, loftier, more exacting, more exciting venture? Was there anything that better deserved, more loudly demanded, the consecration of a life? 'Who will penetrate through Africa?' asked Livingstone.

With this question already answered in his heart, he made the first of his longer and more dangerous expeditions in 1849, when, in company with William Cotton Oswell and Mungo Murray, who were spending some years in Africa hunting big game beyond the borders of Cape Colony, he passed through the Kalahari drought-belt which had baffled previous explorers and reached Lake Ngami, 870 miles north of Kuruman. Next year, accompanied this time by his wife and three small children, he again visited the lake, but soon came to the conclusion that the country in its neighbourhood was too malarious for a missionary settlement. 'A more salubrious climate must exist farther up to the north,' he wrote; and farther up to the north, accordingly, he made his way in 1851. At the Chobe River, some 200 miles beyond Lake Ngami, he was met by Sebituane, the chief of the Makololo, who, after a desperate and not uneven conflict with Mozilikatze and his dreaded Matabele, had secured the mastery of a wide sweep of country on both sides of the Upper Zambesi. Unfortunately Sebituane, who had been frankly delighted to see a white man, had welcomed Livingstone's idea of a missionary settlement in his country, and had promised all the help he could give, fell a victim to pneumonia very soon after Livingstone's arrival. His daughter, however, who succeeded him, was no less friendly; and with her permission to explore any part of her territory Livingstone pushed on another 130 miles to Shesheke on the banks of a 'glorious river'. Above, he was told, there were rapids; below, a great waterfall. In fact, though he did not know it at the time, he had lighted on the Zambesi at a point farther west than the Portuguese had ever reached. But a good site for a settlement was still to seek. The banks of the Zambesi and all the country south of it were flat and marshy. Northwards still—perhaps in the Batoka uplands which rose to over 4,000 feet between the Zambesi and the Kafue—the search must be continued. Livingstone's return to Kolobeng, therefore, was not a home-coming. Kolobeng had been, it was to be, the only home he ever had—the only place he ever lived in with his family for any length of time. But any kind of settled life had now become impossible for Livingstone; and since his experiences had taught him that he could only keep his wife and children with him on his wanderings at grave peril to their health, he decided to send them back to Scotland. So firmly fixed now was his resolve, and so great the personal sacrifice it entailed.

The master-idea of Livingstone's life had, in fact, been reinforced, stiffened, and clarified by his experiences in the north. Already he had penetrated Africa far enough to discover something which made its penetration a more necessary, a more urgent duty than even he had hitherto conceived it. He had raised a corner of the veil that hid the heart of Africa and seen the Arab Slave Trade feeding on it. Not long before he came up from the south, the Arab traders, pushing from the east ever deeper into the interior, had trafficked with the Mambari, neighbours of the Makololo; and among the products of civilization which they had exchanged for African children had been a number of old Portuguese firearms. Some of these—so Livingstone was told—had been offered by the Mambari to Sebituane on condition that he paid for them in the same coin. The temptation was too great. Any scruples the old chief may have had grew faint when he thought of the Matabele. He had to get the muskets, and eight of them he got for eight boys of about fourteen—not Makololo boys, be it said, but sons of prisoners captured in intertribal war. The next step was as obvious as it was easy. Chiefs who want more muskets must steal more children. A joint raid was accordingly arranged by the Mambari and the Makololo on some tribes to the eastward. Some two hundred slaves were secured. According to Livingstone's account it had been agreed that these were to be the Mambari's share of the booty, the Makololo taking the cattle. But he also records that the latter, as they marched triumphant homewards, fell in with some Arab traders from Zanzibar and sold them thirty slaves for three English muskets.

Thus, inevitably, the black history of the West-coast plague-belt was beginning to repeat itself in those central areas, hitherto immune, into which the fatal infection was now spreading. And Livingstone was quickly forced to the same conclusions as the philanthropists who had studied and combated the disease in the West. Memories, no doubt, came to him of that meeting in Exeter Hall, of the objects of the Niger Expedition, of the programme of the African Civilization Society; but in any case his mind was bound to follow the same logical path to the same end. The Slave Trade would only cease when 'legitimate' trade supplanted it. The necessary conditions for the establishment of such a trade were, first, the discovery of a not too difficult route from the centre of the continent to the sea, and, second, European settlement in some healthy inland district both for trading with the natives and for teaching them how to develop their resources. Missionary enterprise would proceed side by side with commercial. Livingstone, in fact, had taken the old positive policy from the shelf where it had lain for a decade in disrepute. And, unlike Wilberforce or Buxton, he was in a position to be himself the first instrument of its execution. 'You will see by the accompanying sketch-map', he wrote to his Directors in the autumn of 1851, 'what an immense region God in His grace has opened up. If we can enter in and form a settlement, we shall be able in the course of a very few years to put a stop to the slave-trade in that quarter.' He then suggests devoting himself for about two or perhaps three years to this task. Whatever his private inclinations, he cannot settle down with his family in the south. 'Providence', he says, 'seems to call me to the regions beyond.' That so bold a proposition would have its critics he was well aware: and voices were soon raised against it, not all of them in moderate or kindly tones. The headstrong father was

orphaning his children. The missionary was forgetting himself in the explorer. He was out for the worldly glory of
discovery. But such comments—it was characteristic—
merely stiffened Livingstone's resolve. His consciousness of
a definite call deepened. 'I will go', he said, 'no matter who
opposes.'

So it was that a new chapter began in the history of Africa.
For, when Livingstone made that resolve, he started a process
which was destined to move, slowly at first and with long
pauses, but presently with a steadily gathering momentum,
until, at the close of the century, British policy in Africa had
become 'positive' beyond anything the great humanitarians
had imagined, until at least a quarter of Mid-Africa had
come, directly or indirectly, under British rule.[1]

---

[1] Livingstone, *Missionary Travels and Researches in South Africa*
(popular ed., London, 1912), chaps. i–ix. W. G. Blaikie, *Personal
Life of David Livingstone* (6th ed., London, 1925), chaps. i–vii, xxii.
W. E. Oswell, *William Cotton Oswell* (London, 1900), chaps. vii, ix, xi.

II

JOHN KIRK

I

LIVINGSTONE, Maclean, Mungo Park, Macaulay, Macgregor Laird—these notable Scottish names have already figured in this record of Africa; and it so happened that the man who was to serve as Livingstone's lieutenant in Africa for more than five years, to become his trusted friend, and to do more than any one else after his death to serve the cause which had inspired his life, was also a Scot.

Along the road which follows the bleak coast of Forfarshire east and north towards Aberdeen, about eight miles east of Dundee and two miles west of Carnoustie, lies the village of Barry. Here, at the manse, on December 19, 1832, John Kirk was born. He was the second of the four children of the Rev. John Kirk, a citizen of St. Andrews, and of Christian Carnegie, a member of a cadet branch of the Southesk family whom he had married in 1818. The third child, Elizabeth, died in her 'twenties'. The fourth, James, was weakly and migrated early in life to South Africa. The first-born, Alexander, was more vigorous and distinguished. After a successful career at Edinburgh University, he was apprenticed to engineering at the yards of Napier & Sons, then the great ship-builders of the Clyde. His first responsible position was that of manager of the Bathgate paraffin works, established by James Young, who—so the threads of life are interwoven—became one of Livingstone's greatest friends; and he soon proved his ability by inventing various improvements in the process of separating the paraffin from the lighter oils. Later he returned to Glasgow as head of the Napier firm, where, as a supplement to his duties as a 'captain of industry', he directed his inventive genius to the application of the principle of triple expansion to marine engineering. He died in 1892.[1]

[1] Among other things, Alexander Kirk invented ice-making

KIRK'S PARENTS

Photograph by Kirk

The father of these four children was a remarkable man. Born in 1795 and educated at St. Andrews University, he was admitted a licentiate of the Established Church of Scotland in 1820, and on his ordination five years later was presented by the Crown to the parish of Barry. At the end of 1837, when his son John was just five years old, he was promoted, by the patronage of Lord Panmure, to the more important and remunerative living of Arbirlot, some three miles inland from the seaside town of Arbroath. And there he was caught in the historic storm of controversy which shook and split the Scottish Church. A few months after the move the prologue to the impending drama was spoken by Dr. Chalmers when he declared, in his famous lectures in London, that the business of the State was merely to maintain an established Church and that in all matters ecclesiastical the latter's authority was supreme. At the same time the first of a series of disputes as to the right of a congregation to reject a minister nominated by the patron was being diversely decided by the Scottish ecclesiastical and civil authorities. For the next five years, all over Scotland, the battle raged. It was a battle of principles, of which the question of patronage was only an illustration. One party, the 'moderates', upheld the authority of the State, the validity of the historic constitutional settlements, and the supremacy of the civil power as the final arbiter between ecclesiastical factions. The other party—a minority, but intensely serious and powerfully led—clung to the watchword of spiritual freedom. It was, in fact, a revival in modern shape of a quarrel that went back to the roots of Scottish history. It was a domestic quarrel now: no alien enemy was involved; but there was much in this nineteenth-century conflict of high ideals and stubborn wills that went back to the time when the struggle for national and religious liberty was one and the same, back to the days of the Covenanters. And it was with something of the Cove-

machinery. The first machine was erected at Hong Kong and is still there.

3531

nanters' spirit, of their dogged determination, their contempt
for argument or compromise, their readiness to suffer all
things for conscience' sake, that these modern zealots fought
their fight. There could only be one end to it. In the spring
of 1843, at the opening of the General Assembly of the Scottish Church, the retiring Moderator, followed by more than
four hundred ministers, left the Assembly Hall and proceeded
through the crowded streets to another hall at Canonmills.
The schism of the 'Kirk' was thus accomplished. Three-
eighths of its ministry had seceded. And since the controversy had centred, as it happened, on the question of
patronage, the seceders were bound in honour to resign the
livings which no spiritual authority had bestowed.

Amongst them was the minister of Arbirlot. Without hesitation, in June 1843, John Kirk removed himself and his
family from the pleasant manse and, since no other residence
was available in Arbirlot, betook himself to lodgings in Arbroath. This did not mean, of course, the abandonment of
his congregation—at least of those among them who shared
his convictions, elected him their minister without any patron's initiative or intervention, and did what little they
could to support him from their own slender purses. Meantime Lord Panmure, whose sympathies were strongly with
the other side, filled the vacant manse with another *nominee*
and, not unnaturally, did nothing as a landlord to facilitate
the rebel's poaching on the preserves of the Established
Church. Kirk, indeed, would have found no building in
Arbirlot in which to carry on his ministry if he had not
happened, while at the manse, to obtain from Lord Panmure
the lease of an adjacent piece of land in order to increase the
modest acreage of the glebe. On this land, a romantic object
in that plain rural landscape, stood the ruins of Kelly Castle.
There, better than anywhere, the Kirk children had loved to
play. There, as they grew older, in the gaunt, dismantled
banqueting-hall, young John's tutor had been inspired to
construct a miniature shooting range. And thither, since the

lease had still some time to run, the sturdy father now trudged from Arbroath to worship in that same hall in freedom, as he saw it, no less than in truth. Those were lean, hard years. One wonders, indeed, how the children would have fared if Kirk and his wife had not both possessed little incomes of their own to augment the efforts of his followers. As it was, he could manage to hold his ground until, at last, a new Lord Panmure, of opposite sympathies, ruled in place of the old, and the 'Free Kirk' was enabled to obtain a status and security comparable with those of its 'Established' rival.

Young John, it may be assumed, knew little or nothing of the storm that crashed about his childhood. But if the seeds of his father's character were already planted in him, their growth must have been fostered by intimate association with that single-minded, stiff-backed, indomitable fighter in those testing days. And there was something closely akin to the qualities of the Rev. John Kirk of Arbirlot in the fidelity, the strength of will, the stubborn devotion to a cause, which in after years distinguished Sir John Kirk of Zanzibar. But that was not all the son acquired from the father. The latter's 'conversation', so the *Fasti* of the Scottish Church record, 'was good to the use of edifying'.[1] And the subjects of it were by no means so limited as the phrase suggests. The graduate of St. Andrews was a scholar as well as a parson; and, especially after the abdication, when a tutor could no longer be afforded, he doubtless took a hand himself in his children's literary education. But literature came second in his heart to natural history. He was an enthusiast for botany, both theoretical and practical; and he inspired in John the second a similar passion, which was to play a large part in directing the course of his career at an early stage of his life and to burn on undimmed till its end. Nor was botany the only field of science to which the country-side invited him and teachers led him. A mile or two to the east lay the cliffs and sand-dunes and beaches of the coast. Westwards were quar-

[1] *Fasti Ecclesiae Scoticanae*, H. Scott, 1871 ed., part vi, p. 790.

ries of old red sandstone, rich in fossils. And when the move was made to Arbroath, the sea was so near at hand that the hours away from school could be easily and gloriously spent in scaling the cliffs in search of wild-fowls' nests, while inland, filling the background, stood the Grampians, a wonder-world of grand, unsullied nature, not too far off for an occasional holiday within the family means. Finally, at the Arbroath High School, an ancient and distinguished institution, none the less efficient for its purpose because, in the Scottish manner, it did not cater for the tastes or purses of a single class, John Kirk was initiated into the mysteries of chemistry —seductive enough when taught by a master who never tired of repeating those simple, yet surprising experiments which every boy delights in, still more seductive when the boy is encouraged to perform the experiments by himself.

Good teaching was not wasted on young Kirk. After four years at Arbroath, when he was still only in his fifteenth year, he satisfied the matriculation examiners and prepared to follow his brother Alexander to Edinburgh University. It was an early age to go out into the world, but manse and school and country-side had produced a youth who was very well able to look after himself, a quiet, self-possessed, modest, friendly youth, naturally gifted and capable of steady hard work, very strong and active, not so much of a games-player as English boys, but no less addicted to other open-air pursuits and already a fair shot with gun or rifle, and—not least important—quite prepared, like many another Scot, to 'cultivate the muses on a little porridge' and keep himself at the University on some £60 a year.

2

After two years' work in the Faculty of Arts, Kirk moved on to the Faculty of Medicine; and since the medical course is necessarily lengthy, it was not till 1854 that he obtained the M.D. degree. Of his life during those seven years at the

University little record has survived. It is safe to assume that he worked hard at his subject, and the fact that his thesis for the degree, 'On the Structure of the Kidney', was among the few considered for the Dissertation Prizes is a proof of his capacity; but, though he was doubtless contemplating the medical profession as the field of his future career, he seems never to have felt a strong vocation to it. None, indeed, of the new sciences he now explored awakened quite the passion he felt for his old love. It was the botanical classes he attended with most zest, and the member of the University staff with whom he became most intimate was the Professor of Botany, J. H. Balfour, a teacher of the old school, a little stiff and dry, but not so uninspiring or unlovable as one would infer from his nickname, 'Woody Fibre'. Kirk's training was thus twofold. He became concurrently a qualified doctor and a proficient botanist. While still an undergraduate he was elected a Fellow of the Edinburgh Botanical Society, and that he could speak with no less authority in academic circles on botanical than on medical subjects is evident from a story told of him by a fellow student. In the summer of 1854 the so-called 'Torbanehill mineral question' was being keenly debated at Edinburgh. It was a naturally fascinating question since it not only raised a nice point of law—whether a lease of coal on a certain property could be taken to cover a kind of richly bituminous shale discovered thereon—but also involved the destination of a vast fortune. Every one was talking about it, every one had an opinion on it, but every one was not so foolish as to air his opinion in public unless he were an expert on the legal or scientific issues involved. A certain Professor Bennett, however, rashly determined to read a paper on it to a Pathological Society whose only claim to this honour would seem to have been the fact that the Professor himself had recently founded it. To Kirk's sober scientific mind such amateurish enthusiasm seemed altogether out of keeping with academic standards. 'He has no business to meddle with the subject,' he told his friend, John Beddoe, 'for, though he is a good microscopist, he knows nothing of botany or of the carboniferous flora which is really the crucial matter. I mean to oppose him.' The sequel may be told in Beddoe's words. At the close of the paper 'Kirk rose up in the back of the room and in quite a few modest but clear and firm sentences so completely demolished the Professor and his paper that the former, making some lame and hasty excuse about other engagements, dissolved the meeting without attempting to reply. He never called the Society together again, and we all said that Kirk had destroyed it'.[1]

One other subject, which, if not precisely academic, was by no means unscientific, deeply interested Kirk at this time. Photography as we know it was one of the creations, and by no means the least interesting or useful, of that extraordinary Victorian Age; and it was while Kirk was an undergraduate that the most important step in its development was taken by the introduction of the collodion process. It was a novel and attractive hobby for any one with a scientific bent, with an adequate knowledge of chemistry, and with a store of patience; and Kirk was one of the earliest amateurs to master the new art. Nowadays, when anybody can make decent photographs by pressing bulbs and turning handles, it is difficult to realize that this was something of an achievement on Kirk's part. His cameras were primitive. The paper on which his negatives were taken was sensitized by himself. He mixed his own chemicals. And he produced, even under the difficult conditions of travel in the tropics, such beautiful and durable photographs as those which have been selected to illustrate this volume. To this hobby—or rather this accomplishment, for it was more than a hobby—he was devoted all his life, eagerly availing himself of each successive improvement in technique and equipment, until in extreme old age he was forced to abandon it by the failure of his eyesight.

[1] J. Beddoe, *Memories of Eighty Years* (Bristol, 1910), 54–5.

THE RESIDENT STAFF OF THE ROYAL INFIRMARY, EDINBURGH, IN 1854

John Beddoe   John Kirk   George Hogarth Pringle   Patrick Heron Watson

Joseph Lister   David Christison   David Struthers

Having obtained his M.D. and in the same year the L.R.C.S. Edinburgh, Kirk was appointed to a resident physicianship at the Royal Infirmary. There were seven residents in all during that year (1854–5) and rarely can a similar group of fellow apprentices to the medical or any other profession have contained so much talent to be so diversely used. Two of the seven died young. The other five were Joseph Lister (born 1827), who, as the founder of antiseptic surgery, ranks among the greatest benefactors of mankind; John Beddoe (1826), one of the most eminent of British ethnologists; Patrick Heron Watson (1832), the finest surgeon in Scotland in his day; David Christison (1826), the archaeologist, well known among antiquaries for his researches on Scottish earthworks; and John Kirk. All lived long—Watson till 1907, Beddoe till 1911, Lister and Christison till 1912, and Kirk till 1922, his ninetieth year.

The professional training which the Edinburgh Infirmary provided for these talented young men was probably the best in Britain. Lister, loaded with London honours, already a Fellow of the Royal College of Surgeons, and a loyal *alumnus* of University College, had, none the less, deliberately come to Edinburgh to learn what more he could about the art of surgery from its greatest living practitioner, James Syme. And he was not disappointed. 'The Infirmary', he wrote to his father, 'is larger than I expected to find it. There are 200 *Surgical* beds and a large number in other departments. At University College Hospital there are about 60 Surgical Beds, so altogether a prospect appears to be opening of a very profitable stay here.' And as to his master, 'Syme is, I suppose, the first of British surgeons, and to observe the practice and hear the conversation of such a man is of the greatest possible advantage'. Nor was Syme's genius by any means the only light irradiating the medical world of Edinburgh at that time. Amongst others, there was Sir James Simpson, the famous gynaecologist and the discoverer of chloroform; Dr. (afterwards Sir Robert) Christison, David's father, the famous

professor of medical jurisprudence; and, not least, Dr. John
Brown, author of *Rab and his Friends*.[1]

To move in such a cultured circle, to live and work with
such gifted colleagues—and especially the brilliant young
Quaker from London—must have been in itself a notable
education for the son of the manse at Barry; and that last
year of Kirk's Edinburgh life was surely the most stimulating
and delightful of them all. 'An almost ideal life,' Beddoe
called it, looking back over more than half a century. 'Regular work and plenty of it, a moderate degree of discipline and
responsibility, the congenial society of one's equals, excellent
plain food with plenty of milk and cream—what better could
have been desired?' And of course it was not all work. There
were the drawing-rooms of Edinburgh: Lister found his wife
in Syme's. There were rambles among the encircling hills,
on one of which, while they were climbing Cat's Nick on
Salisbury Crags, Beddoe dislodged a great rock on Lister:
happily he half avoided it, and they carried him home on a
litter with a badly bruised thigh. And there were sprees, as
when Lister, Beddoe, Kirk, and Christison 'sallied out', as
the last-named recalls, 'and took down the wooden board,
about five feet long, of a quack doctor in Brown Square. . .
We carried it off to the Infirmary and solemnly burnt it.'[2]

3

Botany, as has been seen, was so powerful a rival to medicine in Kirk's heart that it is doubtful in any case whether he
would ever have settled quietly down to a doctor's practice;
but, as it happened, the normal current of his life at Edinburgh was interrupted, his interests diverted, and in the upshot his career determined by the impact and the challenge
of two great events in the outer world. The first of these was

[1] Sir R. J. Godlee, *Lord Lister* (London, 1919), 30, 33.
[2] Beddoe, *op. cit.*, 51, 55–6. D. Christison, in *Looking Back,
1907–1860*, by J. Chiene (Edinburgh, 2nd reprint, 1908).

the Crimean War. The winter of Kirk's residence at the
Infirmary was the glorious and terrible 'Crimean winter' of
Balaclava and Inkerman—one of the noblest pages in the
records of the British soldier, but certainly the most shame-
ful in the records of British military administration. As the
shocking story dribbled home of suffering and death at the
front, due solely to the lack of the most elementary requisites
for a campaign on foreign soil, public opinion grew more and
more inflamed at the criminal incompetence of the Horse
Guards and the War Office. It is indeed a striking instance
of British self-control in politics that nothing more violent
occurred than the fall of the scapegoat Aberdeen Government in the New Year. Meantime, the nation which had
made such a triumph of business in forty years of peace had
set itself to try to be businesslike in war: and among other
obvious measures was the enrolment of a volunteer 'Civil
Hospital Staff' to make good the insufficiency of the regular
military medical service. The volunteers were to undertake
hospital duties at the base, so as to relieve the regulars for
work at the front, and men were asked for who had held
or were holding hospital appointments. The response was
immediate. The applicants numbered, it is said, about seven
hundred. Fifty were selected. Among the fifty were Beddoe,
Christison, and Kirk.

Early in 1855, therefore, the three friends found themselves
in London, where they became themselves the victims of
official inefficiency. For weeks they kicked their heels while
the authorities blundered and wrangled. The friction and
delay were partly due, says Beddoe, 'to the indefinite divi-
sions and unpardonable jealousies between the various
official departments concerned, but a large part of the matter
was summed up in our minds thus: That things relating to
the War would never go on rightly till the War Office was
burnt down, and that if a few of the clerks were inside at the
time it would be ever so much the better'. At last, however,
the Civil Hospital Staff were actually on board the P. and O,

steamship *Candia*, which had been hired to transport a battery of artillery to the Crimea; and in due course they reached Constantinople. They were not warmly welcomed by the principal medical officer and his colleagues—partly, no doubt, because the pay and service-conditions of the volunteers were better than those of the regulars—and it was only by dint of vigorous remonstrances that the new-comers obtained better quarters than the small and filthy house at first assigned to them. Since the great base-hospitals were now in such good order, thanks to Florence Nightingale, that their services were not required there, they stayed idle at Scutari for some weeks, while their chief, Dr. Parkes, was seeking a site on which to erect the squared timber they had brought with them from England into a hospital of his own. During this interval the three friends obtained permission to visit Brusa. A recent earthquake—its last tremors were still felt at intervals while they were there—had sadly damaged the romantic old Turkish town: and all of its clustering minarets save one were ruined or decapitated. Thence they made the ascent of the snow-capped Bithynian Olympus. They camped for the night high up on a little 'alp', fringed with juniper bushes; and, as they sat at supper round their fire, they felt yet another sharp shock of earthquake. They had planned to return to Scutari by way of Isnik (Nicaea) and Isnikmid (Nicomedia); but as Christison sprained his ankle during the descent of the mountain so seriously that he had to be carried in a litter, they made straight for the little port of Ghemlik to catch a boat for Stambul. When they reached the port, exhausted and in darkness, a second and far more serious accident nearly happened. Beddoe was just about to walk off the end of the unlighted pier into deep water, in which, since he was heavily laden, he would certainly have sunk, when Kirk detected the danger and caught hold of him. They arrived at their quarters without further mishap; and to Kirk at least the expedition had been not merely a pleasant diversion but professionally fruitful; for he had brought back with him a valuable collection of plants from the sides of Mount Olympus.

And now at length a site was decided on—near Erenkevi on the Dardanelles, some ten miles below Chanak. It was a fine healthy site. Good water was available from neighbouring springs, and cleansing winds swept up and down the Straits. The hospital began quickly to grow out of the timber. Piers were built at the adjacent bays and connected by a tramway. Nurses arrived from England, shepherded by Miss Parkes. Soon, in fact, all that was needed was patients, of whom the wards were planned to hold 2,000. But there was now no great overflow from the reorganized regular hospitals, at any rate until the assault on Sebastopol swelled the stream of wounded; and according to Christison the staff at Erenkevi never had to handle more than about 600 at a time. For long periods, therefore, of the year they spent there Kirk and his friends again had little work to do. But it was by no means on that account a wasted year. They set themselves to learn Turkish, none more keenly than Kirk, who was to find it a useful acquisition in later life. And there was much else to be learned by any one who used his eyes in that derelict corner of Asia. Beddoe was busy with skull-shapes and pigmentation. Christison was in an archaeologist's paradise: the site of Troy lay, waiting for Schliemann, only fifteen miles away. And Kirk, always interested in his fellow human beings, obtained a knowledge not only of his neighbours' tongue but also of what was to prove still more useful to him in after years, their Moslem faith and customs.

There was plenty of lighter amusement. The friends made a habit of visiting the local coffee-shops and getting into conversation with the queer company that frequented them —Greek sailors and traders, stragglers from the neighbouring camp of Bashi-bazouks, who were reported to be so mutinous that arms were served out to the hospital staff in case of an attack, wandering Arabs, Jewish pedlers, and, once at least, a brigand from the hills. There was plenty of sport, too.

'Kirk was the only genuine sportsman or hunter among us,' Beddoe records, 'and he generally secured a big bustard or a wild swan or two, and some smaller game.' But if Kirk was the better shot, his companions were the better horsemen. Riding, however, was so obviously the best way to get about the country, and horses were so cheap, that Kirk was tempted, like his friends, to buy one. A fine white Arab was paraded before him by the crafty dealer and Kirk succumbed. Borrowing a military saddle and a snaffle, he clambered on to the animal's back. Instantly it sped off at a gallop, jumped clean over a heap of timber, and bolted along the beach. Kirk soon lost his seat and clung desperately to the beast's neck till, as the pace steadied, he was able with an effort to regain his saddle and even presently to control the direction of his flight. He returned from the ride, therefore, in a triumphant mood: and since the price was small—so small as to suggest that the horse was not the vendor's property—he bought it there and then. But he never mastered the equestrian art. He used often to complain that he could not understand the pleasure other people got from riding.[1]

Of several expeditions inland the most interesting was to Mount Ida. While Kirk and Beddoe were sitting at the coffee-house one day in the spring of 1856, they observed a big handsome Turk offering barley and coffee-mills for sale. 'Do you know who he is?' asked a bystander. 'No.' 'He's the most terrible brigand-chief in the country.' The chance was too good to be missed, and the two friends at once invited the new-comer to join them at coffee. 'Why', he asked them in the course of their talk, 'have you not visited Mount Ida?' 'Because of the brigands,' replied Kirk; 'they caught a Turkish officer only the other day and held him for ransom.' 'Oh! that's all right,' said the chief: 'he was no friend of ours. You will be quite safe. I will give the word.' 'But what about the Greek brigands?' 'They are pariahs. They would not dare to touch one of *my* friends.' So at the next oppor-

[1] Beddoe, *op. cit.*, chap. iv, and K. family records.

tunity they set off southwards to the upper valley of the Men-
derek, once the Scamander, and rode up it to the mountain
whence it flowed, and then on foot up steep slopes covered
with slippery pine-needles to the top. The scenery was ex-
quisite. 'It was the season of green leaves and clear rushing
brooks . . . and the country was all carpeted with flowers,
especially anemones, crimson, purple, and blue.' They returned by way of Troy; and presently they met their notorious friend again. They had greatly enjoyed the trip, they
told him, but they had seen no brigands. 'They saw you,'
said the chief; and proceeded to describe their movements
in detail, day by day, to show how well his men had obeyed
his orders to watch over the safety of their master's friends.
Does it spoil the story to add that the local Governor had
provided them with an escort of two Turkish soldiers—for
what they were worth?[1]

Meantime, in March 1856, the ill-conducted war had been
brought to an unsatisfactory end by the Treaty of Paris; and,
as the Erenkevi hospital gradually emptied itself of patients,
the staff began to drift away. By midsummer Kirk was back
in London, but not in Edinburgh. Once the thread of a young
man's career is broken it is not always easy—as this generation knows—to tie it up again; and Kirk was not yet ready
to bind himself for the rest of his days to the narrow routine
of professional life in Scotland. His first experience of foreign
lands had given him an itch for travel. He was to have more
than enough of it before long; but at the moment he was
longing to get back to the dust and sunshine of the East. He
had only seen its decadent Levantine fringe, but he was one
of those children of the West for whom the East possesses a
peculiar fascination. He had tasted, moreover, the delights
of scientific exploration. Already on Ida and Olympus he
had discovered many rare plants and one hitherto quite
unknown to European botanists, and he thirsted to probe
further into the botanical secrets of that Eastern corner of

[1] See preceding foot-note.

the Mediterranean world. When, therefore, he was offered the post of medical attendant for a tour abroad—a 'bear-leadership', Beddoe calls it—and found that his 'bear' was willing to go where he liked, he at once accepted it and set off again for the Levant. Thus in the autumn and winter of 1856 he wandered through Spain and Egypt, improving his acquaintance with Turks and Arabs and Moslem life, and examining and collecting plants and taking photographs. In the spring of 1857 he returned to England by way of Naples and Rome.[1]

And now Kirk could no longer postpone his entry on a profession. But what was it to be? His further experiences abroad had not made him any keener on a doctor's life. On the contrary, they had strengthened the claims of the alternative career. He had come back not only with a deepened enthusiasm for botany, but also with an enhanced reputation as a botanist. When, therefore, his old teacher and friend, Professor Balfour, seriously advised him to become a professional naturalist, he accepted the advice without demur. At the moment no post was vacant, but the untrammelled young bachelor could afford to wait; and in the meantime he devoted himself to a detailed study of the produce of his travels. He had already presented to Edinburgh University his collections of plants from Mounts Ida and Olympus; to these he now added his collection from Egypt; and descriptive papers on all three were published in due course in the records of the Edinburgh Botanical Society.[2] In the course of the summer he visited Kew and consulted Sir William Hooker, the Director, as to a strange species of *Muscari* he had found on Mount Ida; and then he settled down at home at Arbroath to study and arrange his fourth and last collection, the Syrian, of which he had offered a local contribution to Kew. 'The *Muscari*', he wrote soon after to Sir William, 'concerning which we took the liberty of consulting you when in London,

[1] See foot-note on p. 60 above.
[2] *Transactions of the Botanical Society of Edinburgh*, v. 162, vi. 22, 28.

has turned out to be quite a new species to which Dr. Playne Armitage and I have given the name of *M. latifolium.*' Thus opened a correspondence and a friendship which were to last for more than sixty years. A month later came the second letter of the long series, enclosing some photographs of Anatolian trees and announcing that the academic opening Kirk was awaiting had occurred. 'Dr. Balfour', he wrote, 'has advised me to apply for a situation in one of the Canadian Schools as teacher of Natural Science.'[1] It was, to be precise, a Chair of Natural History at Queen's University, Kingston; and since Kirk obtained strong recommendations both from Balfour and from Hooker, it seems probable that he would have been appointed. But before the matter was settled there intervened the second of the two great events in the outer world which diverted and determined Kirk's career.

4

In the course of 1857—as will appear in the next chapter —Livingstone's appeal to his countrymen to save and civilize the peoples of Central Africa had crystallized into a practical project. An expedition, equipped by the Government and led by Livingstone himself, was to ascend the Zambesi and prospect the unknown interior in order to ascertain its possibilities for British trade and settlement. Since the question of profitable crops, especially of cotton, was of vital importance, the staff of the Expedition was bound to include a well-qualified economic botanist. The Director of Kew was approached and promptly recommended Kirk, whose claims were vigorously supported by Professors Balfour and Wilson at Edinburgh. He was a peculiarly strong candidate. Young, very healthy, with some experience of travel already to his credit, he was qualified not only as a naturalist but also as a doctor. So Livingstone, with whom, as will be seen, the

[1] K. to Sir W. Hooker, 17. x. 57 and 12. xi. 57, printed in Kew *Bulletin of Miscellaneous Information*, 1922, No. 2, p. 50.

choice of his staff virtually lay, decided to kill two birds with one stone. He offered to nominate Kirk for the double post of botanist and medical officer to the Expedition. And Kirk, his *wanderlust* still unsatiated, all his enthusiasm for botany, all his scientific zest for new discoveries fired by the thought of exploring a vast and virgin world, at once accepted. It was a momentous decision for him. It meant that the best part of his life was to be spent, the best part of his life's work done, not in Britain but in Africa. It meant that, though his medical knowledge and training might often be of use to him and others, and though his love and practice of his favourite science might continue undiminished all his days, he was to become neither a professional doctor nor a professional botanist, but an officer of the Crown, a diplomatist, and, in the field of international and inter-racial politics he made his own, a statesman.

III

LIVINGSTONE'S LEAD

I

LIVINGSTONE had been as good as his word. 'I will go', he said in 1851; and so, in the following year, he went—up the old, long trail from Cape Town, past deserted Kolobeng, through the drought and the marshes, and so again to Makolololand. His first objective was clear in his mind. He had opened a 'highway into the north', as he called it, but he knew, of course, that his stream of trade and civilization could never flow, at any rate in his day, along that route. He must find a short cut to the sea. The two coasts were practically equidistant. The route from the east coast would have the advantage of the Zambesi, which might well be navigable for several hundred miles. The west coast, on the other hand, was far nearer to the ports of Europe, far better in that respect for the development of trade. He decided, therefore, to aim first at S. Paulo de Loanda. It was, as it happened, distinctly the more difficult alternative; and in any case the prospects of his success were meagre. He was assured of a good start, it is true, for Sekeletu, a youth of eighteen, to whom his sister had now resigned the burden of ruling the Makololo, quickly became even more attached to Livingstone than Sebetuane. He called him 'his new father'. He implored him to stay. But if he insisted on going, he would help him on his road. Promising to keep Livingstone's waggon in safe custody and with it his journals—to be of infinite value one day to the world—most of his books and such other goods as he was forced to leave behind, he provided him with the only vehicles of transport that could be used in the pathless country to the west—oxen and men. But beyond those first essentials, Livingstone's equipment for a long, hard, and dangerous journey was ludicrously inadequate. A little coffee, a few tusks, a tiny store of beads and cloth—that was all: no stores of food for himself or his carriers, nothing to purchase food with when that trifle of ivory and beads and cloth was exhausted, no bundles of gifts wherewith to placate a suspicious tribe or buy a passage through its country. Livingstone himself, moreover, was in wretched health, constantly suffering from fever and dysentery, often deeply depressed. But, as his letters and diary record, there was an unfailing tonic for his gloomiest moods in what he saw about him. 'The Slave Trade', he noted at this time, 'seems pushed into the very centre of the continent from both sides': and one day he witnessed the terrible spectacle of a slave-gang chained together on the march. In truth, however, Livingstone no longer needed inspiration or confirmation. It might well have seemed that the adventure on which he was embarking under such desperate conditions could only have one end; and indeed he recognized the risk and made provision for his death. But the thought of giving it up, of turning back, seems never to have crossed his mind. In a sense his mind was no longer his own. His life's idea had mastered it, obsessed it. The more he pondered that idea, the higher, the truer, the more divine it seemed, as new thoughts illumined and expanded it. 'The double influence of the spirit of commerce and the gospel of Christ', he commented a few days before the start, 'has given an impulse to the civilization of men. The circulation of ideas and commodities over the face of the earth and the discovery of the gold regions have given enhanced rapidity to commerce in other countries, and the diffusion of knowledge. But what for Africa? God will do something else for it . . .' And part of that 'something', Livingstone did not doubt it, was this journey of his to Loanda, whatever its end might be.[1]

So on November 11, 1853, the little party left Sekeletu's *kraal* at Linyanti and, winding up the River Leeba, plunged into the unknown *hinterland* of Portuguese Angola. The

[1] Blaikie, *Livingstone*, 116–27.

detailed story of the delays and hazards and sufferings that followed may be read in Livingstone's own record. Suffice it to say that, after months of sheer endurance, often so ill that he could not move or even think or speak, with nothing to carry him forward but his feet or an unsaddled ox, sometimes obstructed by unfriendly natives, especially in districts infected by the Slave Trade, but always winning through in the end with no gun fired or blood shed, at last, at the beginning of April, with his company of twenty-seven Makololo undiminished, Livingstone reached the outlying stations of the Portuguese. His troubles might not have ended there. Not unnaturally, the Portuguese were astonished at the emergence of this haggard scarecrow from the jungle, and at first, not unnaturally, they were also suspicious. A missionary? And a doctor? Impossible! A doctor of mathematics, perhaps, capable of making a secret survey of Portuguese territory. 'Come; tell us what rank you hold in the English army?' Very soon, however, the questioners were disarmed, their distrust quite dissipated; and though Livingstone saw little to praise in the administration of Angola, though some of the leading residents admitted and deplored to him the lack of all development, though the natives apparently remained in the same barbarism in which the white men had found them three centuries ago, he was deeply moved by the kindness and courtesy of the Portuguese officials. They took him into their houses. They gave him clothing for his rags. They stripped their gardens for the food he so badly needed. They eased, as best they could, the last stages of his journey. And so, a little stronger and much more presentable, he arrived on May 31, 1854, at S. Paulo de Loanda.[1]

The Portuguese head-quarters were as attentive as the out-stations. The Bishop of Angola, who was acting as Governor, sent his secretary to offer Livingstone the services

[1] Livingstone, *Missionary Travels and Researches in South Africa*, chaps. xiv–xix. Blaikie, *Livingstone*, chap. viii.

of the Government medical officer. And now, too, since he was within the orbit of the west coast patrol, Livingstone was among his fellow countrymen again. He struck up a close and lasting friendship with Mr. Gabriel, the British Commissioner for the suppression of the Trade; Commander Bedingfeld of H.M.S. *Pluto* and Captain Skene of H.M.S. *Philomel* invited him on board their ships; and he was offered, as a matter of course, a passage on the next cruiser that sailed for home. It was, he admits, a tempting offer, and any one else would have accepted it. After all, half his task had been achieved. He had survived the appalling risk. He was still alive. Why not take an interval of rest and sorely needed physical recuperation before returning to the toil and the danger? Livingstone's answer was simple. 'I could not allow my Makololo friends to attempt a return to their country without my assistance, now that I knew the difficulties of the journey and the hostility of the tribes living on the Portuguese frontier.' But that, he confesses, was not all. In conducting the Makololo back to their chief, he would also be getting on his way to the achievement of the second half of his task, 'to make a path to the east coast by means of the great river Zambesi'. To do that, and to do it at once, was his heart's desire. The westward entry to Mid-Africa had proved impracticable. He *must* find a better trade-route in the east. And so, though he was reduced to 'a mere skeleton' by a relapse of dysentery in August, he started out again on September 10, cheered on his path by the marvelling Portuguese. The local merchants, hopeful that more trade with the interior would come of it, gave him letters to their friends in Mozambique. Even those of them who had least reason to be kind to any Briton forgot their grudge. 'Though I spoke freely about the Slave Trade,' he wrote to his wife, 'the very gentlemen who have been engaged in it, and have been prevented by the ships from following it, and often lost much, treated me most kindly in their houses, and often accompanied me to the next place beyond them, bringing food for all in the way.' Nor was the Government less benign. The acting Governor seized the chance of establishing a link with Sekeletu, and sent the chief a colonel's uniform and a horse; and for Livingstone himself he did everything he could. He lent him twenty porters for the first part of the journey. He sent out orders that the district commandants were to give him every assistance. He furnished him with a recommendation to the officials in Portuguese East Africa. But, despite all these aids and a better supply of cloth and beads and food, the inward march proved even more arduous than the outward. Crossing a plain that was ankle-deep in water, Livingstone was obliged to sleep in the wet. The result was a severe attack of rheumatic fever. At another time he was nearly blinded by a blow in the eye from a branch of a tree as he rode on ox-back through a forest. But, as before, though feebly at times and very slowly, he pushed on and on. Barotseland was reached in July 1855, and Linyanti in September. Once again Livingstone had emerged from the wilderness alive, bringing all his twenty-seven faithful followers with him.[1]

Sekeletu, though he had heard nothing at all of his 'new father's' fate for nearly two years, seems never to have doubted that he would return. The waggon was there, its contents unharmed, and their savage guardian as friendly as ever. He mildly accepted Livingstone's rebukes for the raids he had indulged in while he was away; pressed him again to stay, or at least to postpone his going; and finally insisted on escorting him to the borders of his realm. So, on November 3, Livingstone left Linyanti and started eastwards along the course of the Zambesi. Some ten days later he beheld the grandest natural spectacle in Africa and named it the Victoria Falls. On an island at the very edge of the Falls, in soil moistened by the perpetual spray, he planted fruit-stones and coffee-seeds brought from Loanda. 'When the

[1] Livingstone, *Travels and Researches*, chaps. xx–xxv. Blaikie, *Livingstone*, 142–5.

garden was prepared', he gravely records, 'I cut my initials
on a tree and the date 1855. This was the only instance in
which I indulged in this piece of vanity.' A few days later
Sekeletu, having provided Livingstone this time with no less
than a hundred and fourteen porters and twelve oxen, not
to mention a store of butter and honey, turned homewards,
while Livingstone, swerving away from the Zambesi some
miles above the Falls, struck out north-eastwards over the
Batoka plateau. This line of march brought him in due
course to the Kafue River, along which he returned to the
Zambesi. After following its left bank, past the ruins of
Zumbo, for about 150 miles, he crossed it, and, a little farther
downstream, diverged again, south-eastwards this time; and
so avoiding the gorge of Kebrabasa by a detour, arrived at
Tete on March 3, 1856.[1]

With the outward appearance of this the most westerly
Portuguese settlement Livingstone was not impressed. He
observed about thirty European houses, rough, untidy, the
cement washed out from between the stones by rain. He
reckoned the number of regular Portuguese residents at
less than twenty, but there were some eighty Portuguese
soldiers temporarily sent upstream from Sena owing to
the sickness and mortality that were prevalent there. But,
as in Angola, the manners of the Portuguese were better
than their environment. Major Sicard, the commandant, set
himself to nurse and nourish his emaciated guest, insisted on
his staying till his strength was quite restored, and when, after
seven weeks, he felt fit to continue his journey, provided him
with a boat and with one of his lieutenants for escort. And
that was not all. As he was now taking to the river, Livingstone no longer needed his little regiment of Makololo porters.
What, then, was to happen to them? This time Livingstone
felt duty as well as inclination calling him back to England;
and without his leadership they dared not attempt the long

---

[1] Livingstone, *Travels and Researches*, chaps. xxvi–xxx. Blaikie,
Livingstone, 148–59.

march back to their own country. The problem was solved by Major Sicard. He gave them land at Tete on which they could raise crops for their maintenance and supplied them meanwhile with food, while Livingstone, his mind already made up to return to the Zambesi, promised them that, as soon as he could, he would come back and lead them home. A month later, on May 20, delayed by yet another bout of fever, Livingstone reached the sea at Quilimane, where he was again most hospitably received. 'One of the best men in the country', he called his host, Colonel Nunez. For six weeks he waited, 'in this unhealthy spot', for the chance of a passage home. At last, on July 12, H.M.S. *Frolic* put in and took him to Mauritius. On December 12 he landed 'once more in dear old England'.[1]

The intervening years have detracted nothing from the greatness of his achievement. Between September 1854 and May 1856 he had done what only one other white man had succeeded in doing through all the centuries of European contact with Mid-Africa. He had crossed the continent from sea to sea. Latter-day travellers, accustomed to speed about Africa by rail or motor-car or aeroplane, might imagine, at first thought, that twenty months were a long time to take over it. But in truth that length of time was the measure of Livingstone's extraordinary endurance. Most other explorers have only ventured on such tasks with substantial backing from scientific societies or newspapers or governments, with careful and costly preparation, and with companions of their own race. But Livingstone had no one to finance him; he depended for his miserable equipment on the generosity of an African chief; and he faced the fatigue and the danger, struggled on through those innumerable miles of wilderness, alone with his African followers. So little did his achievement owe to his times that he might have done very much the same thing in very much the same way in the early days of the

---

[1] Livingstone, *Travels and Researches*, chaps. xxxi–xxxii. Blaikie, *Livingstone*, 159–65.

Portuguese Empire. But if Livingstone himself recognized the importance of it, he did not exaggerate it, nor ascribe it to his own unaided power. It was surely God's doing, and it was only the first small part of what had yet to be done. 'I think I see the operation of the Unseen Hand in all this, and I humbly hope it will still guide me to do good in my day and generation in Africa.' And again: 'The end of the geographical feat is only the beginning of the enterprise.' [1]

2

It was only a beginning; and Livingstone was well aware that, though he might still have a great part to play himself, the enterprise could only be carried through with the active support of public opinion. The British people must share his vision; the business world must bestir itself; traders, missionaries, settlers, must presently set out along the pathway he had opened. His immediate task, therefore, was to capture the attention of his countrymen, impress the importance of his new discoveries on their minds, and appeal once more to their moral and material instincts. And for this his exploit had given him the best possible start. The news of it had thrilled the country. With dramatic suddenness public interest switched back to Africa, and it was a far keener and more general interest now than at the time of the Niger Expedition. When Livingstone arrived in London, he found himself the hero of the day. He was given an enthusiastic welcome by the Royal Geographical Society, with its President, Sir Roderick Murchison, in the chair, and by his own L.M.S., presided over by Lord Shaftesbury; he was summoned to an interview with the Prince Consort 'in presence of some of the younger members of the Royal Family'; and from all parts of the country public tributes and invitations came pouring in. For some months, however, he was fully occupied with the task of writing an account of his travels; and, except

[1] Blaikie, *Livingstone*, 159, 163.

for the bestowal of the freedom of the City of London in May, he remained more or less in retirement till the autumn. In August his triumphal progress began with a lecture to the British Association, then meeting in Dublin. In September he addressed the Manchester Chamber of Commerce, and astonished and excited those hard-headed men of business by explaining that the Zambesi country, which they had supposed to be a waste of swamp and sand, abounded in the raw material of British industries—in oils and fibres and sugar, and especially in cotton. In his native land a stream of honours broke on him. At Glasgow, where he had studied medicine and had already received from the University an honorary degree, he was presented with the freedom of the city, with an honorary fellowship, rarely bestowed, of the Faculty of Physicians and Surgeons, and with a public testimonial of £3,000, besides addresses and meetings of welcome from the United Presbyterians and the Scottish Cotton-Spinners' Trade Union. At Edinburgh he was also made a freeman and spoke at two great public gatherings. Then, 'dead tired', as he confessed to Murchison, of 'public spouting', he visited Leeds, Liverpool, and Birmingham. In November he had a great reception at Oxford. 'They made me', he wrote to a friend, 'a D.C.L. There!!' At Cambridge, a few weeks later, where he spoke to crowded audiences in the Senate House and the Town Hall, the enthusiasm was even greater. On the scientific side, the culminating honour was his election to the Royal Society.

Livingstone, in fact, had become a great national figure. He had gripped the imagination of his countrymen as few other men in any age have gripped it. Every one was thinking and talking and reading about him. A first edition of 12,000 copies of *Missionary Travels and Researches in South Africa* was sold out before publication. The newspapers were full of him. Nor was the autumn of 1857 one of those placid interludes in the course of public affairs when any novelty excites attention. The Crimean War had been quickly

followed by war in China; and, a few months after Livingstone's return to England, Palmerston had fought and won
a general election mainly on the question of foreign policy.
About the same time the first tidings had arrived of the outbreak of the Indian Mutiny; and while Livingstone was
pursuing his great campaign in the north the tragic drama
which stirred the emotions of the British people more deeply
than any other great event since Trafalgar and Waterloo was
fast coming to its climax. That autumn Delhi fell and Luck-
now was relieved. It is a signal proof of Livingstone's power
that he could command so much attention in those days of
suspense and ferment, that he could win a place in the public
interest and admiration beside Nicholson and Lawrence and
Havelock. And it was, in its way, a repetition of history.
The last great swing of public opinion from apathy to interest
as regards the relations of Britain with the backward peoples
of the world had brought the destinies of Asia and Africa
into conjunction. The idea of a positive responsibility vested
in the British people for the good government of India, the
idea of a trust exercised by the strong for the weak, had had
their birth in the scandals in Bengal; but hardly were they
born when they were applied to Africans as well as Asiatics.
It was within a few months of the opening of Warren Hastings'
impeachment in 1788 that Wilberforce made his first speech
for the abolition of the Slave Trade. So now, in 1857, while
the British people were being forced by the shock of the
Indian Mutiny to reconsider their relations with Asia and to
initiate a new era of Indian government, Livingstone was
starting a new era of interest and action in Africa.

He was soon assured of all the practical support he needed.
It was, indeed, almost taken for granted that the work he
had begun in Africa must be continued and that he could not
be allowed to continue it alone. It seemed out of the question
that he should be exposed again to all the hardships and
dangers of his last heroic journey, a solitary Scotsman in the
heart of the Tropics, without any companions of his own

race, without any one to help him not merely in simply keeping alive and moving on, but in all the varied scientific tasks of exploration, the countless observations of position and of climate, the botanical and zoological notes and collections, the keeping of records and the making of maps and sketches. Clearly, too, the results would be far more fruitful if the exploration were conducted by a party of men and not one man only, however superhuman he had proved himself to be. Nor must the material resources, the equipment, the means of transport, the supplies, depend this time on voluntary or missionary effort. It was the nation's business now. If the next step was a further examination of the Zambesi route with a view to a possible settlement in the interior—and this was what Livingstone advised—then the Government should organize and equip a 'Zambesi Expedition' and set Livingstone at its head. Only so could he be furnished with an instrument, so to speak, that was worthy of his work and of the public enthusiasm he had aroused.

Political memories are notoriously short; but it would scarcely have been surprising if the Government, so soon after the tragic precedent of 1841, had hesitated to run the risk of burning its fingers in the same fire. The *débâcle* on the Niger, it is true, had not cooled for long the zest for discovery. Apart from private enterprise in the same field, the Government had dispatched a second expedition to the Niger in 1854, with Dr. W. B. Baikie in command, and in this same year, 1857, was dispatching a third, again under Baikie. It was with the full approval of Government, moreover, that Richard Burton and J. H. Speke had been commissioned by the Royal Geographical Society to penetrate Central Africa from the Zanzibar coast. They were now, as it happened, on the point of discovering Lakes Tanganyika and Victoria Nyanza. All those expeditions, however, were exploratory and little else. They were not associated with schemes of settlement and civilization. They excited small

public attention. But Livingstone was demanding a great
deal more than exploration. The Zambesi Expedition, it was
soon evident, was to be fashioned in range and objective on
the disastrous model of 1841. And it is one more proof,
perhaps, of Livingstone's mesmeric influence that the proposal
should have been so warmly and so quickly welcomed in
ministerial circles. The initiative, of course, was unofficial—
the first steps appear to have been taken at the Dublin
meeting of the British Association—but, as soon as it was
laid before Lord Clarendon, his interest and his sympathy
were instantly engaged. He sent for Livingstone, discussed
with him the precise field and purpose of his scheme, and
then, after consultation with the Admiralty, promptly presented a favourable report to the Cabinet. Shortly before
Parliament rose for the Christmas holidays, the Chancellor
of the Exchequer, Sir George Cornewall Lewis, announced in
the House of Commons his intention to spend £5,000 from
the civil contingencies fund on a Government Expedition to
explore the Zambesi valley under Livingstone's command.
'It is stated', he said, 'that such an exploration might lead
to important commercial consequences and that it is a district
which is well fitted, among other things, for the cultivation
of cotton.' It was hoped that a start would be made early
in the following year.[1]

3

Though the Zambesi Expedition was a Government
Expedition, its organization was more Livingstone's work
than Government's. The Foreign Office was formally in
charge of it, as of the Niger Expeditions. The technical side
was dealt with at the Admiralty, where Captain Washington,
who had a hand in the Expedition of 1841, was still at his
post, still an enthusiast for African exploration, and one of
Livingstone's heartiest admirers. No task could have been

---

[1] Blaikie, *Livingstone*, 166–94. *Hansard*, series III, vol. cxlviii
(1857/8), p. 558.

more to his taste, and he had soon drawn up a plan on a generous scale, with a large staff of naval officers and everything else to match—the sort of plan that the Navy was accustomed to, thoroughly watertight and efficient and rather expensive. But Livingstone was altogether averse to such an elaborate scheme; and Lord Clarendon put himself entirely in Livingstone's hands. 'Just come here', he said to him, 'and tell me what you want, and I will give it you.' And Livingstone, who had doubtless been evolving his own ideas about the Expedition for some months past, lost no time. By the end of the first week of the new year he had set down in a memorandum for Lord Clarendon's information a definite plan of operations and had decided not merely what should be the numbers and qualifications of the *personnel*, but, in all but one or two cases, who the actual men should be. The 'assistants' he would require, said the memorandum, would be '1*st*. A Naval Officer. 2*nd*. A practical mining geologist. 3*rd*. An economic botanist. 4*th*. A general assistant and moral agent. 5*th*. An artist combining the duties of storekeeper. 6*th*. A ship engineer. 7*th*. Ten Kroomen.'

'The persons [he continues] with whom I should like to be associated and with whose characters I am well acquainted through the recommendations of friends and by personal examination are:

1st. Commander Norman Bedingfeld, R.N., as the Naval Officer. His well-known services on the coasts and in the rivers of Africa render him peculiarly elegible for the purposes of this Expedition, and the fact of his volunteering to serve under me from a simple love of the enterprise in which we are to be engaged makes me entertain very sanguine anticipations of his efficiency. I may add that he could effect a rapid survey of the river and also make some observations of terrestrial magnetism.

2nd. Mr. Richard Thornton of the Government School of Mines who is strongly supported by Sir Roderick Murchison.

3rd. Dr. John Kirk who is as strongly recommended by Sir William and Dr. Hooker and also by Professors Balfour and Wilson of Edinburgh on account of his knowledge of economic botany and medical skill. He has travelled in the East and had some medical practice in one of the Crimean hospitals.

4th. Mr. Charles Livingstone as general assistant. He understands cotton and the machinery used in its preparation. He has travelled much, and having great experience is fully qualified to act as moral agent. I place entire reliance on his temper and judgment in dealing with the natives during temporary absences of the other members from the central staff.

5th. In respect to the person who is to combine the duties of artist and storekeeper, I have not yet fully made up my mind as to the best individual, though I am disposed to suggest the name of Mr. T. Baines of the late North Australian Expedition.

6th. A ship engineer having the requisite qualifications has not yet presented himself, but I have no doubt that a suitable one will soon be found.[1]

The plan of operations follows. The Expedition is to pass rapidly through the unhealthy area of the Lower Zambesi, deposit its heavy baggage at Tete, visit the leading native chiefs above Tete, and proceed to the Kebrabasa Rapids to discover whether the launch would be able to steam up there when the river is high. An iron house, to be taken out in sections, is then to be erected on a suitable site above the confluence of the Zambesi and the Kafue to serve as a central depot. This depot will be of great importance 'for depositing collections and its moral influence on the public mind of the country'. Further exploration is then to be undertaken towards the source of the Zambesi and up the rivers flowing into it from the north, 'in order to ascertain whether the network of waters reported by natives exists or not'. Some members of the Expedition are always to be left in charge of the central depot, where they will make experiments in agriculture and give religious instruction to the natives. At

[1] F.O. 63/842 (H. Lloyd, President of British Association, to Clarendon, 14. xii. 57; Admiralty to Clarendon, 21. xii. 57; Treasury to Clarendon, 1. i. 58; Livingstone's memo, 7. i. 58). Blaikie, *Livingstone*, 193–6.

the end of the second year, Livingstone will await the Government's orders, 'the members of the Expedition having then the option of returning to England'.

'This seems a very estimable plan', noted Lord Clarendon on this document; and he at once requested Livingstone to reproduce it in a more detailed form to serve as the Foreign Secretary's official Instructions to the Commander of the Expedition. So Livingstone prepared a draft of his own Instructions, submitted it to Lord Clarendon, and was duly presented with an almost *verbatim* copy of it. It was understood that he would himself draw up the consequential Instructions for the members of the Expedition; and since these repeated the greater part of the original document and Kirk's copy will presently be printed in full, it is enough to say here that, while proposing the same programme as that of Livingstone's previous memorandum, the Instructions by no means tied his hands. 'You are yourself so experienced a traveller in these regions', runs the fourth paragraph, 'that it is hardly necessary to do more than state the general objects of the Expedition and leave it to you to carry them out in the manner most conducive to these results.' Two further points may be noted. The document begins with an enumeration of the members of the Expedition, and then at once a significantly early reference is made to the provision of a paddle-steamer with a two-foot draft of water. There is a further allusion to this vital question of river-transport later on. 'If the steam-launch prove serviceable, of which there is little doubt, you will be able to proceed at 30 miles a day'—and so rapidly escape from the lower reaches of the Zambesi. The other point is concerned with Livingstone's powers of command. 'Should any individual refuse to comply with your reasonable directions, you are fully authorized to send him home at the first opportunity, and his salary will cease from the day you find it necessary to discharge him.'[1]

[1] F.O. 63/842 (Draft Instructions, 20. ii. 58).

Meanwhile the material equipment of the Expedition had been no less promptly taken in hand. Far the most important item, it has already been hinted, was the little paddle-launch. It was this, in fact, more than anything else, that was to render the Expedition more effective than Livingstone's solitary and infinitely slow wanderings in the past. Unless the launch could navigate the shallow Zambesi and its main tributaries at a good speed, not only would the health of the Expedition be endangered at the outset, but, cumbered as it necessarily would be by its stores, its instruments, and its materials for trade, the chances of making any great progress into the vast interior of Africa or of achieving any great results within a reasonable time would be gravely impaired. It was soon evident that a boat would have to be specially built to meet the special need; and Livingstone was not long in finding just the man to build it. Mr. Laird was a Scottish man of business. He professed an ardent zeal for the philanthropic objects of the Expedition. He was prepared to build exactly the craft required. And he would charge only £1,200. So, the design and the cost having been submitted to the Admiralty and approved, the contract was signed; and in due course, the launch, christened *Ma Robert* (the native name for Mrs. Livingstone, derived in native fashion from that of her eldest son), successfully underwent its trials, in the presence of Captain Bedingfeld, but not of Mr. G. Rae, who had been appointed as the Expedition's engineer. It was then split up into three sections to await shipment. The rest of the equipment was an easy matter—preserved foods, medicines, instruments, and many rolls of cloth for gifts to chiefs and barter with their tribesmen. All the expenditure involved, together with the salaries and the passage-money, was at last neatly fitted within the compass of £5,000. As to salaries, Livingstone, as will shortly appear, was to figure separately on the Foreign Office list; Bedingfeld was to receive £450 (in addition to his naval half-pay of £150); Kirk, Thornton, and Charles Livingstone £350; Baines and

Rae £200. Baines promptly protested that his salary on his Australian Expedition had been £300, and this sum was accordingly allotted him. Livingstone also protested, but much later, after the Expedition had already sailed; and when Lord Malmesbury, who had meantime succeeded Lord Clarendon at the Foreign Office, received the protest, he agreed that the sum was 'far too small' and expressed a pious hope that it might be increased at some convenient date.[1]

Such, in brief, was the organization of the Zambesi Expedition. It was a remarkable achievement if only in point of speed. The Government had been as keen as the public. The Foreign Office, the Admiralty, and the Treasury had demonstrated that inter-departmental co-operation could at need be swift and efficient. Lord Clarendon and Captain Washington had given their closest personal attention to the business. Two or three months were surely a record time for the improvisation—programme, *personnel*, equipment—of any such Government operation, and the officials concerned deserve their meed of praise. But it may be said again that their main task was to confirm and carry out some one else's decisions. It was Livingstone who made the Expedition. And inevitably so. It was inevitable, to begin with, and it was perfectly right, that Livingstone should have been asked to lead it. The Expedition *was* Livingstone. The very idea of it had sprung from his own recent exploits and had been fostered by his own appeal to the country. Its *raison d'être* was simply to enable him to continue his career as an African explorer, to repeat with the better status and backing of a Government agent what he had achieved as a missionary, to do with others' companionship and help what he had already done alone. It was, in fact, impossible to conceive of the Expedition with any other leader. None the less, it is worth remembering that, though Livingstone had already proved himself to possess a wonderful gift for managing

[1] F.O. 63/842 (L. to Malmesbury, 22. iii. 58).

Africans, he had had no experience of managing Englishmen; and it was certainly a novelty, an experiment, and a tribute in itself to Livingstone's prestige, to appoint as commander of an official Expedition a man, even a great man, who had never commanded. It seems clear that Livingstone himself was well aware of this new and difficult aspect of his work and was a little uneasy about it. Commenting on his rejection of the Admiralty scheme, his biographer remarks that, 'instead of having to press Captain Washington, he had to restrain him. . . . All was to be plain and practical; nothing was wished for ornament or show.' One may be permitted to suggest that Captain Washington's ideas were also plain and practical and not for ornament or show, and that Livingstone's dislike of them was more probably due to a not unnatural hesitation at the prospect of leading a large body of Englishmen, under his absolute command, into the unknown heart of Africa. Men who have attained to greatness in particular fields have sometimes been infected with a touch of megalomania and imagined themselves capable of anything. But Livingstone was not that kind of great man. He was very self-confident, but also very modest. He knew that he could do again what he had done already. He knew that he could make his way through Africa alone; and there were moments, one suspects, when he wished he was setting out alone once more. Self-made and self-reliant, he had always done things himself in his own way. Could he get others to do them as they should be done? Lacking in social gifts, could he work happily and smoothly with his colleagues? It would be difficult in any case on the banks of the Zambesi, where, as he knew, the climate and the fever might set all men's nerves on edge; but it would be twice as difficult when he was their official master, bound to give orders and to get them obeyed. And if the party were all at sixes and sevens, still more if there was any actual insubordination, not their success merely, but their safety, might be imperilled. In the Makololo country, if they got as far, there would be little danger; but elsewhere they would be surrounded by strange, suspicious, and possibly hostile natives; and one irresponsible member of the Expedition might be the death of all.

It was reflections such as these—it cannot be doubted—that mainly influenced Livingstone in keeping the *personnel* of the Expedition as small as possible. But the fewer they were, the more essential it was that each one of them should be of good calibre; and it is a little surprising, therefore, that they should have been so quickly, almost hastily, selected. Two of them, however, Kirk and Thornton, were strongly recommended to him by responsible authorities. With Bedingfeld Livingstone had become acquainted at Loanda; and his appointment shows that he was fully trusted by Captain Washington. And, if Baines' sponsors were not so personal—he was recommended by the Royal Geographical Society—his record seemed to mark him out as exactly the right man for the post. Born in 1822, he had been tempted out to Cape Colony, in his twentieth year, by love of travel, and had accompanied the British troops as official artist in the Kaffir War of 1848–51. In the same role he had joined Gregory's Australian Expedition in 1855. All four, indeed, and doubtless Rae as well, seemed as good men for their work as were likely to be obtainable. Nevertheless, the fact remains that, except for his brief meeting with Bedingfeld four years earlier, their commander had no personal knowledge of them. Livingstone only knew one member of his Expedition, and that was his own brother. Charles, now 36, was David's junior by eight years. He had emigrated to the United States in 1840, and in 1847 he had entered the Union Theological College at New York. Having qualified for the ministry, he had obtained a pastoral charge in New York State; and it was a mere chance that he happened to be home on leave of absence in 1857. It is remarkable that his elder brother should have succeeded in persuading him to desert his family and his flock and embark on an uncertain adventure in the heart of Africa. It is still more remarkable that of the six men chosen the only one whom Livingstone really knew—or at least had known in earlier years—proved, as will appear, his most mistaken choice.[1]

4

There was another, and by no means unimportant, side to the preparation of the Zambesi Expedition. The barest international courtesy required that the Portuguese Government should be informed of the project; for the Expedition —an official Expedition—was proposing to penetrate territory which the Portuguese claimed to possess, with the purpose of establishing British trade on a river-system the navigation and commerce of which the Portuguese claimed to control. It was essential, too, that the Portuguese should not take unnecessary alarm. They must be told that the Expedition would only operate in the *hinterland* beyond the Portuguese colonial frontier—wherever that was—and that it would only ask for permission to pass and transmit its stores through Portuguese territory. Every effort, in fact, must be made to obtain the Portuguese Government's sympathy and support. Orders from Lisbon could do much to assist the Expedition. Hints from Lisbon could do more to obstruct it. At an early stage, therefore, Lord Clarendon took in hand the task of negotiation with the Portuguese Ministry, or, rather, he set Livingstone's hand to it. Nor was this as undiplomatic as it might seem in the light of after events. For, though Livingstone had remarked on the backwardness of the Portuguese provinces in his book, he had only expressed opinions which were shared by the Portuguese officials on the spot. And of the help those officials had given him he had written in the most appreciative terms. He seems, indeed, during that first Zambesi journey, to have had no suspicion that the officials were implicated in the Slave Trade. He had been not a little impressed, moreover, by recent evidence

[1] Blaikie, *Livingstone*, 196. *D.N.B.*, 'Thomas Baines', 'Charles Livingstone'.

of the sincerity with which the Portuguese Government was trying to combat the evil. In the first place it had agreed, at the risk of displeasing the French, to regard the Free Labour Emigration System[1] as tantamount to a slave trade; and in 1855 and again in 1856 it had issued *portarias* directing that the emigration of negroes under that system from Portuguese territory should be prohibited. Nor had it left the matter there. On receipt of information, mainly from British sources, that the prohibition had not been put into effect, in the summer of this very year (1857) it summarily dismissed Governor-General Menezes and sent out Colonel J. d'Almeida in his place, 'for the express purpose of enforcing that prohibition and of otherwise suppressing the Slave Trade'. D'Almeida at once convinced the British consul at Mozambique of the honesty of his intentions, and within three weeks of his arrival he had proved it by so drastic an interference with the Free Labour Emigration System as to cause a first-rate 'international incident' in Europe.[2] About the same time the Governor of Inhambane was also dismissed for complicity in the Trade. And that was not all. The campaign for the abolition of Slavery in the Portuguese colonies which the Viscount Sá de Bandeira had opened by the appointment of a commission in 1848,[3] had been nearly brought to its conclusion. In the course of 1856 a series of laws had been enacted, liberating slaves belonging to the State or Municipal Chambers or Churches or charitable institutions in the colonies, liberating also any slaves entering Portugal or Madeira or the Azores, declaring that all children born of female slaves henceforth would be free, and abolishing slavery outright in certain districts of certain colonies. Only the final step remained. In 1858 it was enacted that Slavery would cease to exist altogether throughout the Portuguese colonies at the end of twenty years. Finally, the Lisbon Government had made at any rate one little breach in its

---

[1] See pp. 24–27 above.　　　　[2] See p. 266 below.
[3] See p. 20 above.

traditional policy of commercial monopoly. It had permitted foreign trade at two or three of its African ports.[1]

This was a notable record, and it convinced Livingstone that King Pedro V was as enlightened as a cousin of the Prince Consort ought to be and that his ministers were genuine enemies of Slavery and all its works. Livingstone was well acquainted, too, with the Portuguese Ambassador in London, who professed the warmest admiration for himself and his designs; and when the Count de Livadio went home for a time in 1857 he was strongly tempted to follow him to Portugal, and, armed with an introduction from the Prince Consort to the King, to conduct the negotiations direct and in person. Owing, however, to a serious outbreak of yellow fever in Lisbon and the risk of indefinite delay this project was abandoned, and overtures were begun on paper and through the normal diplomatic channels. A memorandum drafted by Livingstone was transmitted through the Foreign Office to Mr. Howard, the British Minister at Lisbon. In the Livingstone manner it went straight to the root of the question. In his eyes the primary purpose of the Expedition was to prepare the way for the destruction of the Slave Trade. That was the first, the immediate objective of all its intended operations—exploration, settlement, commerce. When that was attained, the further process of civilization would be simple and straightforward. Livingstone's memorandum, therefore, forced that issue at once to the front. It baldly declared that the prospects of development and prosperity in Portuguese East Africa were blighted by the Slave Trade and it boldly suggested that Portugal and Britain should act in concert to suppress it. ' I venture to propose a combined effort of these ancient allies to establish new stations on the higher portions of the Zambesi for the purpose of developing the rich revenues of the country.' It insisted frankly, more-over, on the need for free trade. To give full effect to the

---

[1] *State Papers*, vol. 47, pp. 905–11; vol. 49, pp. 603, 611, 1063. L. McLeod, *Travels in Eastern Africa*, vol. ii, chap. i.

policy of the two Governments, 'the river ought to be declared a free pathway for all nations'. Howard was also furnished with all available details as to the size and programme of the Expedition and instructed to express the fullest confidence in the willingness of the Portuguese Government to do everything in its power to assist.[1]

The Portuguese ministers had been uneasily awaiting some communication of this kind from London. And their uneasiness was intelligible. They were aware, though they could scarcely be expected to admit it, that Portuguese East Africa had scarcely proved a model of colonial enterprise. They were also aware that at any considerable distance from the coast the very fact of Portuguese sovereignty might be seriously questioned. On paper, no doubt, their position was strong enough. In a protocol of 1847, renewed in 1850, Portugal had secured, as a condition for permitting British warships to enter the coastal waters of Mozambique in order to suppress the Slave Trade, a definite engagement on Great Britain's part 'not to call in question the claim of Portugal to any territories on the eastern coast of Africa'. Moreover, though the extent of those territories inland had never been officially defined, the limits north and south had been fixed in the Anglo-Portuguese Convention of 1817—in connexion, again, with a settlement of the Slave Trade question—as 'the territory included between Cape Delgado and the Bay of Laurenzo Marques'. Furthermore, over the colony as a whole, a *façade* of government had been erected. There was not only a Governor-General at Mozambique, there were also Governors, no less, at Quilimane, Tete, Inhambane, Ibo, and elsewhere; there were minor Portuguese officials at any place where there were Portuguese at all. But did all this constitute the sort of 'occupation' which would be recognized in international law? Certainly all the native races of the country had never formally acknowledged Portuguese rule. It was

---

[1] Blaikie, *Livingstone*, 194–5. F.O. 63/842 (L.'s memo, 1. xii. 57; Clarendon to Howard, 4. i. 58).

reported that one migrant Zulu tribe, known as the Landeens, levied a regular tribute along the right bank of the Zambesi not only from weaker native tribes but from the Portuguese themselves; and on the left bank and northwards there were constant native wars. The first irruption, therefore, of a wandering British missionary into this particular area must have caused some little disquiet in official circles; and when Livingstone returned to England and opened his campaign the disquiet must have deepened. He was not, it seemed, merely an other-worldly evangelist, intent on nothing but conversions. He was a colonial politican, full of ideas about trade and settlement; and he was making a public scandal of the Slave Trade. Apparently, too, he had caught the attention of the British public; and, once the British public got excited about a question of that particular kind, it might 'run amok'. No one in the maritime states of Europe had forgotten how, in her last humanitarian spasm over the West-coast Slave Trade, Britain had not merely abolished her own share in it but morally compelled all her partners on the Continent to follow her example. True, Livingstone could not charge the Portuguese Government with complicity in the Trade. The files at the Foreign Office bulged with proofs of the efforts it had made to prevent the violation of its treaty faith. But no one knew better than the Viscount Sá de Bandeira how ineffective those efforts had been. *Portaria* after *portaria* had been issued, Governor after Governor dismissed; and still the Trade, in one form or another, continued to exist. And this unpleasant fact the impetuous explorer was not only certain to find out but certain also to make trouble over. A new convulsion of the British conscience might easily result in focusing the attention of all Europe on Portuguese East Africa. Its stagnant condition would be disclosed. Evidence of maladministration might be brought to light and canvassed by jealous critics. The facts about the failure to suppress the Slave Trade would fit into their place. An attempt might even be made, in the last resort, to deprive Portugal of the colonies she cherished so deeply if only as the last concrete symbol of her imperial past . . . Too much, perhaps, could be made of it; but Portuguese ministers need not have been very conscience-stricken nor very faint-hearted to dread the passionate philanthropy of Britain, once it was on fire—they had felt its heat before— nor need they have been over-cynical to suspect that British philanthropy might be more fierce and predatory than it had ever been if it were now united with British commercial and colonial schemes and interests. A British trading settlement, a British colony—it was an old story. What limits would be set to it? How far would the claims of a weaker nation be respected? [1]

The Portuguese, in fact, were in a dilemma from which there was no clear way of escape. The British Government had to be permitted, it could scarcely be forbidden, to send its Expedition up the Zambesi. Its transit through the Portuguese preserves would have inevitable results. The realities of the Portuguese occupation of all that area would be more closely observed. Further evidence would be collected about the Slave Trade. The ultimate effect on British public opinion might be very grave. But, if these dangers could not be avoided, something at least could be done to forestall them. If the worst came to the worst, it would be some years before the international question could become acute; and in the meantime the Portuguese Government must quietly maintain its claims and strengthen them, so that, when the need came, it could take a firm stand on the simple, inexpugnable rights of territorial sovereignty. And, after all, it was and would be much easier to be firm with Britain than with any other of the Great Powers. The idea of the ancient alliance had obtained a curiously deep hold on British sentiment. Because both parties were sea-

---

[1] Protocols of 1847 and 1850. *British and Foreign State Papers*, vol. 36, p. 589; vol. 40, p. 242. Convention of 1817. Hertslet, *Map of Africa by Treaty*, p. 683.

faring peoples with imperial traditions? Because one was now so strong and the other so weak? Because of some romantic suggestion of fealty long unbroken? Or merely because the alliance was so old? No matter: it was an invaluable asset for Portuguese diplomacy. To make the most of it, to be very cordial, yet honourably independent, to deal with developments as they arose and never to yield any vital point—that was the strategy adopted at Lisbon. In the end it proved completely successful.

The assurances which Lord Clarendon had counted on were thus at once forthcoming. The Portuguese ministers promised to give the Expedition all possible support and to send instructions to that effect to Africa, and a *portaria* was promptly furnished, commanding the Governor-General of Mozambique and the Governors of Quilimane and Tete in the King's name to render every assistance to Dr. Livingstone and his companions. At the same time the desire was expressed that some Portuguese might accompany the Expedition. It was doubtless realized in Lisbon that this suggestion was almost bound to be rejected, if only for the difficulties it would raise over the question of Livingstone's authority, and rejected it was at once, with due politeness. But it had been an adroit move. Was it not a step towards that 'combined effort' for which Livingstone himself had pleaded? Undoubtedly the Portuguese had begun their little diplomatic campaign with a tactical success; and on the next issue their attitude stiffened. Lord Clarendon had decided that Livingstone should be appointed to the office of British consul at Quilimane, Sena, and Tete. Writing to inform the Treasury and to propose a salary of £500 a year—the sum paid to the consul at Mozambique—he suggested that such an appointment would enable Livingstone to obtain 'more respect and attention from the Portuguese authorities'. The Queen's Commission was accordingly dispatched to Lisbon to receive the Portuguese *exequator*; but, soon after, a telegram in code arrived from Howard reporting that 'the

Portuguese Government are quite ready to give the *exequator* for Livingstone for Quilimane, which is open to foreign commerce, but not for Sena and Tete, which are not so yet' and asking for another Commission to be sent for Quilimane only. Livingstone, who was at once informed of the hitch, had no doubt as to its meaning. 'In reference to the refusal of the Portuguese Government to recognize the right of free intercourse up the Zambesi,' he wrote to the Foreign Office, 'I beg to suggest that it is very undesirable to admit the claim as it involves the admission of their power over the independent tribes on its banks.' And he suggested that no town or area should be specified in his Commission, but that he should be accredited to Sekeletu, the chief of the Makololo, and to other free tribes beyond the limits of Portuguese East Africa. With the latter suggestion Lord Clarendon concurred; and Livingstone was entrusted with a letter to Sekeletu, based again on his own draft, thanking him in the Queen's name for his previous assistance to her servant, Dr. Livingstone, condemning the Slave Trade, and asking him to keep 'God's highway', the Zambesi, open to the free traffic of all peoples. At the same time Lord Clarendon thought it advisable to maintain the consular appointment, limited to Quilimane, and the new Commission was dispatched to Lisbon, not without a sharp expression, in obedience to Livingstone's protest, of 'the disappointment of Her Majesty's Government on learning that the Portuguese Government should appear desirous to restrict commerce in regions about to be visited by Dr. Livingstone instead of taking this opportunity to encourage and extend it'.[1]

The Portuguese, it was evident, in anticipation of the possible results of the Expedition, had begun to dig themselves in. The declaration that foreign trade was only permitted at the mouth of the Zambesi was, so to speak, the first line of entrenchment. The second was a public reassertion of

[1] F.O. 63/842 (Howard to Clarendon, 7. ii. 58; C. to H. 8. ii. 58. Livingstone to Hammond, 7. ii. 58).

Portuguese sovereignty over the Zambesi area and a definition of its extent. This question of the exact frontier was bound to be raised by the Expedition's transit through the territory; it was raised, indeed, already by Livingstone's protest with regard to the consulship. 'I should like to know a little more clearly', was Lord Clarendon's pencil comment on that document, 'his meaning respecting the limits of the Portuguese territory in order that we may place something on record about it with the Portuguese Government.' Livingstone was more than ready to comply.

'In answer to your inquiry respecting the limits of the Portuguese power in East Africa [he wrote] I beg leave to say that, viewing the subject generally, it resembles our own in China with the important difference that the Portuguese are so few and weak that they can scarcely hold the few forts they possess. They have no authority on the south bank of the Zambesi until we come to Sena. . . . The Portuguese inhabitants of Sena, about half a dozen in number, have several times paid tribute to the independent tribes adjacent. There is a hiatus again in their authority above Sena until we come to Tete, another village and fort. There is a stockade on the river below Tete which commands the river, and this is possessed by a native chieftain who has at different times waged war with the Portuguese. The north bank is under a chief who has also been at war with the Portuguese. Leaving, however, all the territory to which from previous knowledge or relationship they (the Portuguese) may feel disposed to claim the sovereignty of, if we ascend the Zambesi to 30 West (East) Longitude (Greenwich), we enter an immense extent of country of which the Government of Portugal never had any cognizance. . . . The Makololo people possess the chief power therein.'

What action, if any, Lord Clarendon might have taken, in the light of this statement, in order to 'place something on record', must remain a matter of surmise. The Portuguese Government had anticipated him. Just at this time a copy reached the Foreign Office of a decree promulgated at Lisbon on February 4 directing that 'the name of Zambesia shall be given in all official documents to all the territories to which the Crown of Portugal has a right in the valley of the Zambesi from the mouths of that river to beyond the fortress of Zumbo'. By the same mail came a second *portaria*, designed, perhaps, to soften the effect of the firm stand taken on the consulship question; it authorized Livingstone to carry all his goods up to Tete without paying any import duties and thence freely into the interior.[1]

With the arrival of these documents the diplomatic prelude to the Zambesi Expedition came to an end. Both sides were more or less content with it, but the honours lay on the whole with the Portuguese. They had shown all the interest in the Expedition and all the sympathy with its objects and had offered all or almost all the official facilities that could reasonably be expected of them. But they had given nothing important away. They had been firm on the vital points. They had definitely strengthened and safeguarded their position on the Zambesi. The British, on their part, may have hoped, but they can scarcely have expected, that the Portuguese would go farther than they had yet gone in abandoning their time-honoured policy of commercial mono-poly and exclusion. On the other hand, they must have expected, and they could scarcely take objection to, a re-assertion of Portuguese sovereignty; and the form of this reassertion had implied a confession of its limitations. It might very well have been worse. Just as the Portuguese might have proved far more difficult and obstructive than they had been as to the movements of the Expedition, so they might have put forward extravagant claims of sovereignty in the interior. But they had implicitly admitted by a specific, if rather vague, reference to Zumbo, a more or less final limit to their westward advance. As Livingstone pointed out, the frontiers of the new Zambesia almost exactly coincided with those he had indicated as limiting the present Portu-guese occupation, such as it was. Portuguese imperialism, it would seem, was retentive but not expansive. There were

[1] F.O. 63/842, Livingstone to Hammond, 7. ii. 58 (with Clarendon's comment), and 11. ii. 58. Howard to Clarendon, 8. ii. 58.

no wild ideas in the air at Lisbon of linking Mozambique to Angola with a great belt of Portuguese territory across the whole width of Equatorial Africa. So Livingstone was satisfied, more or less. Indeed he admitted that the second *portaria* revealed 'a liberal spirit'. He could cling to his conviction that the Portuguese Government sincerely shared his ideals. His coming experience on the Zambesi would put it to the final test.[1]

And if Livingstone was satisfied, so, of course, was Lord Clarendon. His policy, it has been seen, had been literally Livingstone's. Nothing, indeed, could have been of better augury for the success of the Expedition than the almost automatic co-operation of the Foreign Secretary with its leader. Nor, happily, did the defeat of Palmerston's Government, in February 1858, and Lord Clarendon's departure from the Foreign Office break the accord. 'I rejoice to find', wrote Captain Washington to the Permanent Under-Secretary, a few days before the explorers sailed, 'that Lord Malmesbury will follow up Lord Clarendon's spirited and liberal start of this Expedition which, I trust, is the Pioneer (but only the Pioneer) of Christianity and civilization to a very extensive district. May God speed them!'[2]

5

It is time to return to the Expedition itself and its members, amongst whom John Kirk must now take a foremost place, since it is mainly from his standpoint that the history of the Expedition is to be related. How he was himself engaged in those last busy weeks before he sailed can best be learned from a series of letters which he received from his chosen chief. They may be quoted in full; for they are very characteristic of the man who wrote them and reveal the anxious forethought with which he was contemplating the coming enterprise and the detailed interest he took in all its aspects.

[1] F.O. 63/842, Livingstone to Hammond, 16. ii. 58.
[2] F.O. 63/842, Washington to Hammond, 4. iii. 58.

Hamilton, 4th Jan^y.

1858

My Dear Sir,

It was a matter of regret with me that, in consequence of another matter pressing on my attention when you kindly called at Athol Place, I neglected to ask your company to dinner in order to have more conversation together. I saw you in the distance and the servant gave chase, but she said that you suddenly vanished and your note of the 1st Jany. explained why.

I was absent the whole of Saturday, and now before starting for London (20 Bedford Sq.) answer your questions so far as I can.

The passages out and home will be defrayed by Government. The contemplated length of the Expedition is two years, but there is a possibility of its being prolonged beyond that period by circumstances of which we are not at present aware.

With regard to the 'necessary expenses' I am not quite clear as to what you mean. Suppose you shoot a buffalo, there will be no expense incurred in cooking and eating it. There are no inns or hotels in the country. The lodging will be all free. The Expedition will have supplies of plain food—coffee, sugar, etc.; and anything else will be got, I suppose, in the usual mess fashion, each member contributing a share of the expense of the extras. I shall not be answerable for luxuries of any kind whatever. And expeditions of this kind cannot be successful unless all the members are willing to 'rough it', and it will be well if we all thoroughly understand this before setting out. The salary is £350 per annum.

If you are prepared to rough it when necessary, I shall feel obliged by a note to that effect and will then recommend your name to Lord Clarendon.

I may mention that, as a knowledge of the plants and woods already used in dyeing or suitable for dyestuffs, medicines, fibrous substances and gums is expected from the Botanist of the Expedition, if you are still desirous of serving, additional familiarity with economic botany would be desirable. A Mr. Napier, of Glasgow, known, I believe, to Dr. Wilson, has had his attention turned to dyestuffs, and would be happy to give you valuable hints if you thought them necessary.

I am, etc.

D. Livingstone.

12 Kensington Palace Gardens
14th January 1858

MY DEAR SIR,

As it is desirable to have preparations in as forward a state as possible, I shall feel obliged if you make out a list of the medicines which you may deem necessary for the Expedition, bearing in mind that about £15 will be expended thereon and that Fever will be the most common complaint.

The names given in to the Earl of Clarendon were mentioned at the Royal Society and also at the Royal Geographical Society. Dr. Sharpey at the former spoke in the kindest manner of your qualifications, and it was thought that some questions relating to the Tsetse might possibly engage your attention in addition to your botanical and medical duties. The final decision has not yet come from the Foreign Office, but I have no doubt but it will be favourable in as far as you are concerned, and I shall lose no time in letting you know about it.

I am, Dear Sir,
Yours Faithfully,
DAVID LIVINGSTONE.

Dr. Sharpey mentioned that your father was an old friend of his. If you are at home, please to present my kindest regards to him. I hope you are getting yourself up in dyestuffs, gums, etc. etc.

12 Kensington Palace Gardens
21st January 1858.

MY DEAR SIR,

I found out yesterday that I had made a mistake in saying £15 instead of £50 were allotted for the medicines, and your letter of this morning shews that you felt that the former sum was rather stinted. I return the list, and you will be good enough to increase the quantities and also order them from some man in whom you have confidence. See that they are ready and sent to Liverpool by the 1st February and let the account come to me before that time. Allow me to suggest a good stock of the Resin of Jalap. I found a pill composed of that with calomel and quinine an excellent remedy in fever. Also Fowler's Solution of Arsenic— a larger quantity of soda as it is very useful in allaying obstinate vomiting—a decided increase in Epsom Salts for the natives. The

Quinine is not a whit too large. Increase that too. It will be desirable to give Quinine wine to all the Europeans before entering and while in the Delta.

You will not, I hope, think me inclined to quackery if I mention Warburg's Drops as so highly spoken of in India that I really think them worth a trial. If you agree in this, a little may be added, but they are very dear. Enquire about them, and if you think they merit a trial, we may have some.

Dont stint yourself in anything that you feel assured will aid your researches in dyestuffs and get the best of everything though you exceed £50. A knowledge of the value of gums would be useful.

With respect to the paper for drying plants you will do well to consult Dr. Hooker and make that a separate item. Let me know as soon as possible. I shall submit it to Captain Washington, the Hydrographer, who has a general superintendence of our expenses. Take a sufficient supply by all means and of corr. sublimate any quantity (I have seen a smoothing iron used with great effect in drying plants in humid weather). The only difficulty I fear is transport up the river as our steam launch carries very little, being only 80 feet by 8 ft. If we get up to Tete in the vessel that takes us out, then we can deposit the heavier baggage there. Everything ought perhaps to be packed in two portions. We require to take as little as possible of dead weight consistent with efficiency.

What do you propose as necessary for collecting fruits and seeds? The animal kingdom and fishes are very interesting. I shall meet all your views as far as I can, so write freely. The Commission will be a general one, and following the suggestions of the Royal Society and Geographical Societies, will direct our attention to various departments.

I am etc.
Faithfully yours,
DAVID LIVINGSTONE.

Royal Geographical Society.
15 Whitehall Place
22nd Jany. 1858

MY DEAR SIR,

On consulting Captain Washington about the paper for drying plants, he informed me that he has got five reams of it ready for you. He thinks that, after you have made the list complete, it ought to be sent to the medical department of the Navy and that the medicines should be furnished by them. So, if you have not already ordered any, you had better just send me the list, and if you should come to London, you could see to the packing of them as you desire. If convenient, it would be well for you to see Captain Washington before we go. He likes to be *acknowledged* and is also very useful in getting anything for you in his power.

A quarter or half a year's salary may be obtained.

Hoping that this is not too late for reversing any decision about getting the medicines in Edinburgh,

I am etc.
DAVID LIVINGSTONE.

Please name arsenical soap, corrosive sublimate etc. in your list.

50 Albemarle St. London.
26th January 1858.

MY DEAR SIR,

Your name was handed in by me to Lord Clarendon with the statement that you were highly recommended by Sir William and Dr. Hooker and also by Professors Balfour and Wilson. It was approved by Lord Clarendon and sent by the Foreign Office to the Admiralty which has the further organization of the Expedition. You are therefore *appointed*, and all that is necessary now is that you present yourself to Captain Washington, the Hydrographer, for approval in that department, but no objection will be made.

It will be well if you lose no time in making preparations as to outfit as we expect to be off about the 14th of February.

Thanks for the list. I shall order the packing according to your desire, but it would have been an advantage had you been at hand to see that it was attended to.

I am, Yours Most Truly,
DAVID LIVINGSTONE.

Manchester.
28th January 1858.

MY DEAR SIR,

Your salary will commence on the 1st February, and should you want more than a quarter's advance, I shall feel obliged if you let me know. Don't leave your friends in any hurry on account of that. If you can get your things better where you are than in London, by all means do so, and you can remit the money afterwards. We must get all into trim by the 15th.

Anything that I can get for you, please let me know, and if possible I shall do my best to comply with your wishes. The amount of luggage has to be limited, but we shall try and make each other as comfortable as possible.

I am, etc.
DAVID LIVINGSTONE.

I shall be in London on Saturday.

18 Hart St.
17th Feby. 1858.

MY DEAR SIR,

I have not heard whether any arrangement was made for a Ward's Case from Kew. I mentioned it to you, but the subject may have escaped your memory. If we cannot have one from Kew, we can apply elsewhere. I have got another parcel of goods from Rollisson of Tooting and have forwarded them to Birkenhead. Those I gave in charge to you are, I believe, still at the Royal Geographical Society's house.

You will oblige me if you purchase some tincture of myrrh and keep it carefully for the Commandant of Tete who desired me to bring something for fastening loose teeth. If you know anything better or anything of an anodyne nature for his perineum, we may get on the soft side of him. I will repay you.

I am
Yours truly,
DAVID LIVINGSTONE.

London. 22nd Feb^y.
1858.

MY DEAR SIR,

From the present information we have of the sailing of the ' Pearl ' it will be necessary for you to be at Liverpool on Saturday next to prepare for sailing. Should any other information reach me, I will not fail to let you know.

Have we got a peach and apricot tree in the W. cases, and a vine or two ? These seem very necessary.

I am going this afternoon to Glasgow, 4 Athol Place, but do not write if you have got them.

> I am etc.
> DAVID LIVINGSTONE.

> Glasgow, 28th Feb^y.
> 1858.

MY DEAR SIR,

The 'Pearl' will sail from Greenock on Monday next and you will be expected at Liverpool on Tuesday in order to be ready for embarcation.

> I am etc.
> DAVID LIVINGSTONE.

Some things require to be done to the 'Pearl' at Liverpool. I enclose a note for your consideration. Glycerine is, I understand, good for preserving specimens.

IV

OUTSET OF THE EXPEDITION
(1858)

I

THE Zambesi Expedition is well documented. Its leader kept a personal diary of his own[1] and afterwards, in collaboration with his brother and with Kirk, he provided his wide circle of British readers with a popular account of the movements and achievements of the Expedition. Most happily, Kirk also kept a diary. Spread over a dozen note-books of different shapes and sizes, written mainly in pencil but with remarkable legibility, interspersed with frequent scientific calculations of position, with minute botanical and zoological notes, and with lists of native words and their meaning, illustrated now and again with careful sketches of flowers and native weapons and with rough maps and outlines of scenery, it provides a wonderfully detailed narrative of the Expedition and Kirk's part in it and thoughts about it. Through all those years of constant movement and unceasing physical activity, despite the difficulties and discomforts, the fatigue and ill health, inseparable from travel under primitive conditions in a primitive land, nearly every day is faithfully recorded. There is only one serious gap, due to an accident which will be described in due course. All in all, the diary is itself a notable achievement. No indolent or casual or slack-minded man could possibly, under the circumstances, have written it.

The start was delayed, and the first entry is for March 3, 1858. 'Left London and proceeded to Birkenhead, where the *Pearl S.S.*, destined to carry us, had not arrived from Glasgow. She came in on the day following, and all haste

---

[1] The author regrets that he was refused permission to examine Livingstone's private diary. It will often be evident on subsequent pages of this book how much it would have benefited from a knowledge of Livingstone's thoughts. A few quotations from his diary are given in Blaikie's *Life*.

was made to get on board the three segments of the steam launch and stores of the Expedition.' But, almost immediately, Kirk's thoughts were distracted from these dockside labours by grievous news from home. 'On the evening of the 5th my brother came and gave me the sad news of my father's sudden death. How sudden and unexpected! In his former letters he spoke of himself as almost quite well and ashamed to be regarded as under medical orders. My brother must be off to ease my mother during this time of affliction. As we expect daily orders to sail, I cannot accompany him, which I should so like to do.... What a change when I return; until then I cannot hope to fully realise it.' A shadow had thus fallen over the outset of Kirk's great adventure; and the blow and the separation from his mother were the harder to bear as days passed and the *Pearl* still did not sail. It was not till March 10 that she left the Mersey. It was a damp, cold afternoon, and from time to time a scurry of snow swept over the sea.[1]

The fifth day out was a Sunday, and Livingstone 'performed service'. 'Having now recovered from sea-sickness in general', adds Kirk, 'we have morning reading and prayer daily.' On the 18th Livingstone read the Foreign Office Instructions to the assembled company. 'They seem sensible', notes Kirk, who was doubtless unaware that Livingstone had drafted them; 'but the most sensible part is that we are left very much to our discretion. The sum of them is—live at peace with the natives, obtain all the information we can, and try to begin civilisation among them by introducing arts and commerce as far as may seem proper.' He might, perhaps, have added that the programme was ambitious, could he have foreseen how much the time and strength of the explorers would be exhausted by the mere physical task of exploration; but none of them, except perhaps their leader, can have had any but the vaguest ideas of the toil and hardship that awaited them. A little later Kirk was given his

[1] K.'s *Diary*, 3–10. iii. 58.

own personal Instructions, drafted in Livingstone's big, clear, level writing.

> Screw Steamship 'Pearl'
> at Sea off Madeira.
> 18 March, 1858.

Dr. John Kirk.

SIR,

The main object of the Expedition to which you are appointed Economic Botanist and Medical Officer is to extend the knowledge already attained of the geography and mineral and agricultural resources of Eastern and Central Africa, to improve our acquaintance with the inhabitants, and to engage them to apply their energies to industrial pursuits and to the cultivation of their lands with a view to the production of raw material to be exported to England in return for British manufactures; and it may be hoped that by encouraging the natives to occupy themselves in the development of the resources of their country a considerable advance may be made towards the extinction of the slave trade, as the natives will not be long in discovering that the former will eventually become a more certain source of profit than the latter.

(2) It is intended that the Expedition should pass through the malarious district at the lower portion of the Zambesi river as quickly as possible, and it will be necessary for you to put into practice those precautionary measures against fever by the use of Quinine which the experience of the Niger Expedition and your own judgement may suggest as likely to secure the health of your companions.

(3) The efforts of every member of the Expedition will probably be required to facilitate the transport of the luggage to and beyond Tete, the most advanced post of civilization, but the chief power in the country adjacent being in the hands of two or three influential chiefs, it will be our duty to visit them and turn the attention of their people to the cultivation of cotton by giving them a supply of better seed than that which they already possess, and also to explain the benefit that they would derive from an exchange of the natural productions of Africa as ivory, cotton, oil, beeswax, buaze etc. for the manufactures of Europe, and generally to hold out every encouragement in order to induce them to give up their warlike and predatory habits and substitute the more peaceable pursuits of agriculture and commerce. The time occupied in attending to these matters will enable you,

if we find it to be consistent with your personal safety, to glean a general idea of the resources of the country to the north of Tete, and to ascertain in as full detail as the time will allow the nature of the plant called Buaze, paying particular attention to the probable amount to which it and any other fibrous substances might be obtained. You will be good enough to furnish me with a Report thereon for transmission home to the Foreign Office.

(4) Your attention is particularly requested to the discovery of dyestuffs, gums, and medicinal substances, in the hope that should either these or fibrous tissues exist in quantities sufficient to warrant commercial enterprise you may aid in the great work of supplanting by lawful commerce the odious traffic in slaves. It is gratifying to me to feel assured that this object commends itself to your mind as a most important and noble one, and I have the pleasure of handing you a copy of a sketch of the principal duties expected of you in the botanical department drawn up by the eminent traveller and botanist Dr. J. D. Hooker, whose success in reflecting honour on our country I heartily wish you may equal, and requesting, for this part of our travels at least, your earnest and exclusive attention to the same. Other objects of interest will no doubt press on your notice, but considering that the botany of this region is nearly unexplored—that there is a danger of over-working yourself—that your energies will be greater in the second than in the first year—and that the primary objects of the Expedition are to gain accurate information respecting the vegetable and mineral resources of the country, I trust you will see the propriety of limiting for a time the range of your pursuits.

(5) Our stay in the vicinity of Tete must necessarily be short because it is essential to proceed at an early period to the rapid Kebrabasa or Chicova to ascertain the possibility of passing it while the river is still comparatively high, and thus avoid the necessity of taking the launch to pieces for porterage. The people near to the Portuguese settlements who have been in contact with slave traders not being so trustworthy as those farther inland who have not been subjected to the prejudicial influence of such communications, it will be unadvisable to make any distant excursions. Our energies must be bent to the establishment of a depot at some eligible spot beyond the confluence of the Kafue and Zambesi. Having reached a tolerable elevation and examined the country adjacent it will be advisable after obtaining the consent of any natives who may lay claim to the soil to set up the iron house to

serve as a central station. As the spot selected will probably be on the side of one of the hills which flank the river and sufficiently high to secure salubrity, a small plot of ground may at that altitude be planted with wheat and European vegetables as an experiment, and also in order to promote the comfort and health of the Expedition; while another small spot at a lower level may be planted with cotton and sugar cane, and given in charge to the headman of any village adjacent in order to induce the natives to take an interest in the result.

(6) The central depot once established and intercourse with the natives set on foot, a more extended range of scientific observations will then be advisable. You may then follow out as opportunity offers the instructions on Zoology from Professor Owen contained in Appendix No. 2, and without discarding your botanical labours collect any new or rare animals, birds, fishes or insects that may be met with in excursions which in company with the Makalolo may safely be made, and the results deposited at the central station.

(7) Although these explorations and collections are very desirable, you will understand that Her Majesty's Government attach more importance to the moral influence which may be exerted on the mind of the natives by a well regulated and orderly household of Europeans setting an example of consistent moral conduct to all who may congregate around the settlement—treating the people with kindness and relieving their wants—teaching them to make experiments in agriculture—explaining to them the more simple arts—imparting to them religious instruction as far as they are capable of receiving it, and inculcating peace and good will to each other.

(8) One especial means of gaining their favour will be by giving them the benefit of your medical skill and remedial aid. They possess medical men among themselves who are generally the most observant people to be met with. It is desirable to be at all times on good terms with them. In order to this, slight complaints, except among the very poor, ought to be referred to their care, and severe cases before being undertaken should be enquired into of the doctor himself and no disparaging remark ever made on the previous treatment in the presence of the patient. This line of conduct will lead to the more urgent cases only being referred to you; time and medicine will both be saved while your influence will be extended. Never neglect the opportunity which the bed of sickness presents of saying a few kind words in a natural

respectful manner and imitate as far as you can the conduct of the Great Physician whose followers we profess to be.

(9) The Expedition is well supplied with arms and ammunition and it will be necessary at times to use these in order to obtain supplies of food as well as specimens of animals for the purposes of natural history. In many parts of the country which we hope to traverse the larger animals exist in great numbers and being comparatively tame may be easily secured. I would earnestly press on you the duty of a sacred regard to life and never to destroy it unless some justifiable end is to be answered by its extinction. The most vital part ought to be aimed at, and no shot fired unless the animal be within a range that renders it probable that the mortal part will be struck. The wanton waste of animal life which I have witnessed from night hunting and from the ferocious but childlike abuse of instruments of destruction, as well as the wish that the habits of certain races of animated creation, which are evidently destined at no very distant date to extinction, should be calmly and philosophically observed while there remains the opportunity, make me anxious that none of my companions should be guilty of similar abominations.

(10) It is hoped that we may never have occasion to use our arms for protection from the natives, but the best security from attack consists in upright conduct, and the natives seeing that we are prepared to meet it. At the same time you are strictly enjoined to exercise the utmost forbearance towards the people, and while retaining proper firmness in the event of any misunderstanding, to conciliate as far as possibly can be admitted with safety to our own party.

(11) It is unnecessary for me to enjoin the strictest justice in dealing with the people. This your own principles will lead you invariably to follow, but it is decidedly necessary to be careful not to *appear* to over-reach or insult any one. Care must be taken in every case in which a native is to be employed that the terms be well understood and a little patience in settling the amount of remuneration in the presence of witnesses and the exact number of persons engaged will prevent that heartburning and discontent which may otherwise ensue. Let the payment be invariably made into the hands of the man who has performed the work. Unless this is done, the idea of property in the labour of the lower classes of the population is apt to be engendered in the minds of the underchiefs, but by direct payment a most important doctrine is widely inculcated and in process of time each man

comes to feel that he owes subjection to the head chief alone and is otherwise a free subject.

(12) The chiefs of tribes and leading men of villages ought always to be treated with great respect and nothing should be done to weaken their authority. Any present of food should be accepted frankly. It is impolitic to allow the ancient custom of feeding strangers to go into disuse. We come among them as members of a superior race and servants of a Government that desires to elevate the more degraded portions of the human family. We are also adherents of a holy benign religion and may by wise patient efforts be the harbingers of peace to a hitherto distracted and trodden-down race. No great result is ever attained without patient and long continued efforts. In this enterprise in which we have the honour to be engaged, sympathy, consideration and kindness which when viewed in detail may seem thrown away, if steadily persisted in, are sure ultimately to exercise a commanding influence. Depend upon it a kind word or deed is never lost.

(13) You will have access to Koelle's Polyglotta Africana, Bleek's vocabulary of the languages of Mozambique and an Analysis of the Sechuana tongue, and you are to endeavour to master the latter language as it is generally spoken in the Makololo country and its acquisition will materially aid you in all your pursuits. Should opportunity offer, you are expected to collect vocabularies of other dialects using the system already employed in the Sechuana—taking the English consonants and giving the vowels the sound they have in Italian, Spanish and in most European languages.

(14) You are distinctly to understand that your services are engaged for two years unless any unforeseen accident should happen to the Expedition, when you will be set free as soon as an opportunity is afforded for returning to England.

(15) In the event of my being prostrated by illness or by accident rendered incapable of conducting the Expedition, the charge of it will devolve on Commander Bedingfeld. If he too should fail it will devolve on you, and then on Mr. Charles Livingstone, but immediate information of such an event is, if possible, to be transmitted to England for further instructions.

(16) You are at liberty to consult a copy of the original instructions I hold from Her Majesty's Government, and it is hoped that you will enter cordially into the spirit of them and so far as circumstances will allow, endeavour to carry them into effect.

(17) Finally, you are strictly enjoined to take the greatest care

of your own health and that of the Expedition. My own experience teaches the necessity of more than ordinary attention to the state of the alimentary canal. Constipation is almost sure to bring on fever, and it would be well if you kindly explain to the different members the necessity of timely remedial aid to overcome any tendency to it, especially if accompanied by dreaming, drowsiness, want of appetite or unpleasant taste in the mouth in the mornings. If Quinine combined with a mild aperient be administered, this precautionary measure will often ward off an attack of this formidable disease. Feeling the fullest confidence in your zeal in the great cause of African civilization and rejoicing in being associated with you in this noble work, I heartily commit you and the cause in which you will, I hope, be an influential Pioneer to the safe keeping of the Almighty Disposer of Events.

I am your
Most Obedient servant
DAVID LIVINGSTONE.

Besides the technical Appendices, these Instructions were accompanied by the following short letter.

Private   'Pearl', 15th April, 1858.

MY DEAR SIR,

In handing to you the accompanying letter of instructions I may be allowed to suggest that, when you write the report required, you will do it as carefully as possible as I intend to send your own manuscript to the Foreign Secretary. I think it is my duty to promote the interests of my companions as far as lies in my power, and by thus bringing you as it were into direct contact with the Government it may ultimately tend to your benefit. If you make it as clear and simple as possible, it will secure attention.

I shall try and get your plants home to Dr. Hooker as soon as possible, as it is important to get them into the hands of your friend before the German of Angola.

Believe me yours
most truly
DAVID LIVINGSTONE.

At the date of this letter the *Pearl* was slowly approaching Table Bay. The monotony of the voyage had been broken by a stay of six days (March 25–30) for taking in coal and stores at Freetown, the capital of the famous colony of Sierra Leone and now the head-quarters of British administration on the west coast of Africa. It was Kirk's introduction to the continent to which his life was henceforward to be devoted; and, in the light of after events, it was not inappropriate that this first contact with Africa should have occurred at a point so closely associated with the group of philanthropists who, half a century ago, had brought about the abolition of the English Slave Trade.[1] An opportunity to see something of the country was soon provided by an invitation from a Mr. Campbell to accompany him on an official visit to some native villages up the river. The best part of three days was spent on the trip, and several pages of the diary are devoted to a description of the scenery and vegetation, the dense jungle and the seeming scarcity of animal life, the coloured crabs and jumping fish, and the vast stretches of malodorous mud left stewing in the sun at low tide. Kirk was fortunate in finding a half-caste Frenchman living on Rotumba Island 'beyond the power of any European laws' and exercising a 'sort of chieftainship over the natives', who 'was extremely well-informed on all matters'; for, like all explorers before him, he soon discovered that it was almost useless to question the natives on scientific subjects. 'My short experience of the natives', he notes, 'leads me to put no faith in any information obtained from them; for they seem not to have any knowledge of plants or native products, and yet they invariably give some sort of definite answer which you find on further examination to be quite false.' Kirk seems, however, to have taken a liking to these first African villagers of his acquaintance, at any rate by contrast with the inhabitants of the colonial capital, of whom his impressions were not all that Wilberforce or Zachary Macaulay would have wished. 'They are a petted saucy lot of vagabonds at Free Town,' the diary roundly declares, 'a contrast to the up-country

[1] See p. 31, above.

people.' And he betrays a little impatience with the philanthropic traditions of the local government. 'If they are called a name, however stupid and insolent they may be, there is a risk of being fined or bothered by the authorities.' A dinner with the Bishop and another on board the *Calcutta*, homeward bound from India with several refugees from the Mutiny on board, were the only other incidents of the stay. On March 30 the *Pearl* left Freetown; on April 21 Table Mountain was sighted; and that evening they cast anchor off Cape Town.[1]

Missionaries had never been popular in Cape Colony. The bitter controversies of the early years of the nineteenth century were not easily forgotten: Vanderkemp and Philip were hated long after they were dead: and in 1852, when Livingstone had last visited Cape Town on the eve of his first historic journey, he had found that colonial opinion, excited by the Kaffir war, was more than usually hostile to members of his calling and especially to those of the London Missionary Society. An unknown man, regarded with grave suspicion, capable, it might almost have been supposed, of intriguing with the natives against British rule, he had had the greatest difficulty in obtaining the supplies he needed and had met with nothing but obstruction in official quarters. But it was now a very different story. Important events in the great tropical belt to the northward have always and naturally attracted attention in South Africa, and on the news of Livingstone's achievement a great meeting had been held at Cape Town. The leading officials, scientists, clerics, and business men of the Colony, headed by Sir George Grey, the greatest of all its Governors, had vied with each other in praise of Livingstone's work and character; and now that he came himself, no longer unknown and a suspect, but the hero of the British world and bearing the Queen's commission, Cape Town rose to welcome him. Sir George Grey again led the popular demonstration and presented Livingstone with a silver box containing a public subscription of eight hundred

[1] K.'s *Diary*, 15. iii–21. iv. 58.

guineas; and the members of the Expedition were entertained at a public dinner with the Attorney-General in the
chair. Nor were the naval authorities more backward. Of
the commanding officer, Captain Lister, and his colleagues
Kirk reports: 'We have the good fortune to meet sensible
men, willing to help in anything; but had we found red-tape
buffers, it would have made a deal of trouble and cost us
time.' Of Captain Skead, R.N., the Government surveyor,
who was seconded to accompany the Expedition for the
survey of the Lower Zambesi, he observes that every one speaks
well of him and that 'he goes at it with much good-will'.[1]

The *Pearl*, meantime, had steamed round the Cape to
Simon's Town to take in stores from the naval depot; and
from there, on May 1, the last stage of the outward voyage
began. On the 7th they passed the beautiful estuary of the
St. John's River, on the 10th they were crossing Delagoa
Bay, and on the 14th they anchored off the mouth of a river
named, in the imperfect maps then in use, the 'West Luabo'.
Next morning the captain of the *Pearl*, undeterred by the
misgivings of his two naval colleagues, set his ship boldly
at the bar, rode safely through it, and anchored within.
While the other European members of the Expedition,
assisted by the twelve Kurumen whom Livingstone had taken
into service at Sierra Leone, set to work to fit together the
sections of the launch, Kirk and Skead were commissioned
to ascend the river in a row-boat and begin a survey of its
course. After two or three days thus occupied—pleasant days
for Kirk, who describes with a fresh enthusiasm the natural phe-
nomena of this delta-country, soon to become all too familiar:
the hippopotami 'swimming in the water and crawling up
to the mud . . . most uncouth beasts', the buffaloes and buck,
the pelicans and storks on shore, the palm-groves and belts
of reed and innumerable unknown plants—the *Ma Robert*
was duly launched; and when Rae, the engineer, with Kirk's
assistance, had fitted up her engine, the whole party steamed

[1] K.'s *Diary*, 22. iv. 58. Blaikie, *Livingstone*, 207.

up-stream. But they soon met their first disappointment. On the second day, after the boat had grounded more than once and for several hours on mud-banks, the river was found to end in a small, sticky, and impassable channel. On the morrow another branch of the river was examined. A native village was discovered on its bank, and its inhabitants, though at first they had fled from the new-comers, were persuaded, after a long palaver intelligible to neither party, to provide a guide in a canoe. He proved useless enough. 'After continuous steaming, we at last opened into a new sort of scenery, the whole expanse as far as could be seen consisting of one immense meadow of grass about 4 ft. high, growing among water. . . . As we went on, our paddles were working among this long reedy grass, but at last we came to a standstill and could go no further. . . . Jumbo [the head Kuruman] was sent on to see, but only found barrier after barrier and eventually an impassable mass. So much for this fine river, its branches ending in a swamp of reed and in a mud ditch full of alligators, and sending out mosquitoes in such tremendous numbers and of such a virulent sort that he who had not a tight mosquito-curtain was in a bad fix. Poor Rae got into this scrape and I never saw a man so marked with anything before with the exception of small-pox.'

The West Luabo, in fact, was not, as the explorers had thought, one of the mouths of the Zambesi, like the East Luabo, but a distinct river—the Luawe. There was clearly nothing for it but to rejoin the *Pearl*, recross the bar, and sail along the coast in search of another opening. On June 3 they reached the Kongone, one of the four true mouths, and, as was presently proved, the best of the four for navigation. Next day the *Ma Robert* steamed some distance up it. The exploration of the Zambesi had at last begun.[1]

    [1] K.'s *Diary*, 1–25. v. 58. D. and C. Livingstone, *Narrative of an Expedition to the Zambesi and its Tributaries* (London, 1865; henceforward cited as Livingstone, *Narrative*), 14–17. Blaikie, *Livingstone*, 208–10.

2

A preliminary survey made it clear that the river was too shallow for the *Pearl* to steam far up it. It was decided, therefore, to unload the stores, send the *Pearl* home, and rely on the *Ma Robert* for the journey up-stream to Tete. A site was selected on an island within the bar for depositing the stores and for the erection of the portable house as a coastal base for the time being. 'The house is rather a puzzle', notes Kirk, who was put in charge of the building party, 'as we have to pick out all the pieces which have been packed more with a view to storage than for facility in erecting.' But within a week the building was completed. Its composition was not, perhaps, exactly what its designers had intended; but it was a servicable structure, none the less, with walls of wood, 'impregnated with some abomination to keep off the ants', a roof of corrugated iron plates, and a thatched verandah. On June 26, the stores being all ashore, a farewell dinner was held on the *Pearl*, and next day she sailed for home, conveying Skead back to his official duties at the Cape and carrying, too, the first-fruits of Kirk's botanical researches, a box of dried maritime plants addressed to Sir William Hooker. It was the breaking of the last link with the outer world. Between Kirk and his companions and their homes and friends in far-off Europe a curtain of silence had fallen, only to be broken through when, at long intervals, a British ship-of-war, with mails on board, sought out their base on that dismal and deserted coast.[1]

Young Kirk would have watched the departure of the *Pearl* with a sinking heart if he had known all that lay ahead of him. From that first moment of isolation the strain on the constitution, physical and moral, of the members of the Expedition began. And very soon, though there is nothing as yet to suggest any sense of uneasiness for the future, Kirk's diary begins to chronicle the three main troubles of the

[1] K.'s *Diary*, 26. v–26. vi. 58.

coming months and years—disease, disharmony, and the conduct of the *Ma Robert*. Disease, indeed, had made its first assault before the party landed, Livingstone having suffered from a painful intestinal attack during the voyage up the coast; and in the course of the second week at Expedition Island both Baines and Charles Livingstone, who had been left at the base with Kirk and a few Kurumen while the rest of the party went up-river with the first load of stores, were down with fever. Baines, it appears, was not over-strong, yet he was unwilling to spare himself or to make terms with the climate. 'Mr. Baines is a trump and does more than anyone else', Kirk had observed on the *Pearl* in mid-Atlantic: 'if anything is required from any case in the hold he is down working and sweating. . . . I am sorry he is not very well as he has caught cold working in the hold.' And now, on the island, he did more than his share of rough work besides his painting, in the glaring sunshine and often without a hat. 'Baines, good-natured soul', reports the diary on July 9 '. . . complained of feeling no desire to work: I wished him to take [a] rest, but he has queer notions about hardening himself, and work he would. However, he had to lie down at noon, looking very ill indeed, his pupils contracted, tendency to shivering, and severe headache.' For the next few days both Baines and Charles Livingstone were 'very ill, with vomiting, purging and delirium'. But before the *Ma Robert* returned, on July 19, both patients were off Kirk's hands, Livingstone shooting wild-fowl from the boat, Baines 'at his pictures again'.[1]

The two other troubles, meanwhile, had been coming to a head. 'For some time', Kirk notes on June 10, 'there have been differences and some words with Captain Bedingfeld who comes out as perhaps the great man and forgets that he is but the equal of others when the Doctor is present. . . . The worst disputes have been with Skead and the Captain of the *Pearl*. The result is that he is left this morning to navigate

[1] K.'s *Diary*, 27. vi–19. vii. 58.

the launch alone, all others being, or finding engagements, on board the *Pearl*.' Before long Livingstone himself had been involved in these altercations. 'There is an evil spirit between the Captain and the Doctor, and I rather think the Captain does not try to make matters go smoothly. In fact also I rather think Bed. is tired of the service; he seems to have expected to live the life of a man-of-war commander and has no idea of being a subordinate. He also feels that he has done nothing but act sailing master of the launch, but I do not see much desire for scientific observations, and of surveying he has no more knowledge than any other man with a little common sense.' 'I heartily wish all this dispute were settled,' says Kirk a little later, 'as it is very disagreeable to all others and makes work far from pleasant.' At last Bedingfeld tendered his resignation; and Kirk, after a long talk with him, was convinced that, since the quarrel was 'past mending now . . . the sooner it comes to a separation the better'. Livingstone, however, hesitated to part with the only member of the Expedition who was technically qualified to navigate the launch; and it was not till the return of the *Ma Robert* from her second voyage up the river that the final rupture occurred. The experience of those voyages was certainly not conducive to the restoration of harmony. 'From what I hear,' notes Kirk after the first voyage, 'the steaming of the launch is a failure.' It was indeed. So far from easily raising steam with any wood, as the philanthropic Mr. Laird had guaranteed, it had been found that only the fine hard woods such as African ebony and *lignum vitae* were of any use at all, and that many a ton of it was required for a day's voyage. It presently appeared that it took the party a day and a half to cut enough wood for a day's use, and the fires had to be lighted at two o'clock in the morning to get up steam by six. What this meant for the speed and success of the Expedition was only too clear, and Livingstone was bitterly disappointed. In such an atmosphere there was little prospect of peace-making, especially as Bedingfeld had been associated with the trials of the launch. Another open quarrel began in the presence of Kirk and the Kurumen over a question of working on Sunday. 'The Doctor then broke out on Bedingfeld (still before the hands) stating that he had deceived him regarding the steaming of the launch at Liverpool when fed with wood. Bed. stated that he had seen the trial and the wood put in, and Mr. Laird stated that steam had been got up with wood. Mr. Rae believes that it was got up with coal, but he was not consulted or requested to see the trial at Liverpool.' One more voyage with the same infuriating results and the dispute flared up to its *finale*. Bedingfeld again tendered his resignation and now Livingstone accepted it. 'He shewed me a copy [of his reply]', says Kirk, 'before giving it over. . . . Some of the things seemed to me a little hard.' Arrangements were made for Bedingfeld to proceed to Quilimane and await a ship for England.

In this, the first but not, unhappily, the last personal dispute in the history of the Expedition, it seems fairly certain that Livingstone was in the right. He was afraid, none the less, that Bedingfeld might win the ear of the Foreign Office and not merely justify his own conduct but also, by exaggerating the difficulties of the Expedition, try 'to prevent our getting any fresh grant for what we shall need'. He was anxious, therefore, that his own account of the case should be confirmed by other members of the Expedition. 'As you are now second in command,' he wrote to Kirk, 'your opinion expressed to me when I shewed you my acceptance of the resignation that it was absolutely necessary to save the Expedition from complete disorganization or words to that effect would prove of no ordinary value to the Foreign Secretary.' 'I am not conscious', he adds, 'of anything disagreeable or harsh in my conduct, nor have I been quarrelsome with anyone ; and in sending evidence to the Foreign Office I do so with extreme regret and sorrow that public duty requires it to be done against any of our members. I earnestly hope and pray that nothing may arise to disturb the harmony which has hitherto existed among the rest of us.'

Kirk's response, if not quite so sweeping as suggested, was definite enough. 'I consider the acceptance of Capt. Bedingfeld's resignation as necessary under the circumstances to prevent further disorganization to the Expedition.' This document, together with a statement by Charles Livingstone that Bedingfeld had used insubordinate language, accompanied Livingstone's dispatch; and, though the defendant could and did make out a case for himself, Lord Malmesbury, after consultation with the Admiralty, decided that the officer had failed to clear himself, and Livingstone's action was formally approved. But it had been an unfortunate beginning for the social life of the Expedition. 'The Doctor's brother has made a private quarrel of it', the diary had observed, 'and does not speak to Bed.; and the Kurumen, as might be expected, are rather insubordinate when there are so many differences among the masters.' But at least Kirk himself had kept free of the feud. Both the disputants, indeed, had taken him into their confidence; and while the diary clearly condemns Bedingfeld, it clearly also makes allowance for him. It was a small thing, perhaps, in itself, but by no means of small importance for the future of the Expedition, that one of its little isolated company had thus shown himself at the outset so good-natured and so level-headed. It would be easy enough to quarrel, when nerves were frayed by heat and fatigue and fever, but it would never be easy to quarrel with Kirk.[1]

Kirk had now been more than a month at Expedition

---

[1] K.'s *Diary*, 10. vi–16. viii. 58. Livingstone to K., 25. viii. 58, in which L. says: 'H.M.'s Government, in order to prevent insubordination such as Baikie suffers from in the Niger Expedition, invested me with magisterial power as a consul expressly to meet such a case as Bedingfeld's.' The official documents are in F.O. 63/843 and 63/871 (L. to Malmesbury, 31. vii and 8. viii. 58, with C. L.'s certificate. K. to L., 27. ix. 58, in which K. says the dismissal was 'necessary under the circumstances'. B.'s protest to L., 11. vi. 58.

Island. He had occupied himself with his botanical researches and the quest of meat for the pot. He had secured several buck and had had a shot at bigger game. 'Fire at hippos. but they show no signs of becoming beef and give decided indications of intentions of making a personal attack.' But he was naturally longing to get up the river and to see for himself what the prospects for the Expedition were. One serious piece of news had already reached him. Not many miles inland the country was in a state of war. A Portuguese half-caste, called Mariano, a scoundrel of unusually bestial cruelty even for a half-caste of that country, had been engaged for some time past in raiding for slaves in the interior and selling them at Quilimane. The Portuguese authorities had not interfered with him until he began to steal slaves belonging to their own countrymen. He was then declared a 'rebel', and on his rashly venturing to Quilimane with a view to bribing the Governor, he was seized and imprisoned, while the Governor set out with a body of troops to round up and suppress his followers, who, led by his brother and armed with muskets, were defending a stockaded camp near the confluence of the Shire [1] with the Zambesi. As the head-quarters of their operations had been fixed at Shupanga, Livingstone had found the Governor in the neighbourhood with several Portuguese officers, among them Major Sicard, who had entertained him so hospitably on his way down the Zambesi in 1856. It was the first contact between the Expedition and the Portuguese Government; and Livingstone was not displeased with the result. 'All seemed friendly', he recorded afterwards in his book, 'and expressed their willingness to assist the Expedition in every way in their power.' [2]

One of the two or three letters written by Livingstone to

B.'s full defence, 29. i. 59). The F.O. referred the matter to the Admiralty (16. i. 59), and Capt. Washington reported that B. had 'failed to clear himself' (31. iii and 10. vi. 59). B. at the Royal Geographical Society, *R.G.S. Proc.*, iv. 23–6.

  [1] Pronounced 'Sheery'.
  [2] K.'s *Diary*, 11–24. viii. 58. Livingstone, *Narrative*, 24–32.

Kirk during the course of the Expedition belongs to this opening period.

21st July, 1858.

Off Shupanga.

MY DEAR DR. KIRK etc.

We came to Mazaro this morning about 9½ and, on going ashore among a crowd of natives and Portuguese, were sickened by the sight of headless mutilated bodies lying about. The Governor having fever, the officers begged me to take him on to Shupanga. I consented, and while waiting for him the firing began a short distance off. Everything was in confusion and the commandant of Tete and Mr. Azevedo and Colonel Nunez all told me that the man at Shupanga was a thief and would connive at the Landeens robbing us of the goods we intended to leave. It seems therefore decidedly necessary for us to go on to Sena. It would be throwing them away here. We shall be three days to that place, now that we know the way.

My Dear Friends, you must exercise patience. I would remain at the island myself, but feel my presence necessary, when either natives or Portuguese come to us, to make our objects understood. If you see any plan by which we might hasten our departure from the island, let me know when I come down. I still think the Portuguese may help us, but war engrosses every thought. I go ashore here to try and get some fowls sent down to you. Examine all the things and use by all means everything you like. I forgot to say before leaving that you ought to make fresh bread for yourselves, the flour is under my boxes. God bless and preserve you all. Baines is quite well now. May I suggest a short morning prayer again? We have been unable to attend to this for some time past.

My kindest salutations to you all.

DAVID LIVINGSTONE.

At last, on August 2, Kirk started up the river. Livingstone himself took Bedingfeld's place as navigator of the launch. 'I would as soon drive a cab in November fogs in London', he wrote home, 'as be skipper in this hot sun. . . . My great difficulty is calling out "starboard" when I mean "port", and feeling crusty when I see the helmsman putting the helm the wrong way.' Kirk, meantime, was occupied in taking soundings and charting the river's depth and course—a task which he found Bedingfeld had virtually neglected. 'The Doctor took command on the way up while I made corrections on the map and kept a look-out as he told me I should bring her down on the way back. . . . The water requires a sharp eye to see the ripple of calm which indicates the channel; the whole stream is full of banks. . . . The lead is kept going constantly, but it is often too late in its indications.' So, for some sixty or seventy miles, they pursued their slow zigzag course between the sandbanks through the vast grassy levels of the delta, till, on the third day, the lie of the land began to change, a wooded ridge appeared on the left and far beyond, in the blue distance, the mountains of Manganja. 'At half-past one we landed at Shupanga island and paid our respects to the officers and gave Major Sicard a loaf of sugar. They have a great pile of wood cut in small billets for us, the best *lignum vitae*. The soldiers were a ragged set, only about thirty Europeans, the others being native levies. The Commandant sent us hands to help at unloading the pinnace.' Having stored their goods in a room provided by the Portuguese authorities in the old stone 'House of Shupanga', they were off again on August 5. 'The Doctor puts me on as skipper on the voyage down, which is rather a new line of life for me and takes up all my time, with the launch and pinnace and a huge native canoe all in line, going sometimes 10 knots and between sandbanks.' Whether it was due to Kirk's handling of the launch or not, they made a quick passage and reached Expedition Island before night. They found Baines ill again—'another touch of his old complaint from too much exposure to the sun'—and complaining that the others had given little help in taking down the house for removal. 'Young Livingstone and Thornton are not of much use, he says, when it comes to a day's hard work.'[1]

On August 9 the launch and its appendages were off again for Shupanga, 'skippered' by Livingstone, with Kirk and

[1] K.'s *Diary*, 2–8. viii. 58.

Baines, 'much better', on board. 'Baines and I take up
quarters in a room with Colonel Nunez and mess with him
and one of the Portuguese officers. The House of Shupanga
is about 150 yds. from the river's edge and elevated above
the present level of the water. It is an old house—about 150
years old—built of stone and brick with mortar; the walls
are of great thickness; the roof is of the stems of the palmyra,
squared outside and covered with tiles; in front is a verandah
with seats, a very pleasant place to sit and talk with the
Portuguese. Our room is a back one and the only objection
I have to it is that the window looks into the court where are
all the slaves who keep up singing and shouting their war-
songs all night and day. Col. Nunez makes us very comfortable; he is always moving about and at work; he has a
slave to bring his pipe when he goes to bed, and if he wakes
up with the rats or mosquitoes, it is another pipe.' In these
quarters Kirk stayed for some weeks while the other members
of the Expedition were occupied in moving part of the stores
a further stage up-stream. It was another rather tedious wait,
but the conditions were comfortable and Kirk evidently
enjoyed talking to his Portuguese hosts on the verandah,
with its view across the river of the great palm-forests stretching northwards to massive Mount Morambala and away beyond, against the sky-line, the outskirts of the Shire Highlands. From one of many such talks Kirk learned something
at first hand of the realities of the sea-trade in slaves. 'Sr.
Vienna is an old slave trader,' he reports, 'but seems to have
reformed, finding it rather unprofitable. He has shipped
4,000 slaves, some from Angola, some from Quilimane. Out
of twelve ships he has been in he has had five taken as prizes.
He is very indignant at one of the prizes which he considers
as being taken unjustly; the others, he says, were fair prizes,
he ran the risk and lost them in a contraband trade. He
says that, when well supplied with food and water, they lose
almost none except from a skin disease, but, when water
runs short, the mortality becomes enormous. Steam vessels

do not suit for the slave trade, nor yet do steam condensers
for water, the heat killing the slaves.' During these weeks,
too, Kirk made acquaintance with the Landeens who were
paying one of their regular visits to Shupanga. 'They were
active men, but by no means well-favoured; they had all
shields made of cowhide, oval and about $3\frac{1}{2}$ ft. long, that of
the chief being small and circular. Their arms are a bundle
of assegais, and a few had battle-axes. The Portuguese are,
as far as Shupanga is concerned, tributaries of the Landeens
. . . so that the poor people of the villages pay to both Landeens and Portuguese.'[1]

After a fortnight's inaction Kirk attempted a little exploration on his own. He made his way across country through
grass-land and forest to Lake Bove, about twenty miles
south-east of Shupanga. 'The chief lake', records the diary,
'is after all nothing remarkable. It seems to be about one mile
across and three in length, lined with papyrus and with water-
lilies floating on the surface.' Here he fell in again with the
Landeens, on their tribute-round among the neighbouring
villages, and found them 'quite civil'. The villagers, too,
were friendly; they provided a hut for Kirk and his companions to sleep in and 'would not receive anything for the
food they gave'. On his return he found a letter from Livingstone, written at Pita Island above Sena. It reported that
Sena had been reached in four days, but that the water was
'now getting very shoal', and *Ma Robert* betraying all her
vices. 'The slightest touch [on a sandbank] makes the launch
show her want of power by slewing round. Three times she
has done that with me (Bedingfeld did it often), and when
she goes on a shoal, the current keeps her on and much time
is lost'—a whole day, on one occasion. 'Should you be
desirous', the letter ends, 'of getting away before I come,
and can arrange with the Portuguese to take you and cargo
for say £20 or £25, pray dont hesitate.'[2]

[1] K.'s *Diary*, 9–24. viii. 58.
[2] Ibid., 25. viii. 58.   L. to K. 25. viii. 58.

FIG. TREE AND NATIVE CANOES AT SHUPANGA

Photograph by Kirk

But Kirk now found himself tied to Shupanga by duties which no doctor could evade. The Portuguese had opened their campaign against the 'rebels'. 'The camp is taking quite a warlike aspect', says the diary on August 18; 'the slaves are cleaning their guns and making preparations for the march in the direction of Morambala where the rebels have their chief stronghold. The Governor orders all across to the island by night to be ready for the departure. Col. Nunez sets off with all his men, leaving us a cook and servant to attend us, and having orders to supply us with all things.' The course of the Portuguese advance could soon be observed from the verandah. 'The march of the army to the north is distinctly marked by the line of smoke, as the whole country is covered with long grass which they burn off, destroying all villages etc. in their way. The policy is to drive the rebels up to Morambala.' But the advance was not unopposed, and casualties were soon trickling back to Shupanga where there was nobody but Kirk to deal with them. 'Have a large hospital of sick and wounded from the front', he coolly chronicles on September 2. It was certainly a fortunate accident for the Portuguese that a European doctor should have chanced to be at Shupanga; and in due course Kirk received a letter from the Governor of Quilimane, 'giving an official acknowledgement of my services to the sick and wounded of the army. He enclosed also a copy of General Orders in which my services were particularized and which were to be sent on to the Mozambique Government.' The Portuguese officials, indeed, whatever their failings otherwise, were not lacking in courtesy. On receipt of the report from his subordinate at Quilimane the Governor-General wrote to Admiral Grey, in command of the British naval station in those waters, expressing his gratitude for Kirk's conduct, *conduite qui honore son caractère*; and a formal acknowledgement of Kirk's services to the subjects of the King of Portugal was printed in the Government Gazette.[1]

[1] K.'s *Diary*, 8. viii and 2. ix. 58. Gov.-Gen. J. S. de Almeida to

Meantime an opportunity occurred for the Governor of
Quilimane to give practical and immediate expression to his
gratitude in a small way. While Kirk was resting on the
verandah—his patients comfortably provided for and no
fresh ones coming in, since the fighting was now over—'a
slave announced the approach of an English boat coming up.
We walked down to the landing-place and found two officers,
Mr. Medlicott and Mr. Cook of the *Lynx*, gunboat, with
a crew of two whites and three Kurumen. They delivered a
letter from Capt. Berkeley, informing Dr. L. that he had on
board provisions and other stores from the Cape and that he
would like us to come and take them at the mouth of the
river. . . . As Dr. L. was now somewhere above Tete and
Mr. Baines was with the pinnace between Sena and Tete
and both were laden with things that could not safely be
trusted in the hands of natives and as it would take some
time to communicate with Dr. L., I determined on applying
to the Governor for the loan of canoes to bring up the stores
from the sea. Mr. Medlicott consents to go with me to the
headquarters of the army which is somewhere near Morambala hills.' Setting off up-stream, they reached the mouth
of the Shire on the second day, and, about two miles up it,
'we saw the Portuguese flag and knew that we had at last
found the Governor. This was the more consoling as we saw
smoke in almost every direction except the rear.' Mariano's
chief stronghold, a 'town' of many houses surrounded by a
strong stockade at least a mile in circumference, had been
captured without a shot being fired in its defence. 'The
Portuguese officers were in high spirits. . . . How the rebels
could flee off without fighting for a place which could have
kept the army out for many a day, I cannot tell. It must
have been some panic, probably from having no confidence
in their leaders. If Mariano had been there, I daresay it
would have been otherwise. I saw many of my old friends

Admiral Grey, 16. xi. 58; Gov. C. J. da Silva to de Almeida, 9. ix. 58.
Boletim do Governo General, Mozambique, No. 49, 4. xii. 58.

and took up my quarters with Sen. Guilleomi Olivera, and called on the Governor who made himself very agreeable and said at once I might have 4 canoes to-morrow. We dined with him and he set before us about twelve sorts of flesh besides soup.' Next day, 'Breakfasted with His Excellency and had another astonishing show of meats, finished off with tea, raisins, figs, and cheroots. He walked down to the Shire to see personally to the canoes being sent off, and we started at 10.15 a.m.'[1]

On September 11 they were back at Shupanga. 'I have great difficulty', Kirk notes, 'in finding crews to go to the sea, as they know how few come back again'—a grim sidelight on the Slave Trade. Two incidents on their way downstream are worth recording. One was the capture of a young gazelle, which laid down on the approach of its pursuers and pretended to be dead. 'Within twenty-four hours' it is 'quite tame and eating grass in the bottom of the boat'. The other incident was more exciting. 'I go off to an orange-tree and begin to get up for a fine ripe orange, when something goes at me like a pistol shot in the neck, then a dozen over my chest. Of course I come down the trunk with a run and find I have crushed a large hornets' nest and that some hundred have settled on me. My shirt and breast were covered, and a good many had got down my coat which had most on it. I soon tossed that off and ran into the reeds where I picked my enemies off one by one. It took a little time to get all to rights again and when I came round I took vengeance on them by firing the long grass which did for them and payed them out for old scores.' It had been a nasty experience for Kirk. He might have suffered very serious injury if he had lost his head; but his telling of the story is characteristically simple and cool—and so is its conclusion. 'I then got a couple of oranges, which were first-rate.'[2]

They reached Expedition Island on the 14th, and next day paddled on towards the bar. 'The canoemen think they are

[1] K.'s *Diary*, 7–10. ix. 58.   [2] Ibid., 11–13. ix. 58.

getting too near the sea and talk of being afraid of going adrift, but I suspect they have more fear of being sold as slaves.' So slow was the progress next morning that Kirk and Cook got into one of the canoes 'which gives them confidence', and when they had been beached near the bar and the Europeans set out in the whaler to find the *Lynx*, only 'one of our men accompanied us to see the ship, he was the only one willing to go over the open sea, a thing they had only heard of and of which they had great fear'. That their nervousness was not unreasonable is clear from the following later entry: 'We heard to-day of a large slaver which sailed from the Meviado under French colours. It was said to belong to Mr. Cruz who is believed to be going strongly for the Slave Trade under the name of French colonization. This war gives the merchants opportunities of obtaining slaves; and, if they catch or entrap a few, they all go under the name of "prisoners of war".'[1]

Kirk had already been long enough in the wilds to appreciate this visit to the *Lynx*. 'I take up my quarters in the wardroom in Medlicott's cabin and enjoy a little society again. The doctor was at Edinburgh College when I was there.' It was decided that Medlicott should ascend the river in the galley and meet Livingstone while Kirk and other officers made a closer survey of the creeks and channels of the delta— a business which involved some risky passages over the bars. Six seamen had been drowned on one of them a few days earlier. The survey led Kirk to the conclusion that all the Zambesi mouths in all the maps and charts were wrongly marked. On September 20 Livingstone, with Rae and Thornton, arrived on the *Ma Robert*. He had hastened down on hearing of the *Lynx's* arrival in order to send home dispatches, especially, no doubt, those dealing with Bedingfeld's dismissal. He reported that Baines was working his way up towards Tete in the pinnace and that Charles Livingstone had been

---

[1] K.'s *Diary*, 14–16. ix and 8. x. 58. For 'French colonization', see pp. 24–7 above.

THE PORTUGUESE FORT AT SENA

Photograph by Kirk

'very ill'. Some days were spent in loading the stores; and on October 7 they said 'good-bye' to the *Lynx* and started once more up the river, taking with them Quartermaster Walker. 'From what I have seen', says Kirk, 'I am sure we have got the proper man.'[1]

It took four days to get back to Shupanga and another week to reach Sena, the first place worthy of the name of town which Kirk had yet seen in East Africa. But Sena was now but a shadow of what it once had been—only the ruins of big houses, only an old stone cross where once a church had stood, only a grass-grown mound to mark the site of a vanished monastery, and a fort by the river so dilapidated that cows were grazing over its broken walls. But, as Livingstone remarks in his *Narrative*, 'Sena has one redeeming feature; it is the native village of the large-hearted and hospitable Senhor H. A. Ferrão', the son of a past Governor of Sena. 'The poor black stranger passing through the town goes to him almost as a matter of course for food and is never sent away hungry. In times of famine the starving natives are fed by his generosity.' Kirk immediately paid a visit to this Christian gentleman and was courteously conducted by a fellow countryman of his to inspect the native industries of the town. On the 22nd they took to the river once more and steamed slowly, very slowly, upwards. 'We took the launch over one flat by means of the anchor, but I must say I dont admire the land transport principle in a steam-boat.' Even Livingstone's patience was sorely tried. 'The Doctor is very good-humoured now that we have passed the shoals,' Kirk drily observes, nine days after leaving Sena; 'it was certainly rather aggravating to see his pet river go and dry up to a 2 foot stream; but now it has got to 5 fathoms and 200 yards.' At last, on November 1, they reached and passed through the Lupata Gorge, where the Zambesi, before it emerges into the measureless, monotonous flats, cuts its winding way for some seventeen miles through a group of

[1] K.'s *Diary*, 18. ix–7. x. 58.

lofty hills, whose rocky faces fall sheer at times to the water from a height of several hundred feet. Two days later they were at Tete, a less neglected settlement than Sena, with its houses built on little sandy ridges, the intervening ravines serving as streets running down to the river, and with a church and a fort both still standing and in use. Another stage of the Expedition had been completed.[1]

3

On his previous wanderings, it will be remembered, Livingstone had been accompanied by a company of Makololo natives, about a hundred strong, provided by Sekeletu as baggage carriers, and had left them at Tete in the spring of 1856 with the promise that he would soon return from overseas and take them home. When in England, he had heard, with great satisfaction, that the Portuguese Government had undertaken to provide for them during his absence; but, whether the report was well-founded or not, no orders to that effect from Lisbon ever came to Tete; and, when Livingstone arrived there, he found that their only friend had been Major Sicard, who had continued to do all he could to provide them with a livelihood. Thirty of them had died of small-pox and six had been murdered by a neighbouring chief. The survivors greeted Livingstone's arrival with ecstasies of joy, rushing to the water's edge and trying to embrace him. 'The Tete people often taunted us', they exclaimed, 'by saying "Your Englishman will never return", but we trusted you and now we shall sleep.'[2]

Their leader restored to them, the Makololo had no desire to start off at once for home; many of them indeed had no great wish to return at all; and Livingstone was intent on immediately taking in hand the next item of his programme —a visit to the rapids, some fifty miles above Tete, to ascer-

[1] K.'s *Diary*, 8. x–3. xi. 58. Livingstone, *Narrative*, 35–6.
[2] Livingstone, *Narrative*, 42–5. Blaikie, *Livingstone*, 211–12.

tain whether they were really an insuperable obstacle to the further navigation of the Zambesi. 'The Doctor speaks of remaining only two days at Tete', notes Kirk on November 3, 'and going on then to Kebrabasa to see the rapids which he talks of blasting!! to clear a channel if possible. This, he says, he would spend 6 months over to say that there was water communication all the way to the Makololo country.' On the 8th, therefore, the advance was resumed. Baines was ill again, and Thornton too; so they remained at Tete with Charles Livingstone, who was anxious 'to try and get on with photography'. So far, Kirk comments, 'he has made a mess of it.' Only Kirk, Rae, and Walker, therefore, with some Kurumen and Makololo accompanied Livingstone. On the 10th they 'entered the gorge where the river contracted to about 40 yards . . . confined to a deep trench between the rocks.'

'Further up the hills began to recede, but the sides of this ditch or trench in which we were steaming became higher . . . When we had proceeded up this sort of place for 4 miles, we came to a slight rapid with rocks under water, and a second a little beyond with several rocks showing. We got through the first, but I was glad when I saw the Doctor keep in shore and call for a line ready. . . . Fortunately I had gone forward and with Walker got the things ready as the current began to take her bow round, and the Doctor to save her had to run her port bow against the rock. Although she came gently on and two men were out instantly fending off, we punched a hole above the water line, but by good luck the rock gave way and the fluke of the anchor took the greater part of the shock or it might have been worse. Having secured the vessel I went ashore with the Doctor and walked for about a mile along . . . The overland journey was fearful climbing among the quartz rock which was in large crystalline masses of a beautiful blue colour. The sides of the water-course were almost perpendicular and 80 feet high. The water, when it rises over this, which it does about 10 or 20 feet, flows over a flat rocky space which extends to the foot of the hills. The Doctor wished to take the launch at once back and return with our needful baggage . . . but at my suggestion he determined first to see whether there were more obstacles and whether they could be overcome if they existed. On our return we got out such things as we might require, should we not get back that evening. Mr. Rae came along with us. My equipment was a revolver and prismatic compass, and, considering the heat, which in the densest shade was over 90° and in the sun something a good deal more, I think I carried all that anyone could ask me to, especially as our course also lay among bright black rocks which had become heated so as to make it painful to touch them for any time. The Makololo who followed us carried our blankets and rifles with enough provisions to make two meals. We landed on the right bank and found at the foot of the hills there had been extensive cultivation of cotton, millet, and tobacco. . . . All the rocks which are covered with water at flood are polished smooth and often have a bright surface and resemble blackleaded ironwork. . . . Here the road had taken us a little distance from the river, and on getting a view of it again we found we had passed a rapid which made a great noise. I walked back to see it while the Doctor went to examine another further up. The one I got to was formed by a large rock, the height of the sides of the gorge, which split the water into two halves. The side next to me was about 12 yards wide, and that on the other side I think not more than 14. . . . I descended the face of the rock to the rapid where the water fell over at a considerable angle. . . . It seemed to me that this was an impediment to the further progress of our launch. I went and described it to the Doctor and we went on to see if those two were the last of them. After a difficult walk of several hours we came to another fully as bad, only the space between the rocks was wider. After examining this we continued our walk and towards sunset encamped by another rapid. . . . Our camp was on a firm sandy spot between the high rocks, where we had our tea, a bit of pork, and a smoke, those of us who indulged in that luxury. The Doctor took a latitude, and we turned in and slept soundly without any covering besides what we wore during the day.'

Next day they pushed on a little farther, observing one or two more minor rapids, and then, their food exhausted, returned on their tracks. On November 12 they were on board the launch again and on the next afternoon they were back at Tete.[1]

This first piece of real exploration—for Livingstone had diverged from the course of the river on his way to the sea

K.'s *Diary*, 3–12. xi. 58. Livingstone, *Narrative*, 53–5.

in 1856—had been short but stiff. And the results of it had been a bitter disappointment. Livingstone had hoped against hope that the rapids would be far less formidable than their name and fame suggested. But it was obvious now—to Kirk, at any rate—that all river-transport must be interrupted at that point—at least 160 miles inside the putative Portuguese frontier at Zumbo. A *portage* system would, of course, be possible, but laborious and costly; and Livingstone must at last have suspected that his dreams of easy navigation up 'God's highway' into the very heart of Africa might have to be abandoned. And what then would happen to his scheme of making the friendly Makololo the first centre of British commerce and civilization?

Disappointment, with fatigue and ill-health to sharpen it, again bred disharmony within the little circle; and it is not an accident that Livingstone's frankest account of the psychological effects of fever occurs in this part of his own narrative of the Expedition. 'At such times', he declares, 'a man feels very much like a fool, if he does not act like one. . . . If a party were all soaked full of malaria at once, the life of the leader of the Expedition would be made a burden to him.' And indeed, at one time, life seems to have been burdensome for all of them. 'Things are not going on well here', notes Kirk soon after his return to Tete, 'between young Livingstone and the others [Baines and Thornton]. On the one side they have been sick and are more sensitive on that account; on the other he is one who has never had anyone under him and is awkward and ungracious in his dealings.' And presently there is another entry which reveals how far all the party were already feeling the physical and moral strain.

'The Doctor's skin disease is getting better and we may expect things to improve soon. It is a curious fact that everyone I have met here with the least fever or sickness of any sort becomes very irritable, and thus I can now tell the state of health and foresee a coming attack. This state is of little consequence with one who comes out with it, but becomes a serious inconvenience in such as the Doctor who never says much but often thinks a great deal. All the way by river to the interior is a serious thought with the Doctor; indeed the further progress of the Expedition becomes only a flying visit into a new country; and, as matters look now, if it is impossible to get the launch up, which I believe it to be, I think the Doctor will as soon see us all back again and go on alone with his brother.' [1]

These are gloomy meditations—one wonders if Kirk himself has a touch of fever on him—and presently the shadows deepen. The rainy season had begun; and Livingstone, still clinging to his dream, decided that one more visit should be paid to Kebrabasa to see whether the rapids might be navigable when the river was in flood. This time all the members of the Expedition, though some of them were still far from fit to stand fatigue, accompanied their leader. Before long they came again to a point at which the rocks, emerging from the flood, appeared to bar all progress. Even Livingstone could no longer deceive himself. 'The Doctor changed his appearance completely from the first time he saw the rocks . . . and in the shaking of his head we could see that things were not working well.' A little later the storm broke on Baines, who was taken to task for not seeing to the regular rationing of the Makololo—a trifling incident, but it is the first occasion on which Kirk, who evidently had a liking for Baines and had already commented in the diary on the complexity and difficulty of his storekeeper's job, feels that his great leader is not being scrupulously fair. He wishes 'the Doctor would explain more fully what he wants. Baines, too, is scarcely off the sick-list and has been, I should say, the hardest worked member of the Expedition.' And he expresses doubts as to how the party will stand the overland journey to the western end of the rapids. 'Thornton is well, but not long off the list, Baines is certainly weak, and the Doctor's brother never does very much.' These doubts were quickly justified. Before the end of the first day's march

[1] Livingstone, *Narrative*, 73–4. K.'s *Diary*, 14–19. xi. 58.

Baines was so exhausted that Kirk had to carry some of his *impedimenta*; but even Baines, in Kirk's eyes at any rate, was not the weakest link in the chain. The unfavourable opinion which Kirk had formed of Charles Livingstone is clear enough by now to any reader of his diary. He obviously thinks him lazy. He is irritated by his careful dress, and his 'lounging indoors and never exposing himself without an umbrella and felt hat with all the appurtenances of an English gentleman of a well-regulated family.' 'I fear most of us are not too particular about appearances when there is work doing.' And it is Charles Livingstone's fatigue, even more than Baines's, that now hampers the party's progress. 'Mr. L. has become so tired with the walk as to be fit for little more than sleep.' 'He being too tired to continue the march, we are to remain until to-morrow *in situ*.' 'Mr. L. is again very tired and scarcely able to walk, so we rest for an hour.' 'The day is fine and the road good, so that we get over some distance, although more than half the time is occupied allowing Mr. L. to have a snooze every half hour or so. . . . At each of these rests Baines and I practise at the hippopotami.' [1]

It is easy to imagine how Livingstone must have chafed at these delays. All his misgivings as to the difficulty of taking Europeans with him into Africa were coming true. Bedingfeld had been a failure, and he was beginning to distrust Baines. Quarrels, no doubt, were almost inevitable when fever was abroad—it had been hard, indeed, to control his own irritability at times—but even in good health the members of his little party did not seem to make the best of friends. And now, at the first real test of physical endurance, at least half their number had more or less broken down. If the Expedition was to proceed as a body, if Livingstone had to keep step with the laggards, its range of exploration would be miserably limited. For many days these thoughts must have simmered in Livingstone's mind, and at last his longing for speed and freedom broke out. It was, in truth,

[1] K.'s *Diary*, 22–28. xi. 58.

a crisis in the development of the domestic relations of the
Expedition and particularly of the relations between Kirk
and the man whom he never ceased, as will be clear, to
respect, and indeed to admire, and with whom he had so
far never openly disagreed. Let the diary tell the tale.

'Dec. 1st. Thornton is better, Livingstone is fatigued, and so
is Rae; indeed we have all had a good deal of hard tramping. At
5 a.m. when at chocolate, Dr. L. says that he will go back again
and explore the river himself as someone has told the men of
a waterfall in front of where we have been. He says that all the
members shall return to the ship. On this I suggested that it
was an insult given to the members, that there were some who
had not been sick nor been behindhand with any work and had
kept up with anyone there as far as we had gone. I made no
application to go, but simply thought it better to show Dr. L. the
light in which I looked on any such thing as the leader of the
Expedition going off alone on a difficult service and sending the
others to smoke their pipes and wait for his return. Certainly
the sick should never be expected to go on and the sooner back
the better. Dr L., reflecting a little, said that, if I chose to
volunteer, I might go: so of course I was only too glad of the
chance not only of seeing new country but also of avoiding the
slur offered to us by the Doctor. In fact all felt their honour
rather touched by the insult which after all, I believe, was
not meant for anything more than that he could do it himself
and was doubtful if anyone else could. (However, as it turned
out, I stood the work which he said was the hardest he ever had
in his whole lifetime quite as well as he.) I soon bundled up my
things and off we went, retracing our steps for Tshiperiziwa,
and were both of us as good friends as could be. I was pleased
at carrying my point and he was very well content to have me
with him.'

The outcome of the little dispute, in fact, had been admir-
able. Livingstone was incapable of artifice; but, if he had
employed the most adroit diplomacy, he could not have succeeded better in securing, without invidiously choosing, as
his companion the member of the Expedition whose strength
and resolution were least inferior to his own. And, as it
happened, this natural comradeship between the two best

KEBRABASA GORGE

Sketch by Kirk

men of the six was at once confirmed by a common ordeal. On the second day, after passing two more rapids, they reached a peculiarly difficult bit of country.

'Dec. 2nd. . . . We descend the hillside and come to the river, but such a river bank it is! For several miles it is confined between mountain sides, each 2,600 feet high. The actual channel occupied by the river seems about 70 yards wide, with a slope on either side of 30 feet, covered with gigantic rocks as of all the sphynxes and statues of Egypt. . . . Many of the single rocks, disjointed and pitched one over the other, were 20 feet high and polished and coated with a black skin, as if rubbed with plumbago, from the action of the water. The men were thoroughly done up now; the heavy marches and the burning heat of these stones (which was fearful) had blistered their feet, and we accordingly left them to rest, for what else could be done? They were unable to proceed. The Doctor and I went on, accompanied by one of the men, and spent several hours in getting about a mile further on. Such climbing I never had seen. We had to find our way among these gigantic stones, while every step was as if we should slip and go down some great crack out of which it would be no easy thing to extricate oneself, even with all the bones entire. It was then a question what was to be done; go on we must, that is we must see the end of this. Dr L. wished to pass over the hill from where we were while the men should take the old road and join [us] at last night's sleeping-place. I persuaded him rather to return to the men now and make the attempt again to-morrow. We found the men trying to come on, but as they had gone no distance we turned and slept at the river side. As the river rises 80 feet in flood, there will then be no possibility of getting along: it is bad enough among those burning stones, but in the bush it will be worse. The heat, however, now is like Hell if that place is what I imagine it—you cannot hold on any time by the rocks.'
'Dec 3rd. We try all we can to get out of the men whether there are any bad places in front or no, and it seems that there are. With great difficulty we get them to promise to go on one day more, but they do so saying they will die with us but there is no path. As they start, we watch them; if they had gone up the hill, I fear we should have followed them, but they take the way of the river. It took us a forenoon to gain the corner in front, not more than a mile and a half off. But such a way! Dr. L. never knew such work all his life. We passed among and over and under

these slippery hot rocks, then ascended what was practically a precipice, chiefly by the roots of bushes, for 200 feet. If one had fallen, all under must have gone to the bottom. At length we came to the bend and had before us a rapid, falling about 30 feet at an angle of 30°. This fall is named Morumva; on either side are steep inaccessible rocks through which the river makes a double bend. . . . We took over the hills on our return and found the way truly as it had been described. The people told us that no elephant or hippo ever passed and even an alligator could not. It was true we had to cut our way, and it was dark before we got back to the water we slept by 2 nights ago.' [1]

On December 6 they rejoined the launch, and the Expedition then turned its back on Kebrabasa and steamed down to Tete. A fortnight later Livingstone wrote to Lord Malmesbury to describe the results so far achieved. They were, it had to be confessed, merely negative. The Kebrabasa obstacle had been examined—and found to be an obstacle. Yet, even now, Livingstone would not abandon hope. On the contrary, in a report to Lord Malmesbury (in which, by the way, he expressed his gratitude for Kirk's assistance) he went so far as to say that 'we are all of the opinion that a steamer of light draught and capable of going 12 or 14 knots an hour would pass up the rapids without difficulty when the river is in full flood in January or February'. *All* of that opinion? 'The Doctor', commented Kirk on seeing the dispatch, 'gives a very favourable account of the rapids, much more so than I could do.' But, even on Livingstone's estimate, the Zambesi could not be regarded as an easy or regular waterway into the interior. An alternative must be looked for. The Zambesi's main tributaries must be examined. The second part of the plan of campaign—the search for that 'network of waters' in the north—must be put into operation, and without delay. Within a fortnight of their return from Kebrabasa Livingstone and Kirk, leaving the weaker brethren at Tete, had started to explore the Shire. [2]

[1] K.'s *Diary*, 2–4. xii. 58. Livingstone, *Narrative*, 59–62.
[2] L. to Malmesbury, 17. xii. 58 (F.O. 63/843). K.'s *Diary*, 26. xii. 5.

THE RIVER SHIRÉ

V

THE DISCOVERY OF NYASSALAND
(1859–1860)

I

LIVINGSTONE and Kirk left Tete on December 20, and, 'with only a moderate use of the anchor', arrived at Sena on Christmas Day. 'Enter the Shire river', says the diary on December 29: 'where it joins the Zambesi, the waters are very different, that of the Shire being clean and black, the Zambesi being very muddy.' Next day, while the crew were employed in wood-cutting, Livingstone and Kirk ascended Mount Morambala. Its top, about 4,000 ft. high, proved to be an undulating, highly cultivated plateau; and its sides were covered with vegetation, changing with the levels and, as Kirk, who was busy collecting specimens, remarks, 'by far the richest I have seen in the country'. For the next few days they made good progress. 'All the way', says Kirk on January 3, 'the river has continued as before, clear and deep. . . . Under proper care this would be a splendid plain, far before that of the Nile, with a fine navigable river winding through it.' They passed numerous villages; but the natives, though food seemed to be abundant, were not always ready to barter it for the white men's cloth. Sometimes 'they entered keenly into trade'; but more often they were shy, aloof, and even hostile. All carried bows and arrows, usually poisoned; and it was soon evident that, partly no doubt owing to the recent fighting, but also to past experience of slave-raids, there was much more suspicion of the new-comers and their astonishing steamboat than in the Zambesi area. One day Livingstone and Kirk found a village utterly deserted at their approach except for two men, one of whom kept flitting from bush to bush and taking aim at them with drawn bow. 'I dont know whether he would have picked off the Doctor or me,' says Kirk; but happily, at a hail, he lowered his weapon and made friends.[1]

[1] K.'s *Diary*, 20. xii. 58—4. i. 59. Livingstone, *Narrative*, 75–6.

On the sixth day up-stream they entered a belt of malarious marshland, 'exhaling at sunset a very offensive smell'. All over it, herds of elephants were moving, 'always accompanied by white birds which perched on their backs'; and, since one of the herds was close to the launch, Livingstone and Kirk ventured on a big game hunt. It was a lively experience. Kirk wounded an elephant in the head, at about eighty yards' range, 'and it instantly turned to us, spread out its enormous ears, curled its proboscis up like a butterfly, and raised its tail in the air like a bull. . . . With an elephant about to charge in long grass where running is impossible, there is little time to think or rather thought works double quick.' Fortunately perhaps, the animal was frightened by further shots, gave up its meditated charge, and lumbered off. On the way back to the launch, 'the Doctor and I were going after a low growl which made the air shake but nothing in itself to be dreaded—indeed we thought it was the wounded elephant groaning—when one of the Makololo called us back'. It was a lion hidden from them in the grass. 'We were not twenty yards from him and should never have seen him, till within two or three, for the reeds.' 'The ground', Kirk coolly continues, 'was very uncomfortable for hunting on foot on account of the long grass.'[1]

On January 8 they reached a village called Chibisa from the name of its chief, and, hearing of a 'small lake' some few days' journey off and a 'great lake' beyond that, they pushed on up-stream, 'the banks on either side . . . covered with niggers, each with his sheaf of arrows and bow in hand'. But, the very next day, they came to an end of navigation. A series of magnificent cataracts—which Livingstone named 'The Murchison', 'after one whose name has already a world-wide fame and whose generous kindness we can never repay' —barred all advance to steam-vessels, though 'perhaps', says Kirk, 'something like the *dahabeahs* of the Nile might be taken up'. Nor were the native reports as to the flow of

[1] K.'s *Diary*, 5–6. i. 59.

ELEPHANT MARSH

Sketch by Kirk

the river above the falls encouraging. As far as 'the lake ', which was five or six days' march, it was 'all of the character we see, continual rapids and one large waterfall'. It was decided, therefore, to return for the present to the base; and, having replenished the supply of wood and set their explorers' mark—'V. R. Jany 10, 1859'—on 'a large rock on the N.E. bank', they began the descent. Its only incidents were another elephant-hunt and a collision with a rock in midstream which knocked in one of the *Ma Robert's* paddles 'like a cracked nut'. By the middle of the month they were back at Shupanga and by the end of it at Tete.[1]

In the middle of March Livingstone and Kirk set out once more for the Shire. Quartermaster Walker and the seaman Rowe accompanied them, but again the other members of the Expedition were left behind. Although, since their experience at Kebrabasa, the advantages of this arrangement seemed obvious enough, Kirk was rather uneasy. 'My meditations on this trip are far from sweet,' he confides to the diary, as he sits in the cabin off Sena, 'but I hope things may with our usual good luck ... not turn out so bad in the end.' They were to be away as long as four months; their previous visit to Chibisa had been merely a *reconnaissance*; now they were to establish contact with the natives along the river and then to proceed overland to the lake-country. Was it wise for so small a party to plunge into the unknown, specially as a report had come in that the Mang-anja believed the *Ma Robert* to have caused the drought which had recently destroyed their crops, and regarded the white men as 'evil witches'. Rowe, moreover, had declared the *Ma Robert* to be unsafe, and yet they were going off in it for a long period without an engineer. Lastly, the unhealthy season was coming on. 'Bad health and a touch of fever is nothing, were it not for the bad humour it puts anyone in, and sickness is a thing with which the Doctor has no patience, either in himself or

[1] K.'s *Diary*, 8–22. i. 59. Livingstone, *Narrative*, 78. L. to Malmesbury, 14. ii. 59 (F.O. 63/871).

anyone else. I have no particular wish for a row with the "Manganja gents", but if the Doctor keeps good health one can manage them . . . but, if his digestive system dont go alright, he loses his diplomatic power wonderfully. But of all the miserables, that of being alone in the cabin for 4 weeks with millions of cockroaches and not a single companion to speak to, if I dont work at botany like mad in desperation——.'[1]

This time, at any rate, Kirk's misgivings proved unfounded. They travelled smoothly and kept well. They were robbed of their sleep, indeed, for three successive nights by swarms of mosquitoes—'they have fairly done me up and the Doctor too looks desperately seedy'—but they escaped an attack of fever. Kirk, moreover, had the satisfaction of shooting his first elephant in the marsh-belt—a young cow, nearly seven feet high to the shoulder. Nor were the natives troublesome. At one place, 'they were at first suspicious of our intentions, but on understanding us became friendly. The Doctor and I landed and walked with them to their village, explaining our objects and what we were. They replied that, when they saw white men, they were afraid, as the people of "Matakenia" (Mariano) had done so much mischief and killed so many in the lower country. . . . They sold us small beans. . . . There seems to be little communication from one village to another; we arrive unexpectedly everywhere and have to give the same story. In most other countries word would spread ahead of us much faster than we travel. Patience is needed to stop anywhere and buy a little to show our good will.' At all these villages, curiosity and acquisitiveness soon conquered suspicion. 'If there is trade going or anyone getting a present—in fact as long as the idea of Manchester is in any way before their minds —every other idea vanishes. . . . They receive a piece of cloth as a child would a toy, holding out their hands long before it is ready to give to them. When in this state of mind they can give no answer to any question beyond "Ey-ah", "Yes".'[2]

On March 29 they reached Chibisa, where they stayed five

[1] K.'s *Diary*, 14–17. iii. 59.   [2] *Ibid.*, 18–27. iii. 59.

MOUNT ZOMBA FROM THE EAST

MONGAZI VILLAGE

Sketches by Kirk in April, 1859

days making preparations and inquiries for their overland journey. The chief himself was very friendly. 'He is a hearty fellow, and likes a good laugh,' says Kirk. He paid several visits to the launch, which Kirk or Livingstone duly returned. 'Chibisa came off with us and dined—he would soon become civilized.' 'Looked in upon the Big Lion; we are always sure of a glass of "pombe" from him.' 'In the morning the chief comes on board bringing as usual native beer which I like now almost as much as he likes my tobacco.' All this time Chibisa was holding interminable 'palavers' with his councillors as to the character of the Expedition and its object in searching for the lakes, until, at last, he declared himself satisfied and provided the guide he had promised. On April 3, a Sunday, Livingstone conducted service, Chibisa attending; and, early next morning, leaving Walker and Rowe in charge of the *Ma Robert*, he and Kirk struck off to the north-east in quest of the nearer of the two 'great lakes' of which the natives spoke. Sixteen natives accompanied them—fourteen Makololo, an interpreter, and the guide.[1]

This last-named individual soon belied his title. 'It is quite clear', Kirk records of the very first afternoon, 'that the guide does not know the road or dont intend taking us, for here we are making a loop going back on our morning march.' Nor could they obtain other guides at any of the villages they passed or only such as deliberately led them astray. 'No one will guide us; they seem afraid of being blamed by their neighbours if we should turn out bad.' One volunteer, indeed, they found, but he was 'rather mad'. In the end they were obliged to trust to the compass and to the sight of the Shire below them on the left. After several days' march along devious native tracks, they sighted Mount Zomba, which rises to 6,000 ft. about fifty miles south of Lake Nyassa; and, at last, on April 16, from a high point, they 'got a fine view of what we were in search of. Before us was a long line of blue water; between us and it a wide plain.... Now

---

[1] K.'s *Diary*, 28. iii–4. iv. 59. Livingstone, *Narrative*, 79.

we can say, beyond all doubt if the eye is to be trusted, we have seen the Lake.' Two days later they reached its shore; and Kirk, one of the first two Europeans to see Lake Shirwa, enjoyed the first real thrill of discovery. And there were greater things to come. Beyond this lake, the natives told them, not more than a day's march northwards, 'begins "Ninyessi", the Lake of Stars, which goes on for so far north that they had never heard of anyone who reached the end of it. . . . They speak of this [Shirwa] as nothing in comparison with the other, and yet this is like a sea, the finest I have seen, surrounded with mountains on two sides . . . with an open sky against the water to the north, and islands with wooded hills and bold precipices in the midst of the water.' [1]

Content for the time being with the discovery of Shirwa and postponing the quest of Nyassa for another expedition, they retraced their steps to Chibisa. Their return was timely, for they found Quartermaster Walker very ill with fever, which, owing to the ignorance of his only white companion, Rowe, had not been relieved by the appropriate drugs. In Kirk's hands he soon rallied, and by the time the launch reached Shupanga he was well again. From Shupanga they proceeded, according to plan, to the sea, where they hoped to find a ship awaiting them with stores and mails. For more than a week they lingered there, surveying the mouths of the Zambesi to occupy their time; but no ship arrived, and, concluding at last that the admiral had not received Livingstone's letter fixing this period for a meeting, they decided to return up the river and make another assignation for the following month. On June 23 they reached Tete.[2]

Despite Kirk's dark anticipations, this four months' trip had proved a success—the first real success which the Expedition had achieved. The discovery of Lake Shirwa, it is true, was only of geographical importance; with its

[1] K.'s *Diary*, 4–18. iv. 59. L. to Malmesbury, 12. v. 59 (F.O. 63/871). Livingstone, *Narrative*, 79–82. *Ninyessi*, see Preface.
[2] *Ibid.*, 19. iv–23. v. 59.

LAKE SHIRWA

Sketch by Kirk, April 18, 1859

swampy banks and bitter, brackish waters it could not be regarded as a favourable site for European settlement. But on the way thither the explorers had crossed the hill-country, now known as the Shire Highlands—fertile, healthy, and clearly beyond the frontiers of Portuguese 'Zambesia'. That they had quickly recognized this area to be precisely what the Expedition was in search of is clear from the letters Kirk wrote to Professor Balfour and 'a medical friend at Edinburgh', both of which were published in the newspapers:

'The Shire flows for 100 miles nearly north in a plain of about twenty miles wide. There is a district near the middle which is marshy and cut up into islands overrun by elephants; but the greater part is fine land for the growth of cotton, sugar-cane, and rice. All these are now cultivated, and we can see at once the capabilities of the country. The cotton is of two sorts, one very fine with good staple. The sugar-cane is chewed, but the people do not know the art of extracting the sugar. Two crops of maize are obtained each year; and probably many other crops might be grown during the cold season, such as wheat. On either side are mountains—those of the north-east reaching 4000 feet. This would be a healthy position for Europeans. These highlands also yield crops of cotton, sugar-cane, and cereals, with various kinds of pulse; but more care is needed for their growth than in the valley. It seems a great thing to find this healthy region so near the coast, with a rich plain of enormous extent, and a navigable river leading without obstruction to the sea. . . . We were out twenty-three days, and very seldom slept under cover; we were wet every morning with dew, and our clothes dried as we marched in the burning sun; yet we were never delayed a day by the sickness of any one of the party, although often fatigued by evening with the heat and the heavy road. . . . We inquired whether any white man had ever been seen in these regions, but all agreed that we were the first ever seen; nor did the elders have any tradition of having seen any other than a single half-caste, with woolly hair, who once came near the lake to trade. This is very singular, as the region is so near to the Portuguese settlements, but is quite unknown to them; or, if it is, the discovery must have been kept a dead secret from all foreigners. Even now they don't profess to have heard of it.'[1]

[1] Letters of 11. iv and 4. v. 59, printed in *Proceedings of Botanical Society of Edinburgh*, vi. 317–21.

This first European penetration of the Shire Highlands was, in fact, a notable event in the history of Africa. From the seed sown that spring by Livingstone and Kirk grew the British Nyassaland Protectorate as we know it to-day. Hundreds of British colonists have now settled on the land they found. Blantyre, the business centre of the Protectorate, stands about twenty miles north-eastwards of Chibisa, whence they started on their march. Zomba, the official capital, lies on the slope of the mountain, close to the route they took. And from Blantyre now runs a railway down beside the Shire to the Zambesi and the sea.

2

'On landing at Tete [says the diary] we found all well, but there had been a good deal of sickness in our absence and things had not gone smoothly. Poor Baines has had many touches and his head seems often to have been quite out of equilibrium; he has done many things which, without this excuse, would have been very difficult of explanation. Thornton has no doubt been sick, but he is now in excellent health, and, although he often complains, yet I could not venture to prescribe for his most anomalous symptoms, many of which are only expressions of giving in to the feeling of lassitude which all have felt and which, if once yielded to, become daily more difficult to overcome. His geological work has been very limited indeed, and he can say very little, even in respect of the coal fields which it was his especial work to examine minutely. Mr. Rae has been very busy at a hundred little jobs; he has had many touches of his old fever. Mr. Livingstone has had the same; he has made a good collection of Birds of which I am right glad, as Botany keeps me well occupied. He has had an unenviable post, and being on no good terms otherwise with some of the others it has been doubly so. I am very glad I was not tried in his position.'[1]

Clearly Kirk's return to Tete was not altogether a happy home-coming. The cracks in the social structure of the Expedition were fast widening. And it was fortunate, perhaps, for Kirk that he could immerse himself in botany

[1] K.'s *Diary*, 23. vi. 59.

during the subsequent weeks of tedious waiting for the next move. 'My time', he records, 'is mostly taken up sorting my plants; they have all to be poisoned. Although no artist, I find my dissections of great use; I wish I had twice the number of them. My collection is very small; the flora of the lowlands is not numerous and on the high tablelands I could not gather many. First explorers must be content with gleanings only; another time I hope to do more to illustrate this flora which, if it does not show many new forms, will at least form an important contribution to the geographical distribution of plants.' On July 11 the *Ma Robert*, whose hull, as will be seen, was by no means in good condition, once more steamed off. Charles Livingstone and Rae now accompanied Kirk and 'the Doctor'; Walker and Rowe with thirty-six natives made up the party. 'We are bound first for the sea to try our luck again in meeting a ship; afterwards we go to make our way as far as possible to the Great Lake.' Thornton remained 'working on the other side [of the river] among the mineral veins of the opposite hills. A sharp letter and a little advice seem to have roused him, and for his sake as well as the credit of the Expedition I hope he will really work hard. . . . Baines is left with the things, but he is under restrictions such as his state renders absolutely necessary for the preservation of the Government goods.' [1]

In conversation with his companions on the voyage downstream Kirk discovered that some, at any rate, of the cracks were opening to a final break-up. In six months' time the two years' contract to which the original members of the Expedition had committed themselves would expire; and then, though the official programme seemed to have been only just begun, it would be open to any member to return to England. Walker and Rowe, who had been temporarily seconded from their service on ship-board, could, of course, apply for their release at any time; and both were now, it seems, quite 'fed up' with the life of the Expedition. 'Walker

[1] K.'s *Diary*, 23. vi–11. vii. 59.

the Quartermaster is still of a mind to clear out if he can. If he asks to be invalided, I think we can [authorize it] on a clear conscience as he has had bad health; but the Kroomen are at the bottom of it, they are a bad insubordinate set and, if possible, do things to annoy him. Nor can officers' authority do much for it, the Doctor has done his best.... It's even worse, however, when Rae tells me that Rowe is sick tired of this also, and it's only the hope of being promoted in case another ship comes out that keeps him up. I thought he was liking it, and he is just the man to suit the Doctor.' And that was not all. 'Rae is keen to get off and has given in his resignation to the Doctor, or rather he does not wish to renew the engagement beyond the two years. He will be a loss, as he can do many things and is a fine fellow. I think he may be prevailed on to remain, that is if they raise the salary, a thing which none of us would be the worse of, but he is most in need of it.' And then the diarist, who has had, it seems, a touch of fever, lapses once more into a transient fit of gloom. 'My £350 p. ann. minus income-tax (especially if there is war going on) wont be much to go ashore with, after one has had one's liver fried for 2 years and no one knows how much longer. We certainly understood we should have a decently healthy country upland; possibly the Government may take a thought upon two years in delta jungle being not the most salubrious place. But I must go to some of those horrid things I have got to write, and cease yarning a lot of grumbles which is my way of working off fever. It's a very innocent one, I hope, as it's the fault of anyone who reads it and not mine for exercising the English privilege.' A few days after this unusual effusion Kirk was smitten with a sharp attack of ague. 'Hope I shant have any more of that sort of thing, it pulls one down at a great rate, but it's after all better than the other sort of fever.' [1]

On July 29 they reached Expedition Island and next day they sighted the hoped-for ship. 'The captain of the *Persian*

[1] K.'s *Diary*, 18–27. vii. 59.

comes in with the stores he can spare which are very acceptable to us. . . . The Kroomen are all sent off. Walker goes invalided to the Cape and we get one seaman in his place, so we are now with Rowe as leading stoker and the seaman with the Makololo for crew, "Bahallum". The seaman we have got is a young active fellow of the name of Hutchins.' Meantime the wretched *Ma Robert*, which Rae had declared to be in a dangerous condition six months earlier, was badly in need of repair. 'We get the vessel beached and dig out the sand underneath to examine the bottom. The plates were only $1/16''$ thick at first, and now they are so worn through by wear and rust that, when touched, the water springs. . . . There is nothing left but to puddle the bottom over with clay in bags and keep the water out as long as possible; but it is a feeble thing we are trusting to; and, when she goes, it will likely be in large holes now.' While Rae was occupied with these repairs, Kirk was no less busy 'filling the pot'. 'I had a long hunt for some fresh meat . . . and got a waterbuck, but hunting is killing hard work and I have had all forenoon spooring among mangrove swamps which stink and make one feel squeamish. But someone must get food for the party, and all the luck of killing has been on my side, so it falls to me, that department. Last night I had to sleep out without a coat by the side of a swamp, being caught by the rising tide. . . . If I keep clear of the fevers, I must be very thankful.'[1]

The ship had brought a piece of stimulating news. 'From the captain of the "Persian" we heard of the splendid discoveries of Burton and Speke inland from Zanzibar. This will pull us up to do something more. . . . The Lake Tanganyika is surely the source of the Zambesi, but we have no particulars. The map of Africa has been pretty well filled in within the last two years; it cannot be long before the whole is settled now.' But, as the *Ma Robert*, puffing and leaking, steamed slowly back through that torrid Zambesi plain, Kirk's thoughts of the future were once more overcast.

[1] K.'s *Diary*, 29. vii—2. viii. 59.

Livingstone, it appears, had made up his mind, since he last left Tete, that Thornton and Baines must follow on Bedingfeld's tracks. He seems to have ascribed Thornton's failure to do his allotted work mainly to sheer lethargy; but he took a far more serious view of Baines's case. Kirk, as has been seen, was quite ready to believe that the unfortunate artist had proved a very incompetent and casual storekeeper; but nowhere in his diary does he suggest that the irregularities complained of were anything more than were to be expected from one who was very frequently confused in mind, and sometimes delirious from repeated attacks of fever. Livingstone, on the other hand, though, when he left Tete, he had made some allowance for the state of Baines's health, wrote from Sena charging him with deliberate appropriation and disposal of large quantities of the public stores—'a fact which lays you open to prosecution'—and informing him that he would be sent home at the earliest opportunity.[1] As to the justice of this decision Kirk is significantly silent; but it is clear from earlier pages in the diary that he liked Baines and was sorry for him. It is not surprising, therefore, to find his reflections taking a despondent turn again.

'The rapids of Kebrabasa have kept us from fulfilling our proper work and whether we shall ever reach the interior as an Expedition seems very doubtful. Baines and Thornton are to be sent home the first opportunity. Rae is sick tired of this and only wishes to clear out with a clean bill and nothing against him. As to exploring on foot I cannot be of much use. Mr. C. L. is very weak, and if he does not pick up a little more spirit than we have seen, he will not stand out; but I think he would be different if he were off alone with the Doctor as I shall not be astonished to see him before many months.

'I hope that, while here, I have done my duty; at least I have tried. When out of sorts in this climate, like my comrades, I have been short in the temper; but the vessel and the many other duties

---

[1] L. to Malmesbury, 26. vii. 59 (F.O. 63/871). L. to Baines, 21. vii. 59. This last and other letters on the case are printed (with a leader favouring Baines) in the *South African Advertiser and Mail*, 6. ii. 1861.

and the duties of first explorers overland have not permitted me to make the connected series of observations which are required and which those who may criticise our work at home will unmercifully expect from us. But a steam vessel of the feeblest sort, without naval officers and proper staff, involves on others many extra duties for which they are not qualified.

'Here is another of the outpourings of a fellow under the influence of mangroves and headache. I am very glad that my fevers are nothing more than a general shade of gloom over the outer world which passes off on the way.' [1]

A shade of gloom, certainly, but no peevish revilings of his fate, no suggestion of flight, as soon as his contract has expired, from the heat and the fevers, from the ill-assorted company and the uncongenial work, if he can still be useful. With no thought that any other eyes will see what he is writing, he sets down his own shortcomings, such as they are, and his doubts, strange enough to those other eyes, as to his fitness for the task of exploration; but if 'the Doctor' needs him, it is evident he will not leave him in the lurch. And then at the end, as before, he makes apology to himself, as it were, for his passing fit of pessimism. Apology? Every reader of these rather moving passages in the diary will surely feel that, under all the circumstances, this young untried Scot has, so far, stood the physical and, still more, the moral strain as few could hope to do. Of the severity of that moral strain a good example is afforded by an incident that occurred a few days after the last-quoted entry in the diary was made. One feels that Kirk himself would hardly have desired the reproduction in cold print of his account—typically restrained as it is, though written at the heat of the moment—of what was, in itself, a petty little affair. Suffice it, then, to say that Kirk, having gone off collecting specimens one morning, returned twenty minutes behind the time fixed for the starting of the launch. He found it gone and had to run along the bank in the heat of the sun to catch it up. It appeared that Charles Livingstone had prevailed on his brother to give Kirk a lesson

[1] K.'s *Diary*, 3. viii. 59.

for going off 'sporting' for 'hours' without a thought for the convenience of the other members of the Expedition. 'In the afternoon', Kirk concludes, 'I spoke to the Doctor and came to a distinct understanding with him; he knew it was quite an accidental mistake as to time. . . . I hope it is explicable on Mr. C. L.'s part by a general bad stomach or fever, although medically I see no such thing about him. We are here cut off from the world and cannot choose our companions or he should not be one of mine; but here I should endure a good deal rather than make an open split which would cause dis-peace the remainder of the time; and, knowing that the Doctor does not in the very least participate [in] the mean feelings of his brother, I dont care very much.' Again one's respect for young Kirk rises.[1]

Meanwhile the *Ma Robert* and her human freight, both showing signs of wear and tear, had come slowly up past Shupanga and for the third time entered the Shire. A change, much needed, was coming for that sore-pressed little com-pany—a change from the close confinement of the damp cabin, from the mangroves and malaria, from the tiresome shallows of the Zambesi and the deadly monotony of its banks, a change to the more tolerable fatigues of an overland march, the refreshing climate of the hill-country, and all the new interest and excitement of setting out to find the Lake of Stars.

3

On the way up the Zambesi the *Ma Robert*, leaking from below, had also been drenched from above by heavy rain, which penetrated the roof of the cabin in such volume that any one who wanted to write had to use an umbrella, satur-ated the cushions on which the voyagers slept, and destroyed, as Livingstone's *Narrative* records, 'many of the botanical specimens, laboriously collected and carefully prepared by

[1] K.'s *Diary*, 15. viii. 59.

Dr. Kirk'. But once up the Shire, the rain was left behind
and Kirk had only to complain of a lesser plague. 'Such a
nuisance the cockroaches are. They eat everything. My
specimens are going under to them.' The *Ma Robert*, however, had not yet exhausted her capacity for evil. She had
been guaranteed to carry from ten to twelve tons and about
thirty-six men. On this trip, though there was very little
baggage, the load of forty-four men was found to be too
heavy; and some of the Makololo were therefore transferred
to the two boats which were towed behind. All went well for
a time; but on August 17, Livingstone having rather rashly
decided to push on after sunset, the *Ma Robert* struck a sand-
bank and, as a result of clumsy navigation in the dusk, one
of the boats was capsized. 'She was overloaded', says the
diary, 'and down by the bow, and may have had a much
greater weight on one side than on the other, for the men
knew nothing about water and canoes, and the mosquitoes
and chill of the night had induced them to get their mats over
their heads.' Most of them reached the bank or were dragged
on board the ship, but one was drowned. 'No word has come
of the missing man', notes Kirk next morning. 'Dr. L. gives
him up. It is a great wonder we saved so many of them. . . .
Steam on. Dr. L. sick with anxiety and vexation at the un-
lucky accident.' 'His loss', wrote Livingstone afterwards,
'threw a gloom over us all, and added to the chagrin we often
felt at having been so ill-served in our sorry craft by one of
our own countrymen.' [1]

Even with the lightened load constant pumping and bail-
ing were needed to keep the 'sorry craft' afloat. 'This morning', Kirk records four days after the accident, 'the middle
compartment has been pumped twice—it was up to the
lockers in the stokehole—and by noon the fore compartment
had been bailed twice also.' And a little later: 'Yesterday
the engine-room was pumped eight times. The leaks are
increasing.' Not unnaturally Kirk began to wonder whether

[1] K.'s *Diary*, 17–19. viii. 59. Livingstone, *Narrative*, 85, 92–3.

the vessel might not sink while the exploring party were away in the interior. And what would happen then? 'We are . . . amongst those whose monopoly of the river we have broken up, and we cannot expect them to do any act of kindness in the event of a weak party falling into their hands. . . . We shall be guided by circumstances, and the Commander is a much more adventurous person than myself, and in him I have the greatest confidence from his past experience of native character.' Boat or no boat, Livingstone was certainly not going to abandon the search for Lake Nyassa. On arrival at Chibisa, the *Ma Robert* was left there in charge of Rae and Hutchins, and on August 28 the rest of the party started to follow the course of the river northwards across the plain.[1]

For the first few days the route led through well-cultivated country, rich in iron. 'Every village has its forge and in the forest are the smelting furnaces.' The Manganja in this district, having seen or heard of the explorers before, were friendly, if unhelpful. Kirk noticed that the men were much addicted to their native beer which 'has a pinkish colour and the consistence of gruel'—in one village they were all hilariously drunk—and that the women were all disfigured by the *pelele* or lip-ring, inserted in youth in the upper lip which in time becomes horizontally extended some two inches from the nose. 'Some of these women are very good-looking,' he observes, 'but that horrible lip-ring is the most infernal invention for making all equally ugly that ever women tried.' But it was not only, it appeared, a universal custom; it was a symbol of sex. 'What', cried an old chief to whom Kirk ventured to criticize it: 'Horrible! Woman no lip-ring! Why, they would then be men, no longer women.' On this chief's own appearance Kirk has an amusing note. 'He seems to have a superstitious veneration for bits of old clothes hung about his person, and what he wears as a cap is on a par for dirt with any engineer's working-cap. His general physiognomy reminds me of Ld. Brougham as seen in *Punch*.' Mean-

[1] K.'s *Diary*, 22–24. viii. 59.

time, the travellers were steadily leaving the low country behind them; the nights were getting cooler and dew falling; and presently they reached the highlands south-westwards of Mount Zomba. 'Where is there a better land for a colony?' Kirk asks. 'Fine soil, growing many things now, and fit to grow anything including wheat, with abundance of water available for irrigation or water-power. And below a still richer valley where cotton and sugar would flourish. There is no tsetse fly to destroy the cattle, while the native grasses are those chosen by them.' 'Up to this', he goes on, 'we have had no difficulty. . . . We knew the country and the people knew we did. We had also made friends, and none of the obstacles which we had to overcome formerly were thrown in our way. Now we begin new ground.' [1]

The chief difficulty of the new ground was the ignorance and timidity of the natives. How, indeed, could they be expected to understand what these alarming white strangers wanted? 'The truth is the best', says the diary. 'We always tell them that we are a great people who make cloth and guns and gunpowder and sell these to others for cotton and corn and sugar and other things; that this country seems good for growing such things as we wish; and that, if we tell our countrymen that the people here are willing and able to give them cotton, they will come and sell goods regularly.' 'Of course', Kirk drily adds, 'some politicians believe this is all nonsense.' But it was not always possible to give these reassuring explanations. The party was now within the area of the slave-raids. 'No doubt', notes Kirk, 'many a child or unarmed person has been carried off and never heard of again.' And so some villages were deserted by all their inhabitants as soon as the new-comers were sighted, while at others they were told that it was not a 'head-village' or that the headman was not to be found; and at all they were unwelcome guests, to be passed on as quickly as might be. 'Our course was to

[1] K.'s *Diary*, 30. viii.–5. ix. 59. A sketch of the *pelele* is given in Livingstone, *Narrative*, 115.

find out the general direction of the "head-village", and then, going on without any guide, to enter the largest and most respectable and ask for the public sleeping-place for strangers where we would squat; and it would have required more arguments than ever were brought to bear to make us move, once settled to our mind.' At one point there was 'a general panic'. 'No one will give any information, there is no headman with whom to reason, and the rabble without a leader, who rush out from several villages, press in amongst us with their bows and arrows, each one more terrified than another. They will not listen to reason and sit down, so we start off, keeping to the paths which lead to the north, while the frightened natives remain, some stupid, others thankful that we have passed their village at least, while others again run on before shouting to all to flee.' At another village, on the other hand, the natives were aggressive, threatening the strangers with knives and arrows and apparently bent on provoking a quarrel; and, when the party moved quietly off, they hung for a time on its heels, muttering, 'the whites are no men'. At this time the explorers were passing through a thickly peopled valley, but presently they emerged into a vast grassy plain on higher ground and here they found 'a new people who had not received any bad accounts of us'. At the first village, Mikena, 'the chief was very civil, rather inquisitive, and laughed (a good sign). The presents we gave pleased both him and his wives who came clapping hands and praising his good looks, rigged out in a bit of blue cloth, value 4d.' None the less, when all the party were taken ill that night with something like dysentery which lasted for several days, Kirk, who had suffered least, was quite uncertain whether it was due to their own cook who had used such an excessive amount of peppery Mulligatawny paste to make their soup that it had blistered their mouths, or whether the chief had doctored the beer he had given them with *muave*, a poison used for trial by ordeal and for testing suspicious characters. And suspicion, after all, could scarcely be avoided by any stranger in any part of that tormented country. It was only a little farther on that Kirk had his first sight of a gang of slaves on the march, laden with ivory, malachite, and copper. Their Arab captors offered to sell the explorers some children; but, 'on understanding that we were English, they made off during the night, although the[y] must have been above a hundred strong with several guns among them. The slaves were forced on by a long pole forked at one end in which the slave's neck was fastened while the other was carried on a man's shoulder behind; at night the free end was fastened to a tree.' 'The flight of this party was of little use', adds Kirk, who is describing this incident in a letter to Sir William Hooker, 'as, on reaching the coast, they were seized by H.M. gunboat *Lynx*, and the slaves recognized us on seeing us at the mouth of the Zambesi several months afterwards.' A day or two later a villager offered Kirk a slave for a fathom of red cloth. 'He says the price of one at the coast is two pieces of cloth of 8 fathoms each, a bunch of beads, and a necklace or two.' [1]

The march had now lasted about a fortnight and there was still no certain news to be got of any great lake ahead. They could only plod on beside the Shire, now flowing 'smooth and seemingly deep, confined by reedy and papyrus banks'. On September 14 they sighted at last what they supposed to be Nyassa; but it proved to be only a lakelet, called Pamalombe, some ten miles long by five in breadth. Next day the natives assured them that no lake had ever been heard of and that the river ran on to where, at 'two months'' distance, it issued from between two gigantic vertical rocks. When, however, it was explained to them that the white men knew of the lake's existence from a book, they blandly confessed that it lay only a few miles ahead. And so, on September 17, a little before noon, the Expedition discovered the Lake of

---

[1] K.'s *Diary*, 6–15. ix. 59. K. to Sir W. Hooker, 26. ii. 60 (Kew, *African Letters, 1859–65*, No. 156). For a sketch of the slave-stick or *goree*, see Livingstone, *Narrative*, 125.

Stars—only just in time to win the credit of discovery, for
Dr. Roscher, a German explorer, who had followed the Arab
route from Kilwa and was murdered on his way back to the
coast, reached the north end of the Lake, two months later,
on November 19. 'A splendid lake', notes the diary; 'cranes,
reeds on bank, sandy at places, 2 islands visible, mountains
on either side white spots in the distance, general bearing
little W. of N. true.' Kirk also observed that this south end
of the Lake was a natural focus of trade-routes. One party of
traders, who again offered slaves for sale, was going east.
A second party, composed of Swahili, was coming up from the
coast and trading in malachite. Copper ornaments were
another article of trade, and a native copper-mine was seen
working in the neighbourhood. But the chief commercial
product of all this locality was unquestionably slaves.[1]

'The trade of Cazembe and Katanga's country and of other parts
of the interior', writes Livingstone at this point of his *Narrative*,
'crosses Nyassa and the Shire on its way to the Arab port, Kilwa,
and the Portuguese ports of Ibo and Mozambique. According
to information collected by Colonel Rigby at Zanzibar and from
other sources, nearly all the slaves shipped from the above-
mentioned ports come from the Nyassa district. By means of
a small steamer, purchasing the ivory of the Lake and the River
above the cataracts . . . the Slave Trade in this quarter would be
rendered unprofitable—for it is only by the ivory being carried
by the slaves that the latter do not eat up all the profits of a
trip. . . . It is only by cutting off the supplies in the interior that
we can crush the Slave Trade on the coast. The plan proposed
would stop the Slave Trade from the Zambesi on one side and
Kilwa on the other; and would leave, beyond this tract, only the
Portuguese port of Inhambane on the south, and a portion of the
Sultan of Zanzibar's dominion on the north for our cruisers to
look after. The lake people grow abundance of cotton for their
own consumption and can sell it for a penny a pound or even less.
Water-carriage exists by the Shire and Zambesi all the way to

[1] K.'s *Diary*, 16–17. ix. 59. Livingstone (*Narrative*, 123), gives
the date of the discovery of the Lake as Sept. 16; but Kirk's diary,
which has an entry for each day after the start from Chibisa, seems
more trustworthy.

England, with the single exception of a porterage of about thirty-five miles past the Murchison Cataracts, along which a road of less than forty miles could be made at a trifling expense; and it seems feasible that a legitimate and thriving trade might, in a short time, take the place of the present unlawful traffic.' [1]

One day this dream was to be fulfilled as completely as Livingstone himself could have hoped; and by exploring the route to Lake Nyassa and the character of the Shire, his Expedition had achieved the first step towards it. At the moment there was nothing more to be done. Later on, of course, the Lake must be surveyed from end to end; but for that it was obviously better to wait and bring up a boat than to attempt the toilsome journey along the shore. So, on September 18, the explorers began their downward march; and on October 8, with no adventures worth recording, they reached Chibisa.

4

The Expedition was fated, it seems, to follow a regular sequence of 'ups and downs'; and the discovery of Lake Nyassa, a real and encouraging achievement, was the prelude to another period of ill-health, friction, and unhappiness. Those six weeks of constant hardship had told on the physique of all the party. Kirk, as usual so far, escaped lightly with a touch of liver trouble. Rae he reports as 'no better than he ought to be'. Charles Livingstone was laid up for several days, 'quite worn out' with fatigue and fever. But 'the Doctor' himself was the most serious case, very sick and feeble for the last part of the march and getting worse on arrival at the base. On October 13 Kirk notes symptoms of dysentery. 'Mr. C. L.', on the other hand, is 'getting better and horribly disagreable company'. 'In fact', he sums up, '250 miles at this season and in this country on foot and on strange food is enough for the strongest; and to have no

---

[1] Livingstone, *Narrative*, 128–9. L. to Lord John Russell, 15. x. 59 (F.O. 63/871).

better fare, not even flour or biscuit or decent sugar, on the return, is more than any one can stand'.[1]

Worse was to come. On October 17 Kirk received from Livingstone written instructions of a distinctly unpleasant kind.

'You are hereby required to pass overland with Mr. Rae to Tete in order to bring away two persons, lately members of the Expedition, in order to send them home by the man of war appointed to meet us at Kongone Harbour in the middle of November next.

'As Mr Thornton, one of the persons referred to, has been honest, and failed in his duties as geologist chiefly from ignorance and a want of energy, he is permitted to take the geological specimens with him, but on the understanding that they are Government property. . . .

'The other individual referred to (Mr Baines), having been guilty of gross breaches of trust in *secretly* making away with large quantities of public property, and having been in the habit of secreting Expedition property in his private boxes, it will be necessary for you to examine his boxes. . . . It will be proper for you to ask him in the presence of Mr. Rae what he did with five jars of butter which he took out of a cask and never sent to table or for cooking. What he did with five barrels of loaf-sugar which he was seen opening and drying, but which were never used in the Expedition. The answers to these and other questions to be put down in the storekeeper's book as soon as convenient and signed by yourself and Mr. Rae. Take possession of this book and of another book of mine in his boxes ('The Plant'), of specimens of brass rings, and of anything else you have reason to believe does not belong to him. If he declines your offer of conveyance he is left to his own resources.'[2]

A disagreeable task; but, as it happened, Kirk was lucky to be able to fulfil it. For, in the course of that overland journey, savage Africa nearly succeeded in killing him. It was a hot time of year; but no one supposed that water, which had been so plentiful throughout the Shire valley, would not be found in quantities at least sufficient to maintain Kirk and Rae, with their guides and a few other natives, on a

[1] K.'s *Diary*, 8–16. x. 59.   [2] Livingstone to K., 17. x. 59.

march of less than a hundred miles. But very soon the party found all the watercourses they met with to be quite dried up; and such water as they could obtain by digging in the beds only served to increase their thirst; natives, indeed, were seen making salt from it. The heat, meantime, was terrible. The tropical sun burned down on the baked earth, from which nearly all the grass had been withered away. 'The men frequently jumped from the path in the vain hope of cooling for a moment their scorched feet under the almost shadeless bushes.' The endurance of the party would certainly have been exhausted if, at long intervals, they had not found water; and this, though it was not salt, was 'nauseous and muddy from the frequent visits of large game'. To make matters worse, Kirk had a sharp bout of fever on the first day; and the supplies of food they carried were soon reduced to elephant's meat and salt pork: 'stiff food', notes Kirk, 'for a fever patient'. On the fourth day, 'Rae suffering from thirst and done up' is the brief comment. But for three more days, still tormented and weakened by thirst and heat, they plodded on, and on October 25 reached Tete. One native, the bearer of the salt pork, had fallen behind and came in two days later 'with nothing but the fibre of the meat left, the fat, melted by the blazing sun, having all run down his back'. But, the ordeal over, Kirk indulges in no reflections on it. Such risks, no doubt, had often enough to be taken by tropical explorers. Yet, had the distance to be covered been much longer, both he and Rae and possibly the natives also might well have perished. As it was, to quote Livingstone, 'the journey nearly killed our two young friends'.[1]

After a day's rest, Kirk proceeded to examine Baines's books and boxes. The result was not very conclusive. No account had been kept of butter, but Baines declared that it had all been used for the Expedition. One cask of sugar could not be traced. The private boxes yielded nothing which could be identified as public property except a small

[1] K.'s *Diary*, 17–24. x. 59. Livingstone, *Narrative*, 132–3.

piece of canvas. Kirk must have felt rather like a suspicious housewife searching the boxes of a distrusted servant-girl, but he could get through the unpleasant job and yet no more quarrel with Baines than he had with Bedingfeld. 'I feel bound to acknowledge', wrote Baines afterwards, that Dr. Kirk 'performed the duty imposed on him in the most gentlemanly and least offensive manner.' Meantime he stoutly protested his innocence. Beyond a few tins of sardines presented to two Portuguese in return for gifts and services to the Expedition, he had given, he asserted, nothing whatever away. And, later on, he obtained written statements to this effect from Major Sicard and from Rae. The former declared that he knew nothing of Baines's disposal 'of any quantities of provisions belonging to the Expedition to present to any person in this town'—a town so tiny that, as Baines pointed out, its commandant must have known most of what went on in it. Rae was still more explicit. 'I do hereby give my word that I have never seen you give away any of the stores belonging to the Expedition, neither have I any reason to think that you did so.' But against such testimony could be set the undoubted fact that Baines, when ill, had made some sort of a confession, though he himself alleged that Charles Livingstone had unfairly interpreted to that end some words he had dropped in a state of 'partial delirium'. All the rest of the evidence against him was Charles Livingstone's. 'The Doctor', however, had made up his mind. He rejected Baines's plea for a formal examination at Tete where alone confirmatory evidence could be obtained. When the whole Expedition was reunited at the Kongone Mouth (November 22)—the *Ma Robert* having come straight from Chibisa and Kirk and Baines, who was ill as usual *en route*, arriving a few days later—the defendant was accorded a final hearing. He did not better himself, as Kirk's brief record shows: 'Dr. L. examined Mr. B.'s case yesterday; he has no presence of mind in making replies.' So when H.M.S. *Lynx*, which arrived according to plan with provisions and mails on November 29 and sailed again on December 11, Baines went with her to the Cape, where he spent many months in correspondence with the Foreign Office, protesting not so much against his dismissal as against the charge of theft, which, unanswered and unproved in any proper judicial manner, had set a slur on his name. But the Foreign Office was getting accustomed to domestic friction in its tropical African Expeditions, whether on the Niger or on the Zambesi; and it had rightly determined to uphold the authority of the men it had put in charge. So Baines was informed that Livingstone had acted in accordance with the full powers he possessed and that Lord John Russell saw no reason to interfere. At the beginning of 1861 Baines published the whole correspondence in a sympathetic South African newspaper. And there, it seems, the incident closed. A nasty little affair, decidedly nastier than the Bedingfeld case, yet one on which the impartial student, at this length of time, must be cautious of committing himself. Baines, on the one hand, had nothing against him in his previous record on the Australian Expedition or elsewhere; and those who knew him believed him incapable of deliberate theft. Livingstone, on the other hand, clearly had no doubts, and not only is his rectitude unquestionable, but also his kindness of heart. Baines himself admitted that Livingstone's refusal to grant him the regular 'prosecution' he claimed was partly due to 'a feeling, which, I feel bound to say, he showed in more than one instance during this affair, that he wished to send me home with as little against me as possible'. One wonders indeed, whether, whatever the truth may have been, those definite charges were really necessary at all. Was not Baines's physical and mental condition the dominant factor in the case? That alone justified his dismissal. Might he not have been quietly sent off and those sordid accusations dropped and forgotten? But Livingstone—it has already been apparent—was not good at managing his fellow whitemen. Unusual or delicate personal relations baffled him. He could not be diplomatic or persuasive. And so, since Baines, in his hectic moods, was undoubtedly a troublesome, obstinate person, he cut the knot and bluntly told him what he believed to be the truth. One wonders, again, how Kirk would have handled the case, had he been in command. Anyway—and this is the justification for giving more than a casual reference to the sorry business—he had once more shown fine qualities of character in a testing situation. Other men's relations with Baines, in those awkward circumstances, might not have been so easy and human; nor might other men's diaries have been so reticent.[1]

One further trouble in this depressing period was the attitude of the local Portuguese. Kirk had not been long in the country before he began to comment in his diary on the degraded life of its European residents, not to mention the half-castes. There were exceptions, of course; one or two have been noticed in this narrative; but in general they seemed to have lost all sense of European standards. Their sexual habits were peculiarly nauseating to the young Scottish doctor. One of the kindliest of the Expedition's friends, he discovered, was accustomed to buy himself native concubines nine or ten years old. 'I believe', he records, 'that there is not one white man or one who may call himself white in the whole district without venereal disease', and he speaks of their wretched, tainted children as 'a disgrace to the European name'. Nor has he any doubts as to their utter incapacity to govern or to develop their great dependency. 'In travelling among the native tribes the Portuguese traders pay for liberty to pass and seem to give in to absurd demands made by any powerful chief.' 'This land will some day make

---

[1] K.'s *Diary*, 25. x. and 24. xi. 59. Baines's letters of protest to Foreign Office in F.O. 63/871 and 894. Partly printed in *South African Advertiser and Mail*, 6. ii. 1861. After his dismissal Baines went to Cape Colony and joined James Chapman in an expedition to the Victoria Falls by the direct overland route from the Cape. Prints of the sketches he made there are still advertised for sale from time to time. In 1868 he explored the route from Pretoria to the Umtali goldfield. He died at Durban in 1876. (*D.N.B.*)

many a fortune doubtless, but it seems as if the present claimants (for owners we cannot call them) must be driven out, and for that no compulsion is needed. Let the Portuguese go on as they are doing and they will soon be extinct or arise as a race of bastards to do the drudgery of some active race. The Slave Trade has brought about this miserable state of things.' On hearing that the Governor desires to discuss the future development of the country with the British visitors, Kirk comments: 'Instead of gaining strength, it seems much more likely that they will be out of this before long, nor should I be astonished to see the French in, although I should be very sorry for it'. But, after all, the immorality and incapacity of the Portuguese did not directly affect the fortunes of the Expedition. What mattered most was their attitude to it. And this attitude, friendly enough, as has been seen, at the outset, had soon begun to stiffen. The exploration of the Shire and the discovery of Lake Shirwa undoubtedly alarmed the authorities at Quilimane, and suspicion and estrangement quickly spread. 'The Portuguese dont like us as an Expedition,' noted Kirk on June 4, 'and some have a personal dislike also. With several of our members the feeling is mutual. All I can say is, they are fools to let us in at all, and it is what we never would have done to foreigners in Australia or the like.' But it was not till Kirk was at Tete after his overland march that the trouble came to a head. Though the commandant was uniformly courteous and anxious to help, the Portuguese townsmen banded together to prevent Kirk obtaining a boat or a crew to take Baines, Rae, and himself down the river. 'The hatred of many Portuguese towards me', he observes (October 30), 'is very distinct.' Two days later, at a meeting summoned by the commandant, 'the whole of the Portuguese present state that they will give us no sailors nor let us have sailors if they can prevent it'. Bold talk, certainly, and malice, but nothing more effective than that. 'Cowardly devils', Kirk calls them; 'if you speak sharp to them, they cringe like their slaves.'

In the end, of course, boat and crew were obtained; but Portuguese hostility, thus clearly manifested, was obviously one more complicating factor in the dark future of the Expedition. And, in the light of events some twenty years later, it is interesting to note the comment Kirk made in his diary on a piece of news—very premature news as it happened— which Livingstone had gleaned at this period from the pages of a Portuguese official gazette. 'There is a German colony on its way out', he writes. 'Well, they will at least break up the exclusiveness of the Portuguese.' [1]

Nor was it only the local authorities that disliked the Expedition. The Lisbon Government had muffled its anxiety and conceded with such grace as it could muster the facilities it could scarcely refuse; but before the *Pearl* had reached the mouth of the Zambesi it had taken steps to forestall or counteract any discoveries which the intruders might make as to the realities of Portuguese sovereignty in 'Zambesia'. On June 5, 1858, it was officially announced that the Governor-General of Mozambique had been instructed to take measures 'for keeping the Caffres in proper subjection . . . and securing at the same time the land and water carriage in Zambesia'. To this end a company of infantry was to be stationed in the country as a 'military colony' to which other colonists were invited. Zumbo was to be re-established as a fortified post—an admission, by the way, of its present derelict state—and sites selected between Zumbo and Tete and between Tete and Sena for the erection of new forts 'for the effectual maintenance of public security in Zambesia'. A custom-house was to be set up on the River Luabo or some other mouth of the Zambesi—a wisely vague allocation. And all craft on the river were to obtain passes and fly the Portuguese flag. Finally, in a dispatch from the Minister of Marine, it was ordered that 'an active and vigorous police' should be established. An ambitious programme, and effective enough on paper; but, like so many colonial projects emanating from

[1] K.'s *Diary*, 15 and 30. v. 59; 3. viii. 59; 6. ii. 60.

Lisbon, it had very little practical result. Nor was the subsequent attempt to 'occupy' Zambesia with more adventurous or substantial colonists than Portugal could supply any more successful. A grant of lands was made to a German 'society of colonization' early in 1859—it was this that Livingstone had read of—but nothing came of it; and a similar offer to French settlers was similarly futile. One might almost suppose that the local authorities were determined to do nothing and rebelliously ignored the orders they received from Lisbon. But that was not so. They attempted at least one item in the elaborate programme of 1858. As Livingstone and his companions made their way up to Shupanga, after the *Lynx* had sailed, they met the Governor of Quilimane coming down with orders to inspect the Kongone Mouth. He was told by Livingstone how to find it; but, catching fever, he turned back, and the inspection was carried out by an officer who, as Livingstone records, '*looked* only, and then made a report, in which our published soundings are used without acknowledgement'. They met the Governor again at Shupanga. 'He is to erect a fort at Shupanga, so he says,' noted Kirk. And presently, as will appear, a flagstaff was erected, the flag of Portugal was hoisted, and four Portuguese soldiers were stationed at the Kongone Mouth. But then, apparently, the effort spent itself; and the exhausted Governor reverted to gloomy acquiescence in the *status quo* and dreamy contemplation of impossible reforms. One night, at dinner at Shupanga, 'His Excellency,' writes Livingstone, 'talking in no way confidentially, but quite openly—indeed it is here the common mode of speaking of lamentable truths—said that the Portuguese in this country were a miserable lot, quite debased by debauchery, and with no enterprise whatever. A few of the large slaveholders, had they any vigour left, might each send fifty or a hundred slaves to the Cape, Mauritius, and Ceylon to learn sugar-making and trades; after which they could manufacture their own cloth from cotton grown on the spot; and make their own sugar too, instead of

importing it from abroad; he saw no reason even why they
should not ere long have a railroad across the continent to
Angola !'

The memory of this conversation spurs Livingstone to a
characteristic outburst. 'It is indeed matter of intense regret
that statesmen, known by the laws they have enacted to be
enlightened men, should be the means of perpetuating so
much misery in this slave-making country by keeping out
other nations, with a pretence to dominion where they have
absolutely no power for good. Is it not paying too dearly
for a mere swagger in Europe to have to bear the odium of
united Christendom as the first to begin the modern ocean
slave-trade and the last to abandon it ?' [1]

5

Since Rae had decided to go home when his two years' contract expired in a few months' time, there would soon be only
half of the Expedition left. What were the three survivors
to attempt? It was clearly the further exploration of Lake
Nyassa, the completion of their one great achievement, that
most attracted them; but they were first bound to consider
the fulfilment of a long-neglected obligation. It will be remembered that, when he left Tete for England in 1856,
Livingstone had promised his Makololo followers not merely
that he would return to them, but that he would shepherd
them home; and their home, the land of their chief, Sekeletu,
lay far up the Zambesi, beyond the Kafue River, more than
500 miles from Tete. If Livingstone's original scheme for
the Expedition had worked out, if they had not found the
navigation of the Zambesi to be interrupted by the Kebrabasa
Rapids, if they had established themselves in the country
above the Kafue River, then the conveyance of the Makololo

---

[1] K.'s *Diary*, 21. xii. 59. Livingstone, *Narrative*, 135–8. Official
orders and announcement (25. v. and 5. vi. 58) in F.O. 63/843: cf.
Howard to Malmesbury (5. v. 58) F.O. 63/831. German colony;
Livingstone to Malmesbury (26. vii. 59) F.O. 63/871.

home could easily have been fitted in. But now the Shire had
supplanted the Zambesi; and the practical objects of the
Expedition would be far better served by further surveys of
Nyassaland than by a long, arduous and profitless march to
the Makololo country along a route which Livingstone had
already explored. Yet could the obligation to those faithful
natives and their friendly chief be evaded much longer?
While he was still at the Kongone Mouth, with the *Lynx* at
anchor, so suggestive of the cool and healthy homeland, Kirk
began to wonder whether he should not follow Rae's example.
'A party with the Doctor', says the diary, is to 'go to Sekeletu's overland. . . . What I do, I know not yet. It seems I
can do very little on a tramping excursion of such duration.
If the Doctor gives the hint that I shall be of little service, I
shall not apply to go on. I wish we were off to Zomba rather
than this place. I should work up the Lake region with much
pleasure or the centre, if I had the least chance of getting
back collections with me. The Lakes are the Doctor's hobby
too. But for the men, he seems little inclined for this tramp.'[1]
    So the question remained for a time undecided while Kirk
accompanied the rest of the party up to Tete and back again
to the Kongone. His experiences were not such as to encourage him to cling to his post; for the *Ma Robert* seemed bent
on making his botanical work impossible—and botany, after
all, was the chief thing that bound him, officially, to the
Expedition. 'This is an awful place to live in,' he complains
on January 8, 'I mean, the ship. My specimens—the result
of five months and including the overland ones—are all wet
and run risk of utter destruction. The water floods the floor
from the windows while the roof leaks at every joint. . . .
Many a pig lives in a better house than we do, and yet we
are in an unhealthy place, with valuable collections, and in
the service of the British Government!' And again: 'People
at home have no idea of the thousand obstacles to making a
collection and getting it safely home. But the vessel is enough

[1] K.'s *Diary*, 11. xii. 59.

to ruin everything.' Nor was this the only trouble. Livingstone was ill again, and Hutchins, the seaman, also. 'Cooped
up in this stinking vessel, what can we expect when in a
region notorious for fever? The food too is against us now;
from the famine in the country we can't obtain fowls or in
fact anything on the way, so that, except what is shot, we
have nothing but salt beef and pork, neither of them good. . . .
The flour also of which the bread is made is sour, two-thirds
of the cask mouldy and wet and full of grubs.'[1]

It was thus during one of the 'downs' rather than the 'ups'
of the Expedition that, on January 31, Kirk's contract expired.

'This day the stipulated time is up. The two years are accomplished. But there is work to be done, and the sooner the better. . . .
I should not think of leaving the Doctor alone at this time—that
is if he wishes me. Mr. C. L. is against going up to Sekeletu's; he
is for risking nothing in the way of health for these men, although
they did bring the Doctor down. They are no worse than most
savages, and it's not with them but with Sekeletu that the thing
stands, and in honour we are forced to undertake a journey which
otherwise I should much rather avoid. I see little but fatigue and
hardship, perhaps sickness, and all for nothing tangible, unless
any one supposes the salary would tempt me there. . . . It is a clear
case of "Kismet", and must be taken as that and patched up as
best I can into something useful. The only thing I care for is the
time my mother will be without letters.'[2]

Thus, though all the selfish factors were against it, Kirk
had decided to stay with Livingstone if he wanted him. But
this essential condition remained vexatiously uncertain.
Livingstone had said nothing. Three weeks passed and still
silence. At length Kirk tackled him.

'Last evening I spoke to Dr. L. regarding the probable duration
of the land journey to Sekeletu. He thinks it may be done in six
months there and back. I asked him also as to the continuance
of the Expedition after the return, as he had told Mr. Rae that
no botanist would be with him in the next boat [i.e. a new boat
expected from home to replace the Ma Robert]. I thought it right
to give him the opportunity of saying so to me. He, however,

----

[1] K.'s *Diary*, 8. xi. and 23. i. 60.   [2] *Ibid.*, 26. ii. 60.

did not continue the conversation, but only remarked that he was ignorant of the intentions of the Government.'[1]

A curious evasion. It is clear from the sequel that Livingstone wanted to keep Kirk, at any rate for some time. Why did he not say so? Was it just his shyness, his incapacity to discuss personal questions? Or did he, in his heart of hearts, look forward to a day when he could shed all his white companions and plunge alone into the wilds again? And Kirk, on his side, shrank from putting directly a question which his chief seemed bent on evading. He would go on up the Zambesi and see what happened then.

On March 17 they left the Kongone Mouth, and, the *Ma Robert* making very little way against the current of the rising river, reached Mazaro, a village below Shupanga on the 25th. From here they escorted Rae for a day's march on the way to the Quilimane river whence he was to catch a boat for England. Rae was taking among his baggage four precious cases of botanical specimens consigned by Kirk to Sir William Hooker at Kew; and, when after many months Sir William reported that they had not arrived, Kirk was inclined to believe that Rae had been criminally careless and somehow lost them. These suspicions were unjust. More than twenty years later, in 1883, Sir Joseph Hooker, who had succeeded his father in the command at Kew, received a rather peremptory note from Portsmouth Dockyard, announcing that four cases addressed to Sir William had been deposited there in 1870 and asking if he would 'kindly take steps to remove them from this yard'. They proved, of course, to be the long-lost cases. Where they had been between the Zambesi in 1860 and Portsmouth in 1870 must remain a mystery, but Rae, at any rate, as Kirk admitted when they met again, had safely dispatched them to England.[2]

Meantime, having parted with Rae, the other members of the Expedition arrived on March 30 at Shupanga and more

[1] K.'s *Diary*, 27. ii. 60.
[2] Correspondence *re* cases at Kew, *Zambesi Expedition*, pp. 42–9

than three weeks later, after a very tedious voyage, at Tete.
'Getting things packed up for the journey', is the entry in
the diary for April 26. And then, for the first time, that
intimate and invaluable record fails. For a reason which
will soon appear, the next note-books are missing, and the
thread is not resumed till November 11. That gap of over
six months can only be filled from one or two of Kirk's letters
home and from Livingstone's *Narrative*.

On May 15, leaving the *Ma Robert* moored to an island
opposite Tete in charge of the two sailors, Livingstone, his
brother, and Kirk started with the Makololo on their long
tramp. 'On starting', Kirk records in a letter to Sir William
Hooker, written on his return, 'we mustered a large party,
but after being a few days on the march our numbers were
reduced by one-fourth by desertion; for, as it turned out,
they [the Makololo] had little desire to go back, nor had they
the honesty to say so, but ran off, leaving us encumbered
with baggage.' The deserters, it seems, were mainly those
who had cohabited with slave-women. By one of the laws
of the enlightened home Government the children of slave-
women were free as soon as they had been baptized; but, as
the local Portuguese averred, 'these Lisbon-born laws are
very stringent, but sometimes, possibly from the heat of the
climate, here they lose all their force', and the children became slaves like their mothers as before. None the less, it
was the children, so Livingstone at least believed, who drew
their Makololo fathers back, though they could never belong
to them, but only to their mothers' masters. Happily the
desertions ceased after the first few days, and the party
emerged from the Kebrabasa hills with sufficient porters for
its necessary minimum of baggage. They now crossed the
Chicova plain, 'a rich flat country . . . covered with scrubby
bush and thorn trees. It is rather poorly watered and would
not suit sugar-cane, but cotton succeeds well, and in ordinary
seasons it yields a magnificent crop of corn.' Under it, moreover, lay an extensive coal deposit which could be seen at

times cropping up at the surface or washed down the river-bed. 'When trade does get into this region', wrote Kirk to his old patron, Professor Balfour, 'there are immense fields of coal ready to take from the mountain side and tumble on board of the vessels.' It was clear from the ruined villages that this fertile plain had recently supported a big popula-tion, but 'desolating wars and slavery', to quote Livingstone, 'had swept away most of the inhabitants'. The heat was now considerable, and the travellers usually availed them-selves of the cooler hours between dawn and a nine o'clock breakfast for their main effort, resting again at mid-day, and breaking off in the early afternoon with little more than six hours' walking to their credit. Even so, they tired the natives out, including the headman who carried little more than they did. 'Our experience tends to prove', notes Livingstone, 'that the European constitution has a power of endurance, even in the tropics, greater than that of the hardiest of the meat-eating Africans.' Thus day followed arduous day, till on June 26 they reached Zumbo, at the confluence of the Zambesi and the Loangwa, having traversed about 250 miles in forty-two days. The so-called Portuguese post at Zumbo had long ceased to exist; but Kirk, like the authors of the Lis-bon programme of 1858, thought that 'the Portuguese would do well again to occupy it', so splendid was its situation.

'The chapel', to quote the *Narrative*, 'near which lies a broken church bell, commands a glorious view of the two noble rivers—the green fields—the undulating forest—the pleasant hills, and the magnificent mountains in the distance. It is an utter ruin now, and desolation broods around. . . .' And the memory moves Livingstone to one of his characteristic and impressive lamenta-tions on the fate of Africa. 'Apart from the ruins, there is nothing to remind one that a Christian power ever had traders here; for the natives of to-day are precisely what their fathers were when the Portuguese first rounded the Cape. Their language, unless buried in the Vatican, is still unwritten. Not a single art, save that of distilling spirits by means of a gun-barrel, has ever been learnt from the strangers; and if all the progeny of the whites were at once to leave the country, their only memorial would be the ruins of a few stone and mud-built walls and that blighting relic of the Slave Trade, the belief that man may sell his brother man; a belief that is not of native origin, for it is not found except in the track of the Portuguese.'[1]

One semi-Portuguese had recently added to the score against the white man in this area by accepting a bribe from one native chief to murder another together with twenty of his followers; and it was as well perhaps for Livingstone and his companions that 'the Doctor' had made himself known and liked by the local tribes on his way through in 1856. 'We are not mixed up with any of these deeds', wrote Kirk; 'the people soon make a distinction, and now the English have a good name and would be well received wherever we passed.' The friendliness of the natives, indeed, was such as to convince Livingstone that they would regard the planting of a British colony in their country as 'an inestimable boon', especially as it would put an end to their desolating inter-tribal strife. 'Thousands of industrious natives would gladly settle round it, and engage in that peaceful pursuit of agriculture and trade of which they are so fond... To the question, "Would they work for Europeans?", an affirmative answer may be given, if the Europeans belong to the class which can pay a reasonable price for labour and not to that of adventurers who want employment for themselves.'[2]

Beyond Zumbo the ground rose and the temperature began to fall at night: it was once as low as 39° at dawn. This swift change from heat to cold may have been the cause of a mysterious illness which fell on Kirk at the Mburuma Pass, though Livingstone thought it might have been due to experiments which Kirk had been making on himself with drugs with the object of discovering some better combina-

[1] K. to Professor H. Balfour, 14. xii. 61 (Royal Botanic Garden, Edinburgh). K. to Sir W. Hooker, 24. i. 61 (Kew, *Zambesi Expedition*, p. 5). Livingstone, *Narrative*, 155–204.

[2] K. to Sir W. Hooker, 24. i. 61 (Kew, *Zambesi Expedition*, p. 5). L. to Russell, 24. xi. 60 (F.O. 63/894). Livingstone, *Narrative*, 193, 199.

tion for treating fever than that which the members of the
Expedition had previously used. Kirk makes no mention
of this attack in his letters, but Livingstone was seriously
alarmed. At the moment of halting by a spring in the Pass,
he records, Kirk 'suddenly became blind and unable to stand
from faintness. The men with great alacrity prepared a
grassy bed on which we laid our companion with the sad
forebodings which only those who have tended the sick in
a wild country can realize.' Next day, however, the patient
was better. On the third he managed to ride a donkey. 'On
the sixth he marched as well as any of us.' And so, without
further incident they reached, on July 9, the confluence of
the Kafue with the Zambesi and saw to the north and east
the wooded mountain-range which Livingstone, before he
discovered the superior attractions of the Shire Highlands,
had marked down as the Expedition's inland base and a
possible site for a British settlement. Then on past the
Kariba Gorge, through the country of the Baenda Pezi or
'Go-nakeds', clad only in red ochre, to the river Zangwe,
along which the travellers, leaving the Zambesi, ascended
towards the Batoka tableland, a 'vast undulating plain'.
'The Batoka lands', Kirk reported later, 'are the only ones
suited for Europeans between the coast and the interior along
the Zambesi. There are many places where people eager to
make money might risk themselves, but this is the only
European climate and here the thermometer sometimes falls
to 30°. Sheep would succeed admirably.' They found the
Batoka to be a friendly, intelligent, and sober people, though
'perhaps the most inveterate smokers in the world', and,
above all, men of peace, in sharp contrast with the blood-
thirsty Matabele on their southern borders. It was all the
more distressing, therefore, to discover, at this far point of
their march into the interior, that the spectre of the coast-
lands was following on their tracks. A party of slaves of
Portuguese or half-caste ownership had been treading in their
footsteps, it appeared, representing themselves to be the

Englishmen's 'children' and buying not only ivory and canoes to carry it, but also 'a number of good-looking girls'. Once more the *Narrative* breaks out fiercely against the Portuguese. 'We were now so fully convinced that, in opening the country through which no Portuguese durst previously pass, we were made the unwilling instruments of extending the Slave Trade, that, had we not been under obligations to return with the Makololo to their own country, we should have left the Zambesi and gone to the Rovuma or some other inlet into the interior. It was with bitter sorrow we saw the good we would have done turned to evil.'[1]

At last, on August 4, the travellers sighted, more than twenty miles away across a great valley, the columns of spray that rise from the Victoria Falls. A few days later they reached what Kirk enthusiastically describes as 'certainly the greatest of all Falls in the world for the mass of water falling, the depth of the fall, and the singularity of their structure. It is a fall in the river without any fall in the level of the country.' Like the many tourists of a later day, coming quickly and comfortably by train from Cape Town, Kirk marvelled at the vast sheet of water, plunging into the sudden chasm and boiling out through the narrow zigzag cleft, and was 'drenched with heavy rain in a minute' from the perpetual cloud of spray. But nothing in all that wonder-spot interested him more than the vegetation which flourished in this perennial moisture. They visited 'Garden Island' where Livingstone had planted fruit-trees and where 'D. L. 1855', carved on a tree, bore witness to the one and only occasion on which the explorer left his personal mark on Africa; and, finding the trees destroyed by hippopotami, they planted fresh ones and tried to protect them, vainly as it happened, with a new and stronger stockade.[2] Before they left the Falls, the explorers

[1] K. to Professor Balfour, 14. xii. 61 (Royal Botanic Garden, Edinburgh). Livingstone, *Narrative*, 205–41. Report by Charles Livingstone 'On the Batoka Country' in *Proc. Royal Geog. Soc.* vi. 32–36.

[2] See pp. 69–70 above. James Chapman, who visited the Falls in 1862 with Baines (see p. 162 n. above), writes as follows in his journal

were surprised to meet a fellow-wanderer, a Mr. Baldwin of Natal, who, fired by Livingstone's previous journey, had made his way up from the south by the aid of his compass. Baldwin was no less surprised at the encounter, and not a little relieved. For he had been disarmed and detained by a local chief for having bathed in the river—a crime which had exposed him to the danger of being eaten by crocodiles and might have exposed the chief to the anger of the English for allowing the tragedy to happen! Asked why he had come, he had tried to explain that it had been Livingstone's doing. The great name had produced an impression, but had not secured his release. And then suddenly, out of the blue, Livingstone had arrived in person, and all was well.[1]

Three days were thus employed at or near the Falls, and then the party pushed on up the river. On August 18 they attained their goal—Sekeletu's *kraal* at Shesheke. Messages from the young chief had reached them on their way, and on arrival he greeted them with the gift of an ox for roasting. But he would not see them. He was suffering from a kind of leprosy and an ancient native medicine-woman had declared he was bewitched and could only be cured by a process of solitary confinement. After a few days, however, he consented to see his old friend and his two companions; and, not without tactful negotiations with the practitioner in charge, European science was brought to bear. 'The disease is one not known at home', wrote Kirk later on, 'and any treatment of it was experimental; yet it seemed to be quite successful as at the time of our departure he was quite a changed man, and from a mass of filthy sores had become a

(August 13): 'A few steps more brought us to Dr. Livingstone's garden—a small circular enclosure of strong stakes in the ground, but the hippopotami had lately broken into it and devoured all the grass; the last flood had been over it, and, according to the boatmen, destroyed everything. The next thing we saw was, carved in a tree, the initials D. L. 1855, and again C. L. 1860.' *Cape Argus*, Feb. 26, 1863. The Author saw what is known as Livingstone's Tree in August, 1928; but, if it is the tree, the growing bark has destroyed all trace of the initials.　　　　[1] Livingstone, *Narrative*, 247–61.

respectable member of society. Yet the disease still remained and I believe will return now that we are gone.' It probably did, for Sekeletu died in 1864.[1]

Already at the Falls the travellers had heard of the sad fate of the L. M. S. party which had recently come out, at Livingstone's suggestion, to work among the Makololo. Mr. Helmore, the leader of the party, and his wife and four of the seven other Europeans had died of fever and the survivors had abandoned the hopeless enterprise. Livingstone was convinced that a little medical knowledge, such as that of his own published prescription for tropical fevers, would have prevented the disaster. 'The blame, I think,' writes Kirk, 'lies much with the Society that sent them out. Surely, if it is worth improving the heathen, it is imperatively necessary to provide those so employed with things and appliances necessary for their health. Instead of which a large body of Europeans and natives are sent off without medical assistance into a notoriously unhealthy country.' At Linyanti, a hundred miles south-east of Shesheke and the most westerly point reached by the party, they visited their countrymen's grave; and here also they found again the waggon which Livingstone had twice left behind him, still standing in its place like some historic monument, its contents a little the worse for the weather and the white ants but otherwise intact. And now there was nothing more to keep them in the interior. The Makololo had been brought home according to pledge, not without some domestic surprises in the manner of Enoch Arden; friendly contact had been re-established with their chief; Lord Clarendon's letter in Queen Victoria's name had been duly presented; and Sekeletu and his principal tribesmen had 'expressed in a formal manner their great desire to have English people settled on the Batoka highlands'. It might well be wished that all invitations or concessions for European

---

[1] K. to Sir W. Hooker, 24. i. 61 (Kew, *Zambesi Expedition*, p. 5). Livingstone, *Narrative*, 265–76. L. to Russell, 6. ix. 60. and 24. xi. 60 (F.O. 63/894).

enterprise in Africa could have been so freely offered, so fully understood, and so genuinely meant as this. Sekeletu, indeed, promised to 'cut off a section of his country for the special use of the English'. And of all settlers none would be as welcome as the young doctor who had so nearly restored the young chief to health. 'Dr. Kirk being of the same age', records Livingstone, 'Sekeletu was particularly anxious that he should come and live with him.' [1]

The trio began their downward march on September 17, and, following a route as near to the course of the Zambesi as the rough country allowed till they rejoined their old track near the Kafue, they reached the pillars of rock which marked the approach to the Kebrabasa Rapids on November 11, without any adventures whatever. But one at least of the party was now on the brink of the most perilous of all his adventures. It can be described in his own words since at this point the next surviving notebook resumes the interrupted diary—this preface only being needed, that, in order to avoid, as Kirk wrote home, 'a most execrable road among 'rocks,' the travellers had decided to take to their canoes for the first stage of the Rapids which they believed to be of a relatively unalarming character.[2]

'Nov. 12. Started in the canoes. For 2 miles we found the way good, the current very strong. Then the river was divided by a long mass of rock ; the sides of the island and of the river were perpendicular and only at a few places could we land. We got up one of these and examined the part in front. On the left the entrance seemed bad; on the right it was very bad, at the farther end so bad that the canoe men desired not to go. The danger on the right was from being dashed against the opposite bank. We crossed to the north bank to examine. In attempting this the canoe of Ramakukan was taken out into the current and almost lost, he however managed to paddle back and leap on a rock thus saving his life although the canoe and all its cargo was swept down. In it went my Enfield rifle and 2 sword bayonets.

[1] K. to Sir W. Hooker, 24. i. 61 (Kew, *Zambesi Expedition*, p. 5). Livingstone, *Narrative*, 278–302. Blaikie, *Livingstone*, 231–2.

[2] K. to Sir W. Hooker, 24. i. 61 (Kew. *loc. cit.*, p. 5). Livingstone, *Narrative*, 303–34. For the 'execrable road', see p. 129 above.

We ordered the cook's canoe now to be abandoned as it was small and unsafe. The things were taken out and it left to float down. On the left bank we found the entrance not so bad as it looked at first. The water flowed along rushing hard on rock (*a*), part flowing by the channel between it and (*d*); a considerable body went down the right channel but a part returned by the passage between (*a*) and (*b*) to the left. The great danger was of being first dashed to pieces on (*a*), secondly of being carried against (*c*). As usual my canoe went first, for mine was the crew with most dash. They went first at all rapids and came through best. We cleared (*a*) in fine style; the water ran hard as the men paddled and had complete command of the canoe. I then said, 'Now avoid (*c*), the water runs hard on it.' They bent the head round and had given one stroke ahead; there was no danger, and we could go through it easily, but at this time we saw Dr. L.'s canoe carried up to the rock (*a*). Every second we expected to see it upset and all in the boiling water. To make things worse Mr. C. L.'s canoe was running as if into them; both would be upset. The only hope was from us. We all looked. Had we paddled on we should have saved ourselves easily, but had the others capsized there was no hope of saving them, for the water boiled up and curved in eddies so that no man could survive. We lost a few strokes of the paddles while thus looking at the almost inevitable destruction of the others.

The next thing I saw was the water rushing over our canoe. We were upset and all in the water. The others told me after that we struck with a loud crack. I heard nothing, the thing was instantaneous. Dr. L., occupied with his own danger still, heard the crash and looked up. The thing was over before he could direct his eyes and we were all under water or clinging on. It is a great thing when these accidents happen suddenly; there is no danger of any one losing presence of mind. The men behaved admirably. We were upset by being carried side on to rock (*c*). The faces of the rocks were perpendicular all along, about 20 ft. deep. The water boiled and rushed past, coming up in heavy masses at times and then subsiding again.

The man at the stern got a hold of the rock; fortunately there was a slight slope where two could hold on. He held the canoe which was pressed forcibly against the rock, from going down; sometimes it was sucked under. The man at the bow at once jumped into the river, his position was the most dangerous, but he held on by the canoe.

the entrance not so bad as
it looked at first

The water flowing
along rushing
band or rock a
past flowing by
the channel between
it & D, a considerable
body went down the river, having
but a part returned by the passage
between a & b to the left.
The great danger was of being
first dashed to pieces on a
2nd of being thrown against b
as usual my canoe went just
for mine was the Crew with
most dash they went first at
all rapids and came through
best. we cleared a in fine
style the water ran hard and
the Crew paddled and

A PAGE FROM KIRK'S DIARY

I found myself in the water with my body sucked under the canoe which was on its side. I managed to drag myself up and crawl along the canoe to the rock. Having ascertained that the bowman was all right, we got a few bundles on the crevice of rock. By this time Dr. L.'s canoe which had escaped by a miracle had come up after landing her goods. We passed what we could catch into her but most of the things had gone. As I got out I snatched up a bag and Lindley's *Vegetable Kingdom* which were sinking; this was an involuntary act. I had not the least feeling of any danger to life until long after, and yet there have not been many escapes more miraculous.

We got the canoe dragged up and baled out. I then found what I had saved was almost all Expedition stores, my own things had gone, and I now possessed the clothes I wore which were in rags, a bag with things for lighting pipes, and a book with a few altitudes worked out, also Lindley's *Vegetable Kingdom* and a rifle. This was my kit. Tooth instruments, surgical case, revolver, bedding, clothes, but of all losses the loss of notes was the greatest— 8 volumes of notes and about 100 drawings of plants, these new ones and of interest, all botanical notes, in fact everything to keep me in mind of the trip, all was gone.[1]

Of all his African adventures this was the one which Kirk was fondest of narrating to his children and friends in after days. And no wonder. For till the end of his life, when he was eighty-nine, he had never been so near death as that day in the Kebrabasa Rapids, when he was only twenty-seven. Yet, as has been seen, he was hardly aware of it at the time. 'The fact was', he confessed to Sir William Hooker, 'I never felt the least danger, although the others who had landed were trembling to see us.' Nor was it the loss of his kit, which he valued at quite £120, that troubled him most. 'If I could have got my notes', he wrote to Sir William's son, 'I cared for nothing else.' 'The loss of my notes seems greater daily', complains the diary, more than a week after the accident; and it may be said in passing that this was undoubtedly the chief reason why Kirk never completed a formal report of his work. But he soon had other things to think of. While they were making their way through those 'execrable' rocks,

[1] K.'s *Diary*, 12. xi. 60.

Livingstone and Kirk found themselves one evening some distance ahead of the others and without food. There was nothing to shoot but a hippopotamus which fell to Kirk's rifle but was carried away in the Rapids. So that night they lay 'alone in the bush without anything to eat'.[1]

Next morning, the diary goes on, 'I felt hunger very keenly, it produced faintness with quick pulse on any exertion. Dr. L. thinks best to go to the Livia [a camping-place downstream] and await the men there. To go back might be to find them gone and to lengthen the journey. And now that we are quite without food and must take heavy exercise in this fearful heat among the rocks, to lengthen our path might be [to] break us up completely. Reached the Livia after a most tedious climb. I felt considerably refreshed by sucking the husk of the *motunda* fruit which some one had eaten before us. I went out to hunt but got nothing. On returning, found Dr. L. gone; and, hearing a shot on the other side, crossed to see if he had gone over in search of food. I found the whole party quietly camped some way off the river, but Dr. L. not there. I sent the men to call him. We were both faint in crossing the river. I did so with my stockings on. Dr. L. not doing so, fell from weakness and bruised himself. It seemed now that Mr. C. L. after wandering up to midday, came up to the party, breakfasted, lay for some hours, then took the men off up the hills. They heard our shots calling them, but took no notice.'[2]

Kirk makes no further comment; but no doubt it was this incident that led his thoughts back to certain episodes which had made the march to Shesheke and back, as he puts it, 'rather a singular one'. Charles Livingstone, it seems, had got on even his hardened brother's nerves. At the outset and at intervals throughout the journey, there were protracted and violent quarrels between them. The provocation, as might be expected, was one-sided. Kirk indeed was startled at the violence of the Rev. Charles's language and confesses that, out of charity, he would have liked to share the natives' opinion that he was mad. The worst scene occurred on the return journey when Charles lost his temper and kicked the

[1] K.'s *Diary*, 20. xi. 60. K. to Sir W. Hooker, 24. i. 61 (Kew, *Zambesi Expedition*, p. 5). K. to Dr. J. Hooker, 13. xii. 60 (Kew, *African Letters 1859–65*, No. 157).   [2] K.'s *Diary*, 17. xi. 60.

headman of the Makololo escort provided by Sekeletu for the first stage. 'Nothing but the [natives'] high personal regard for Dr. L. avoided bloodshed in that case. The spear was poised and needed only a stroke of the arm to send it to the heart... For Dr. L.'s sake he held back.' It was this incident that prompted David, who had already told his brother that the one mistake of the Expedition had been bringing him with it, to remind him of the accusations he had made against his fellow members. Not content, it appeared, with slandering Baines and Thornton—and possibly, Kirk seems to think, himself as well—Charles had actually taunted his brother with allowing Rae to escape with a good character. 'Although Dr. L.', Kirk reflects, 'may know the truth of his brother's insinuations . . . still they have a powerful influence as I have more than once observed. For Dr. L., so remarkable for individual power, is deficient in administrative talent.' 'The character of the two brothers', he concludes, 'is in no respect alike—Dr. L. straightforward, honest, rather shy, unless engaged in his great scheme of opening Africa; Mr. C. L.' —well, perhaps Kirk would have wished this frank opinion to remain buried in the diary. But already, in that day, the world was aware that it had been, in Kirk's words, 'an unfortunate Expedition for quarrels'; and it is only fair to its other members to state the clear fact that the mainspring of those quarrels was the mischief-making of the Expedition's 'Moral Agent'.[1]

Meanwhile the party was at last nearing Tete. 'And time we did', notes Kirk. 'The clothes in which I was when the canoe upset are nearly worn out. The shoes are through and the heels off, trousers torn up to the knees, one arm of shirt nearly off.' But at Tete, he tells himself, his troubles will be over. 'The Expedition has extended a longer time than anticipated, and without the whole concern being on a different footing as to accommodation and time for some sort of packing and arrangement [of plants] I have no desire to be any

[1] K.'s *Diary*, 17, 20, 27. xi. 60.

longer on it.' What use, in other words, was a botanist who
could be little more than a pedestrian? In this mood Kirk
arrived at Tete on November 23. The whole journey had taken,
within a week, just the six months Livingstone had estimated.
'We have kept faith with the Makololo', he wrote to Sir
Roderick Murchison, 'though we have done nothing else.'[1]

6

The Expedition's psychological barometer had evidently
fallen very low when Kirk tramped into Tete; but there it
rose fast and high. For the travellers found a mail awaiting
them and great news in it. In the first place, there was a
dispatch from Lord John Russell, 'seen by Lord Palmerston
and the Queen', which, with no demur whatever, conceded
Livingstone's request for a better steamship to replace the
Ma Robert: it was already on its way out. Secondly, in the
same dispatch, the importance of the discovery of the Nyassa
country was fully recognized, and Livingstone's idea of exploring an alternative route to the Lake by the River Rovuma
so as to avoid the approach through Portuguese territory,
was warmly approved.[2] Thirdly—and best of all—the Universities' Mission to Central Africa had quickly and effectually answered Livingstone's call: a well-equipped party, with
a bishop at its head, might shortly be expected, under orders
to establish a permanent settlement and centre, on Livingstone's advice, in the Shire Highlands. So, at last, it seemed,
the explorers had obtained their reward. Their discoveries
were not to remain dead, unexploited knowledge. In all they
had done their inspiration and incentive had been the hope of
nothing less effective for the civilization of Africa than British
colonization; and now British colonization was actually to
begin, promoted by the Church of England and favoured by
the Government. Secular settlement must soon follow on
religious. The missionaries would need the traders. For the

---

[1] K.'s *Diary*, 21. xi. 60. L. to Sir R. Murchison, 26. xi. 60.
[2] Russell to L., 17. iv. 60 (F.O. 63/871).

Mission to succeed, as Kirk wrote home, 'the country must be opened up and commerce begun; for until the natives can sell their produce, they cannot be expected to give up the Slave Trade.' It seemed, in fact, as if all Livingstone's dream was coming true. 'I cannot tell you', he wrote to a friend, 'how glad I am at a prospect of a better system being introduced into Eastern Africa than that which has prevailed for ages.' And, to cap it all, for Kirk, came at last a definite request from Livingstone that he should stay. The chance of work in the rich and healthy Highlands, which co-operation with the Mission would entail, must in any case have shaken his recent resolve to get away: and, when he knew that Livingstone really wanted him, it instantly decided him. 'Dr. L. desires me to remain', notes the diary briefly; 'I had intended going home, but at once agree to stop.'[1]

There was a fly, however, in the ointment. 'Dr. L. seems to intend sending me up the Shire to Nyassa overland while he will go from the Rovuma and join [me] in the interior.' And then, a few days later: 'I trust that, if I am sent on the overland trip, I may not have C. L. for a companion.' These fears were accentuated by symptoms of a new and dangerous spirit among the native porters—Rowe was seized by the throat one day—which Kirk ascribed to the reactions of Charles Livingstone's worst outbreak. 'They have seen one of our number kick the representative of their chief and think it cannot be much for them to defy those under us.' And so when 'an accidental word'—for 'the Doctor', as usual, kept his own counsel—confirms Kirk's anxious suspicions, the diary boils over. 'The Commander should keep him by himself, for he is utterly unsafe. . . . I shall wish I had kept my former designs and gone home.' But again there was something more immediate to worry about. The whole party was on its way down the Zambesi in a craft that displayed unmistakable symptoms of its final dissolution. 'The bottom

[1] K.'s *Diary*, 23. xi. 60. K. to Professor Balfour, 14. xii. 61 (Royal Botanic Garden, Edinburgh). Blaikie, *Livingstone*, 230–1.

is full of holes', Kirk reports on December 6, three days after leaving Tete; 'and we float by keeping the water out with plugs.' On the 12th: 'The ship full of water all over: one hole closed, another opens.' The end came on the 21st.

'Only got a short way when the vessel grounded on a bank. This was no unusual occurrence. The sand seemed to wash away on the weather side with the current. . . . The two store-rooms being full of water kept her down aft, and the manner in which the chain pulled in trying to get her off helped her over to starboard. The water began to rush into the cabin, and soon it was evident she was gone. We got the things out, but mostly quite wet as boxes floated about in the cabin, and I was working for a couple of hours up to the middle getting all I could get out. Soon the whole vessel went down, showing only the port gunwale, masts, funnel, and upper part of house above water. . . . Camped on a sand-bank, but the water is rising fast.'

Next day, as the river still rose, the castaways moved to a neighbouring island; and Kirk was dispatched in a canoe down to Sena—fortunately not far off—to bring up any boats he could obtain; and since the hospitable Senhor Ferrão at once provided two canoes, the party was soon safe in Sena. 'Last night', says the diary for December 23, 'the river rose greatly, the sandbank on which we camped the previous night being covered, and the masts and funnel with the top of the house all that is visible of the infernal ship'. So, cursed all her life and cursed at her death, the *Ma Robert* perished.[1]

The last week of the year was occupied in moving the rescued baggage down to Sena, mostly in torrential rain. On Christmas Eve the party spent 'a damp night in a miserable native hut' by the river, and the following nights were as bad. 'No sleep going.' 'Mosquitos in thousands.' The new year found them with all their goods at Sena, weary and bedraggled, but cheerfully preparing for the journey to the sea to meet the new ship and the Mission. A new chapter was about to open in the history of the Expedition.[2]

[1] K.'s *Diary*, 6–23. xii. 60. Livingstone, *Narrative*, 338.
[2] *Ibid.*, 24–31. xii. 60.

VI

THE CLIMAX
(1861–2)

I

'THE Mission owes its origin, under God,' said the first
report of the Cambridge Committee of the Oxford and Cambridge Mission to Central Africa, 'to the impression produced
by the visit of Dr. Livingstone to this University.' No one,
indeed, who was present ever forgot that lecture in the Senate
House on December 4, 1857. It was by no means a great display of oratory. The attention of the audience was held more
by the unusual personality of the speaker than by the quality
of his lecture, which was neither very well composed nor very
well delivered, until suddenly, at the very end, his whole
manner changed. In one quiet sentence he foretold his own
death in Africa. In the next, with passionate force and start-
ling effect, he literally shouted his final message at the
crowded benches round him. 'I know that in a few years I
shall be cut off in that country which is now open; do not let
it be shut again. I go back to Africa to try to make an open
path for commerce and Christianity. Do you carry out the
work which I have begun. I leave it with you.' Out of that
appeal, that command, the Mission was born. The latent
idealism of the old Universities readily responded. 'The first
step', continues the report, 'was to invite the co-operation
of the University of Oxford. This was promptly and heartily
accorded.' Dublin and Durham were then approached with
the same result, so that in 1860 the title of the Mission became
'The Oxford, Cambridge, Dublin and Durham Mission to
Central Africa' or, for short 'The U. (Universities) M. C. A.'.
Nor was this academic origin its only remarkable feature. It
was the first Church of England Mission to be founded since
the creation of the great Church Missionary Society in 1799. It
was the first Mission, moreover, to declare at the outset that

its purpose was not exclusively religious; and it is important, in view of the sequel, to observe how closely in accordance with Livingstone's appeal the first Oxford and Cambridge Committees defined their objective. 'It will be understood that the great object of this Mission is to make known the Gospel of Christ; but as the Committees are well aware that, in Dr. Livingstone's own words, "civilization and Christianity must go on together," they think it advisable to state that it will be their aim to encourage the advancement of science and the useful arts, *and to direct especial attention to all questions connected with the slave-trade as carried on in the interior of Africa.*' That last sentence (not, of course, italicized in the original) was the most significant sentence in the whole report. For, just as the chief stimulus to public opinion in Livingstone's appeal lay in his attack on the Slave Trade, so the interest excited in the Mission was largely due to the fact that it was setting out to resume, with the Bible and the Cross, an historic campaign. It was natural, therefore, that Samuel Wilberforce, now Bishop of Oxford, should have taken the lead in most of the public meetings on the Mission's behalf; but it was still more significant that old Lord Brougham, now virtually in retirement and never a votary of religious causes, should have once more mounted the platform to renew the fight he had fought in his prime. And there was one other unprecedented feature of the Mission. To strengthen its organization in the field, its chosen leader, the brilliant and enthusiastic Charles Frederick Mackenzie, who, born in 1825, had been 'second wrangler' at Cambridge, and for the last five years had worked among the Zulus in Natal, was to be consecrated the first Missionary Bishop. Add the essential fact that a sum of £20,000 was quickly subscribed, and it is clear that no similar enterprise had ever made so fine a start. 'I am afraid of this,' said Mackenzie, as he sat in the gallery of the Cambridge Senate House at the 'Great Zambesi Meeting', listening to the speeches of Wilberforce, Gladstone, and Sir George Grey, and noting the

enthusiam of the audience: 'most great works of this kind
have been carried on by one or two men in a quieter way, and
have had a more humble beginning.'[1]

On January 1, 1861, Mackenzie was consecrated at Cape
Town, and on February 7 he arrived, with one of his staff,
at the Kongone Mouth on board H.M.S. *Lyra*. He found
H.M.S. *Sidon* there, a week before him, carrying two other
missionaries and escorting the *Pioneer*, as the new river-boat
for the Zambesi Expedition had been called. There also,
according to plan, were the three survivors of the Expedition
who had reached the sea on January 4, noting on their arrival
what the melancholy Governor of Quilimane had done to
exclude foreign trade from the new waterway which the
troublesome Scotsmen had so needlessly discovered. 'Found
four soldiers established', says the diary, 'and a flagstaff
with Portuguese colours.' No doubt this had accentuated
Livingstone's impatience to explore the possibilities of reaching Lake Nyassa by an alternative route which the Portuguese could not pretend to control. He had heard, too, that
Governor-General d'Almeida had already tried to forestall
him by suggesting to the Sultan of Zanzibar, happily in vain,
that the frontier of Mozambique should be extended northwards to the Rovuma.[2] It was with this specific object, moreover, that the Government had sent out the *Pioneer*; and,
since it was now the unhealthiest season on the Lower Zambesi, the establishment of the Mission inland ought in any
case, so Livingstone thought, to be postponed for a few
months. The Bishop, however, was by no means pleased
with the idea of an immediate exploration of the Rovuma.
He had not yet learned how long it could take to carry out
a simple plan in Africa. Tired of the voyage, full of zeal, he
was itching, fever or no fever, to get his party on the march,

[1] H. Goodwin, *Memoir of Bishop Mackenzie* (London, 1865),
176–89; *Report of the O.C.D.D.M. to C.A. to Dec. 31, 1860* (London,
1861), 19–20. For a full report of the Cambridge lecture in 1857, see
David Livingstone and Cambridge (London, 1908).

[2] Livingstone, *Narrative*, 241.

to establish the settlement, and to begin the great work. He even suggested that they should make their own way to the Shire country and wait for Livingstone to join them *via* the Rovuma and the Lake. But to this Livingstone strongly demurred. Chibisa, he pointed out, had moved from his Shire village to an older home near Tete, and he knew no other chief to whose good offices the strangers could safely be entrusted. And so, after a long discussion, the Bishop yielded. What else could he do? The Mission had come out at Livingstone's call to work where Livingstone wished. His great authority, his expert knowledge, were its mainstay. It was impossible to reject his first advice. Mackenzie, more-over, had been deeply impressed by the tone of a letter he had received from Livingstone on his way out. 'How excel-lent', he wrote home, 'his way of offering assistance, not as if he were indispensable, but might certainly be of *some* use. This is the way real strength and real knowledge always speaks.' And personal contact had confirmed the impression. 'During the discussion Livingstone continued as friendly and kind as possible. . . . He is an excellent fellow, and I have no fear of any difficulty at any time arising between us.' The disappointment, therefore, was soon forgotten; and, while the rest of the Mission party were landed at Johanna, an island coaling-station between Madagascar and Cape Delgado and one of the bases of the British naval squadron on the coast, Mackenzie and one of his staff joined the explorers in the *Pioneer* at the mouth of the Rovuma.[1]

While awaiting the Bishop's arrival the explorers had sur-veyed the mouths of the Rovuma and discovered the main channel, broad, deep, issuing into the bay without a bar, and providing safe anchorage for sea-going ships—in every re-spect an improvement on the Zambesi. About eight miles up-stream the land rose to about 300 ft.—another advantage over the Zambesi as indicating a shorter journey through the

[1] Goodwin, *Memoir*, 251–5; *O.C.D.D.M.C.A. Report for 1860*, 21. Livingstone, *Narrative*, 348–9.

fever-breeding flats. Before long, however, the shoals began. Once more, as on the Zambesi, navigation became intricate; once more there were groundings and long delays. And it had been plain, alas! from the first, that the *Pioneer*, though her construction had been carefully supervised by Admirals Walker and Washington—the latter, as has been seen, one of the Expedition's warmest friends—was not the perfect ship. In strength, equipment, and comfort she was incomparably superior to the *Ma Robert*; but the extra weight put into her to enable her to stand the sea-voyage out had increased her draught from the designed three feet to five. And the waters of the Rovuma, which had fallen a little since the explorers arrived but were still relatively high, were soon found to be only four feet deep or less. So the old delays and labours were repeated. 'Got immediately aground', says the diary one day, 'getting off only at sunset after much work in which the Bishop, who is a trump of a fellow, distinguished himself.' On March 17, five days from the sea, they decided to return. If they had proceeded much farther, with the water-level falling daily, it might well have proved impossible to get the *Pioneer* down the river at all, and, in any case, Livingstone had promised Mackenzie that this little expedition should not delay the settlement of the Mission for more than three months. But the further exploration of the Rovuma was not abandoned: it was only postponed till the next winter. And Livingstone, at any rate, was by no means hopeless of success, provided that a boat of shallower draught were ultimately available. The natives, indeed, had definitely declared that 'a canoe can come out of Lake Nyassa where the Manganja live and reach the sea by the Rovuma'. And natives did not always lie.[1]

---

[1] K.'s *Diary*, 18. iii. 61. K. to Sir W. Hooker, 21. iv. 61 (Kew, *African Letters, 1859–65*, No. 159). L. to Russell, 11. iii. and 16. iv. 61 (F.O. 63/894), 'Bishop Mackenzie now on board and works like a Briton wherever he can'. Goodwin, *Memoir*, 255–9. Livingstone, *Narrative*, 349–50.

On March 23, exactly a fortnight from the start, they were
back again at the mouth. While they were cutting wood and
fuel and preparing for the coast-voyage, Mackenzie had his
first touch of fever. 'It was a very mild attack,' he wrote to
a friend in England, 'certainly no worse than a slight influenza
cold. . . . The cure is worse than the disease.' The Bishop, in
fact, had been quick to underrate the danger of the most
insidious weapon with which Tropical Africa holds or used
to hold her white intruders at bay. But he could scarcely
ignore the ease with which it spread among the new-comers.
In a few days almost every one was sick except the seasoned,
stale-blooded members of the Zambesi Expedition; and,
short-handed as they were, they were obliged to put out to
sea to escape from the noxious lowlands of the coast. 'One
leading stoker', says the diary, 'took the engines and between
us we managed to navigate the ship, the helm being kept by
volunteers. The Commander was sick, but able to look up
occasionally.' Fortunately, perhaps, the weather kept fair;
and to navigators of the Zambesi it seemed a relatively easy
task to navigate the ocean, 'where', as Livingstone confessed,
'if one does not run ashore, no one follows to find out an
error and where a current affords a ready excuse for every
blunder'. It was all good fun, in fact, despite the fever. The
members of the Expedition were busy and happy; and the
Bishop was delighted that the delay was over and his own
real work about to begin. 'I trust that this month will not
end', he wrote from the *Pioneer* on April 1, 'before we are
at the foot of the Murchison Cataract. It is very pleasant
being on the easy terms we are with Livingstone; and as for
Dr. Kirk, we are the greatest possible cronies. He encouraged
me to try my hand at Botanizing, a thing which has been
open to me any time as long as I can remember, but for which
I never thought I had any turn; but now, with his help, I
have settled the order to which each of some ten or twelve
plants belong, of whose nature I had no notion to begin with.
He is an excellent teacher.' Kirk's opinion of Mackenzie has

already been quoted; and the quick friendship was cemented by long walks taken together when the *Pioneer* reached the group of islands to which Johanna belongs. The second of these, a climb across the main island through forest and over mountains 'of perhaps 4,000 ft.', tired the older man and brought on another bout of fever. 'Weak as water for two days, but Kirk set me right.' [1]

On April 22, the *Pioneer* 'very deeply laden', with the Mission party on board, sailed from Johanna; on May 1 she entered the Zambesi; and, after a few days' pause for 'wooding up', she started on her first voyage up the river. [2]

2

'We are now steaming through the delta', wrote Mackenzie on May 8 to his sister, who was waiting at Cape Town to come up and join the Mission as soon as it was settled. 'Livingstone is most kind and excellent. He promises to make a tour with us, as soon as we leave the ship, to look out for a site. We hope to reach the Murchison Cataract in about seventeen days.' But the Bishop's new estimate of the journey's length proved almost as over-sanguine as his earlier hope of arriving at Chibisa by the end of April. The actual date of arrival was July 8. The ascent of the Zambesi and the lower reaches of the Shire, as it happened, did not prove so difficult; but it took more that six weeks to traverse the fifty miles between the Elephant Marsh and Chibisa. The river was at half-flood, and, as Kirk emphatically declares, 'three feet is the utmost of which the Shire is capable in order that a ship should proceed without constant labour'. In the swift current and narrow, winding channel the *Pioneer* was continually in trouble; and hours and sometimes days of the old, wearisome work with anchor and cable were needed to

---

[1] K.'s *Diary*, 29–31. iii. and 4–10. iv. 61. K. to Dr. J. Hooker, 21. v. 61 (Kew, *African Letters, 1859–65*, No. 160). Goodwin, *Memoir*, 262–3. Livingstone, *Narrative*, 350.

[2] K.'s *Diary*, 22. iv.–7. v. 61.

haul her through the sand. So the new-comer's letters repeat
the story which Kirk's diary has told and re-told *ad nauseam.*
'We are now not more than twenty miles from the end of our
river voyage at Chibisa's. It is just a month since we crossed
the bar. . . . The fact is we have been aground about as many
hours as we have been afloat. . . . It has been hard work. My
hands are sore and cramped with hauling cables and handling chains and anchors. They say this vessel must never
come up this river again, and they will be thankful if she ever
gets down.' And then, a fortnight later: 'Well, here we are,
not having made more than six or seven miles in the last three
weeks.' But when he next writes, on July 20, the Bishop's
worst troubles seem over and his spirits are high. 'Last morning we left the vessel and took to our feet. It is a beautiful
country this, as fine as Natal. You would like to see our picturesque appearance on the march. . . . Livingstone in his
jacket and trousers of blue serge and his blue cloth cap. His
brother, a taller man, in something of the same dress. I with
trousers of Oxford grey and a coat like a shooting-coat, a
broad-brimmed wide-awake with white cover, which Livingstone laughs at, but which, all the same, keeps the sun off.
He is a salamander. . . . All these winding along the narrow
path, sometimes admiring the glorious hills, Chiradzura which
we left behind yesterday, Zomba with its flat top, or the distant peaks and precipices of the Milanje mountains on our
right beyond Shirwa. We have not seen its blue waters yet:
we are about 1,000 ft. above it, on a plateau.' 'We were a
strange party', says another letter: 'Livingstone tramping
along with a steady, heavy tread which kept one in mind
that he had walked across Africa.' [1]

Those were happy days for Mackenzie; but it seemed to
Livingstone, looking back a few years later, as if at that
moment the acme of all his own Expedition's work in Africa
had just been reached—and passed. At the time of their

---

[1] K.'s *Diary*, 8. v.–8. vii. 61. Goodwin, *Memoir*, 265–75, 282,
Livingstone, *Narrative*, 351–352.

recent arrival at Chibisa, says the *Narrative*, 'the Expedition, in spite of several adverse circumstances, was up to this point eminently successful in its objects. . . We had opened a cotton field which, taking in the Shire and Lake Nyassa, was 400 miles in length. We had gained the confidence of the people wherever we had gone; and, supposing the Mission of the Universities to be only moderately successful . . . a perfectly new era had commenced in a region much larger than the cotton fields of the Southern States of America. We had, however, as will afterwards be seen, arrived at the turning-point of our prosperous career, and *soon came in contact with the Portuguese slave-trade'*. At the Expedition's brightest moment the old spectre had appeared again, to haunt it now and thwart it to the end.[1]

It was on the day after their arrival at Chibisa that they heard the news of trouble in the Highlands. 'When in the village', Kirk records, 'we saw several people come from Zomba. . . They have fled to tell Chibisa their village has been attacked and their people carried off as slaves'. Their assailants, it appeared, had been the barbarous and militant Ajawa, a tribe located north of Mount Zomba, between Lake Shirwa and the Shire; and they had been instigated, it was very soon evident, by the Portuguese slave-traders at Tete, anxious to obtain a supply of slaves from this new area for the Quilimane market. It was also reported that 'a large gang of recently enslaved Manganja crossed the river, on their way to Tete, a few days before we got the ship up'. On their previous journeys the explorers had never heard of slave-raiding so far up-stream as this; and it was only too clear that once more, as Kirk put it, 'we had been the means of opening a slave-hunting country'. A little later the explorers and the raiders came face to face. On the morning of July 16, the former halted at the village of Mbame, a friendly chief, where, as Livingstone was unwell, it was decided to remain for the day; and Mackenzie went off with two of his missionaries to bathe

[1] Livingstone, *Narrative*, 354. Italics not in the original.

in a neighbouring stream. Presently they were disturbed by strange music from beyond the village. It was the drivers of a slave-gang blowing their long tin horns. 'We heard a sound of penny trumpets', to quote Mackenzie's letter, 'and thought Livingstone had been giving away presents, when shortly Dr. Kirk came and told us that a party of six men with muskets had come flourishing into the village with a train of eighty-four slaves; that the men had run away and the slaves were free; that our guns had all been out, though the conscience-stricken wretches had needed no firing to hasten their flight.' Kirk's diary gives further details.

'The slaves were most of them tied by the neck with ropes in gangs; some refractory ones had beams of wood as thick as a man's thigh and 6 ft. long with a fork at one extremity in which the neck was secured by an iron pin. The party consisted of women and children chiefly, with a few men. They began clapping their hands as soon as they knew that we were their friends, the English. The ropes were cut adrift and the sticks sawn off their necks, while the goods of the traders were seized by our men. Unluckily in the confusion the slave-drivers were suffered to escape. The people of the village looked on during all this with great satisfaction. Before many minutes had elapsed the slaves now free were cooking what was their masters' food with their own sticks which had served to fasten them, and the women clothed with white calico. The atrocities committed on the march seem to have been very great. Two women were shot because they attempted to escape... One woman, who was unable to carry both her load and young child, had the child taken from her and saw its brains dashed out on a stone.'[1]

Thus, at last, the positive conflict, which from the outset had surely been sooner or later inevitable, between the Zambesi Expedition and the Portuguese Slave Trade had occurred. Livingstone's interference with the raiders, it is true,

[1] K.'s *Diary*, 9 and 15. vii. 61. K. to Professor Balfour, 14. xii. 61 (Royal Botanic Garden, Edinburgh). Livingstone, *Narrative*, 354–7 (with a sketch of the slave-gang). Goodwin, *Memoir*, 283. Another account by Mackenzie in *U.M.C.A. Report for 1861*, 6–7; and one by Mr. H. Waller, lay-superintendent of the Mission, *ibid.*, 17–19.

had not been very violent. As soon as he accosted them, they had fled. None the less, it was interference, and it was deliberate interference. Mbame had warned Livingstone that a slave-gang was approaching; and, though he had only a few minutes' grace, it was enough for calculation and decision. 'Although no time was lost in executing the liberation', says Kirk, 'yet it was well considered. Dr. L. suggested that all our goods at Tete would be destroyed by the Portuguese, but that we should take the risk and free the slaves at all hazards.' And Livingstone himself carefully records the reasons that determined him. 'This system of slave-hunters dogging us where previously they durst not venture and, on pretence of being "our children", setting one tribe against another to provide themselves with slaves, would so inevitably thwart all the efforts, for which we had the sanction of the Portuguese Government, that we resolved to run all risks and put a stop, if possible, to the slave-trade which had now followed on the footsteps of our discoveries.' Nor had Mackenzie, confronted for the first time with the grim realities of the Trade, any doubts or fears whatever. 'There had been five or ten minutes' notice of their approach,' he wrote, 'so that Livingstone had time deliberately to take his course—a course which no one can blame; but surely all will join in blessing God that we have such a fellow-countryman.' The Bishop was right. No one of common humanity could have done, if he had had the courage, anything else than what Livingstone did. And though it was doubtless his natural feelings that most influenced him, his quick decision was also the best decision for the interests of the Expedition. To interfere, it was true, with the Slave Trade was a direct challenge to the Portuguese. The Slave Trade was their principal, almost their only economic activity. It was conducted by their agents. The Governor-General of the Province, at the best, was unable to suppress it. The Governor of Quilimane at least tolerated it. Some of the lesser officials almost certainly connived at it. It is significant that among the drivers of the rescued gang was a slave belonging to an old friend of the Expedition, Major Sicard, known as Signor Tito, lately Commandant at Tete. 'One of them', says the diary, 'was Katura, a slave of Sr. Tito, who served as our cook and steward at Tete. He was excessively afraid on being caught: he declared they had been sent neither by Tito nor his agent, Sr. Candido'. Be that as it may, the Portuguese officials, as Livingstone repeatedly declares, were certainly not above suspicion. If, therefore, the British intruders set themselves to stop the Trade, by force or a show of force, in such parts of the province as they chose to traverse, they must expect to find the authorities not merely unhelpful but positively obstructive. And as for the Portuguese colonists directly concerned in the trade, would they not do all they could, by violent means perhaps, and at least by making trouble with the natives, to drive out of the country these canting British busybodies who stole their property and spoiled their game? Clearly, interference would mean trouble, fatal trouble perhaps, or at least serious enough to wreck the Expedition. And yet, no less clearly, it was better to abandon the Expedition straightway than not to interfere. For the ultimate purpose of the Expedition—British colonization and the benefits it would bring to Africa, including, of course, the abolition of the Slave Trade in its area—was uncertain of attainment and in any case could only be attained at some future time: whereas its certain and immediate result had been the spread of the Trade along the paths it had opened into country hitherto unexplored. The dilemma was obviously conclusive. The decision was obviously right.[1]

Obviously, also, Mackenzie was in the same position as Livingstone. What was true of the Expedition was true of the Mission. It could not do its work, it could not exist, in a country ravaged by slave-raids; and its inevitable connexion with the whole question of the Slave Trade had been

[1] K.'s *Diary*, 16. vii. 61. Goodwin, *Memoir*, 283. Livingstone, *Narrative*, 355–6.

made as clear at its inception as at that of the Expedition. With no misgivings, therefore, the Bishop joined hands with the Explorer 'to put a stop to the Slave Trade'. Since his subsequent actions involved him in some criticism, a passage may be given here from the letter already quoted:

'I ought to say a word about the principle of using force, and even firing, if necessary, upon the captors of these poor creatures in order to free them. The objection lay chiefly in this, that having been sent out to this country to bring blessing and peace to the people, I could not reconcile it to myself to kill them even in self-defence: and I still think that if by any possibility the people of this land should attack us, to drive us away or to rob us, we ought not to kill our own sheep. But this is a different case. These are strangers from Tete and beyond Shirwa, coming to make war on our people and carry them off as slaves. This we must help them to resist by every means. Livingstone is right to go with loaded gun and free the poor slaves; and there being so few English here, we are right, though clergymen and preachers of the Gospel, to go with him, and by our presence, and the sight of our guns, and their use, if necessary (which may God avert), to strengthen his hands in procuring the liberation of these people. When Kirk went down last Thursday to the ship where Rowley is, I wrote to Rowley to say, "Do as you think right yourself; but my advice is, that you volunteer to help Kirk by going armed in the boat or by staying armed on board, and use your gun, if necessary, but if you are not required, be glad that you are spared so painful a position. I intend to act on that principle here". I believe some will blame Livingstone, and more will blame me: but I can only act as I think right.' [1]

Meantime, the party, as appears above, had divided its forces. News had come in that other large gangs of slaves were being driven from the Zomba district towards Tete. One of them, a hundred strong, was said to be in the near neighbourhood, hurriedly making for the Shire on hearing what had happened; and Kirk was dispatched with four Makololo to Chibisa to try to intercept it. He reached the *Pioneer* without sighting the fugitives, and there he learned that 'a white man, a Portuguese from Tete, had crossed the

[1] Goodwin, *Memoir*, 285-6.

previous day with about sixty guns'. He had told the Chibisa
natives who had ferried him over the river 'that the English
of the ship were his brothers. . . However, he never came near
it, although he put a bold face on and crossed in sight of the
vessel'. Next day (July 13), Kirk ordered one of the boats
to follow up-stream as far as possible and himself pushed ahead
on foot with eight men, inquiring for news of the raiders at
every village he passed. But the natives, though they were
civil enough and though Kirk had been authorized by Livingstone 'to use bribes to any amount for information', preferred to know nothing, 'partly', thought Kirk, 'from fear of
the Tete Portuguese and partly in order to obtain the profit
of the crossing'. When he returned in the evening from his
fruitless search, Kirk discovered that the boat, instead of
following him up to watch the river between him and Chibisa,
had only 'gone about three miles, making a pleasure trip and
remaining at a village a couple of hours trading for goats
etc.'. Next day he learned that the people of one village he
had passed had waited till he was well out of sight and then
quickly brought the gang, which was in hiding on the other
bank, across the river. 'At this very time the boat lay a few
miles below doing nothing. . . Had its occupants showed the
least activity, they would have come on them in the act of
crossing.' Thus, to Kirk's intense annoyance, the raiders and
their victims had slipped through his net; and it had been a
large party, 'very many slaves and much cloth and goods'.
Pursuit towards Tete was attempted, but soon abandoned
as hopeless; and Kirk spent the next few days in patrolling
the river between Chibisa and the Cataract. But it was
clear from information supplied by some natives who arrived
from Tete that the traders were determined to outdo him.
'The Shire is closed, they say, by many parties up and down;
so they [the agents] are to purchase in the villages away from
the river. . . . They return soon and depend on making many
and small trips.' But Kirk was also a determined man. 'This
must be stopped to-morrow', he notes: 'they must be driven

out of the whole country.' Unfortunately this proved a difficult, in fact an impossible task, because the villagers themselves were implicated. The headman was often only too
anxious to obtain his four fathoms of cloth by the sale of one
of his flock, and only too ready to conceal the trader and to
deny all knowledge of the trade when Kirk appeared. 'It is
curious', comments the diary, 'how all agree on the wicked-
ness of selling people although they still do it'. A few more
days had been occupied in this baffling, thankless work when,
on August 1, Livingstone and his party arrived back at
Chibisa.

They brought exciting news. After Kirk's departure, Livingstone and Mackenzie, leaving the freed slaves at a village in
charge of one of the missionaries, had continued their march
for a day or two to the north, meeting and liberating more
slaves from time to time. These were mostly stragglers from
some large body, but once they came upon a party of fifty.
'The head of this gang', Livingstone records, 'whom we knew
as the agent of one of the principal merchants of Tete [Senhor
Pasqual], said they had the licence of the Governor for all
they did. This we were fully aware of without his stating it.
It is quite impossible for any enterprise to be undertaken
there without the Governor's knowledge and connivance.'
Other captives, indeed, had asserted that His Excellency's
own agents were at work in the neighbourhood. It was so
far only with these agents who had bought slaves for the
Portuguese traders that the explorers had been dealing; but
now (July 21) they were to meet the savage tribe which had
done most of the work of seizure and sale. Kirk tells the story
as Livingstone told it to him.

'Dr. L. and the Bishop went on to Mangazi . . . heard of the
Ajawa ahead, and came up to them. On the western slope of
Zomba, at the pass, they had just taken and burned two villages:
and, as Dr. L. passed, they heard the wail of the dying [1] and saw

---

[1] Or more probably, according to the *Narrative* (360), 'the wail of
the Manganja women lamenting over their slain'.

the smoke of the burning. The country was without population, and food stood untouched in the fields. Grain of all sorts had been thrown away and destroyed. The Ajawa, seeing the party coming down the hill, threw away the booty which they were taking to their camp and fled. . . The people first scattered, and then, on our party retiring in order to induce them to come to terms, they rushed back thinking it was a retreat. The fight now began in earnest. The Ajawa danced about and cut capers, firing their arrows with tolerable aim at 100 yards; none however struck, except one in the arm of a Manganja. . . The rifles took down about 6 men. . . The Ajawa fled to the hills, while Dr. L. burned the village. The huts . . . were full of plunder which all went in the flames. At one time our party was quite surrounded. Had the Ajawa fought at close quarters, it would have been hard for our fellows to stand against them. . . As Dr. L. wound down the hill to the Shire valley, the Ajawa chaffed him—how they would come again after him—but they had lost too much for anything of the sort.'[1]

It was easy, perhaps, at the moment, to make light of this chance encounter with the Ajawa. But it might well have had a more disastrous ending—one of the poisoned arrows had fallen between Livingstone and Mackenzie as they stood together—and in any case it was a grave misfortune for all concerned. It was the first time, as Livingstone rather sadly comments, that he had ever been attacked by Africans. That they were the aggressors was unquestionable. Mackenzie's account of the incident confirms Livingstone's. 'They ran to their camp and we followed,' he wrote home. 'Livingstone in vain attempted to have a parley with the chiefs: the Ajawa drew their bows and began firing poisoned arrows at us. There was no resource but one. It would not do to retreat. Livingstone gave the order to fire, and the struggle continued for about an hour and a half. I had a gun in my hand, but seeing Livingstone without one I asked him to use mine rather than that I should.' But the Ajawa had clearly attacked them in the belief that they were themselves about to be attacked.

[1] K.'s *Diary*, 1. viii. 61. A fuller account by Livingstone in *Narrative*, 360–1. Other accounts cited in next note.

The liberation of the slaves a few days earlier had doubtless been interpreted as the first step in an organized campaign; and unfortunately, when the two parties first met, some of Livingstone's Manganja followers had shouted out exultant taunts which meant, in effect, that a great white warrior had come to lead them to war with the Ajawa. It was thus no longer only a question of conflict with the Slave Trade. The Expedition and the Mission alike had become entangled in the web of native strife.[1]

It mattered less, at the time at least, to Livingstone, whose immediate objective lay farther north, than to Mackenzie, who had planned to establish his Mission in that very neighbourhood. And he could not change his plan. The settlement must be within a fairly short march of the Shire, whence its supplies could be obtained by the river route from the sea; and it must be on high ground. Where else could it be save in this area which Livingstone had chosen? There was a new reason, moreover, against prolonging their explorations much farther. The disposal of the liberated slaves would have been an awkward question if the Bishop had not at once offered to take charge of them. Their acquisition, indeed, had seemed a happy accident. Over a hundred in number now, they would provide so to speak, a ready-made flock for the Bishop, regarding him and his colleagues as their saviours, willing to work and willing to listen. But the sooner they settled down the better. The food question alone would make it difficult for the flock to go wandering far afield. And, lastly, it was hard for Mackenzie to refuse the entreaties of the local Manganja chiefs that he should settle near them, although it was only too clear that they wanted the Mission, to quote Livingstone, 'as a shield against the Ajawa'. So, with 'the Doctor's' full concurrence, the inevitable decision was taken: and the settlement was made at Magomero, about sixty miles north-east of Chibisa and

[1] Mackenzie to a friend, 4. xi. 61, *U.M.C.A. Report for 1861*, 7. Waller's *Journal, ibid.*, 22–3.

fifteen south-west of Lake Shirwa. It was an attractive situation, on a small promontory encircled on three sides by a
winding river and shaded by tall trees; but it lay short of the
real highlands, at a height of about 1,000 ft.; and for that
reason it was regarded as only a temporary home for the
Mission until the Bishop should become himself familiar with
the surrounding country and select at leisure a permanent
site. At Magomero, then, on July 29, Livingstone left them,
in brilliant, healthy weather like an English summer at its
best, already happily absorbed in the work they had so long
awaited, Mackenzie studying the language, one of his staff
planning the lay-out of their village, another building a
stockade across the open end of the promontory, another
superintending the transport of the stores up the long path
from Chibisa, and another beginning a school for the freedmen's children.[1]

'Never had a mission a better start', Kirk wrote home.
But why, he asked, when money was no object, was there no
doctor on the staff?[2]

3

Kirk had no opportunity of seeing the Magomero settlement for himself or of saying good-bye to that 'trump of a
fellow'; for, shortly after Livingstone's return, on August 6,
the old trio, accompanied at first by Dr. Meller, who had come
out as medical officer to the *Pioneer*, started up the Shire.
Their programme was first to carry up a boat past the Cata-

[1] Goodwin, *Memoir*, 287-8, with a sketch of the settlement.
Waller's *Journal*. *U.M.C.A. Report for 1861*, 23-4. Livingstone,
Narrative, 362-4. The following is an extract from Waller to Dean
Goodwin, April 1865: 'It has been questioned whether the determination to settle at Magomero was a wise one. It was at the time
most earnestly considered. . . . It resolved itself into this, and was
thus put by Dr. Livingstone to the Bishop and myself, the only
members of the mission party present: "If you fall back to Mount
Soche, all this densely populated country will go before the Ajawas:
if you take your stand here, it will be saved".' *Memoir*, Appendix, 2-3.

[2] K. to Dr. J. Hooker, 7. iii. 61. K. to Sir W. Hooker, 6. xii. 61
(Kew, *Zambesi Expedition*, pp. 15, 18).

racts; next to explore Lake Nyassa with its aid; and then to return to the *Pioneer* at Chibisa, and take her down to the sea. There they were to meet Mackenzie's sister and Livingstone's wife, who was also coming out *via* the Cape, and bring them up the river.

Dr. Meller turned back on the 8th with a Makololo patient, and on the 16th the hard work began. Sometimes they could force the boat up-stream between one rapid and another; but there were heavy stretches of 'portage' overland, and their rate of progress was only from two to four miles a day. Abreast of Mount Zomba, the lie of the land was more level and the rapids less frequent, and by August 26 they were enjoying long spells of sailing on 'a wide serpentine river, lined with reeds and papyrus, abounding in hippopotami'—one of which opened its vast jaws to seize the stern of the boat and snapped them within a few inches of Kirk's back. 'The men said that *Nampe* (God) alone saved us as it is a common thing for these wild bulls to destroy canoes and kill the crew.' 'The people', notes the diary hereabouts, 'are fleeing from the east bank and bringing corn with them. . . All this day we have passed a succession of temporary huts with stores of corn. . . The chief wishes to go and attack another party of Ajawa opposite. . . It was explained that . . . when we went to the Ajawa at Zomba, it was to try to prevail on them to desist [from] plundering the people. But when they would not listen and attacked us, then in defence we fired. Now we had come on a journey to Nyassa. . . We wished to stop the Slave Trade, not to make war.' It was none the less distressing for two whole days of the voyage to watch that unceasing flight. At one point where Livingstone went ashore, in a forest near the west bank, 'he met with long lines of poor starved fugitives and others resting on the grass without a single thing of their own. Some of the boys were in a miserable state'; while away to the east of the river could be seen the flame and smoke of burning villages. On August 31 they reached Lake Pamalombe, deep and still, encircled by a belt of papyrus so thick that the boat could hardly be got ashore. That night, beside the papyrus, was unpleasant. The ground was black and damp and smelt abominably when disturbed. Myriads of mosquitoes plagued them. Malaria was clearly in the air. By breakfast-time next morning they had left the noisome place five miles behind. On the day after (September 2), they sailed out into the lake.[1]

It would have been a relatively quick and easy matter for the explorers to traverse the whole length of the lake in the sailing-boat; but, since the natives who had accompanied them to assist in the *portage* were unwilling to be planted down alone in a strange land, it was necessary, though, as Kirk frequently complains, very tedious, to proceed in two parties—most of the natives marching along the coast and the boat holding back to keep in touch with them. Thus, at the old slow rate of some half-dozen miles a day, they rounded the noble promontory which divides the southern end of the lake into two branches—they named it Cape Maclear after the Astronomer Royal at the Cape—and then crept up the western coast. They found the shore-line curving in a series of sandy bays between rocky capes. Inland lay a plain, now fertile, now marshy, which stretched at first some ten or twelve miles back to a range of wooded hills. As they sailed north, the hills rose into mountains, drawing nearer and nearer to the lake, till at last they rose in great precipices from the water. The maritime strip was densely populated. Wherever the boat put in, the natives instantly rushed down in hundreds to see its outlandish occupants. 'The banks are black with people,' notes Kirk one day, and grimly adds: 'If the Slave Trade is to continue, this is the best locality; for all the slaves in the world would make no impression on the numbers.' They were not, it seems, attractive folk. 'The people hereabouts are the ugliest I have seen in Africa and the most inhospitable, neither giving nor selling. They were 'miserably clad', ill-nourished and sickly. 'Disease

[1] K.'s *Diary*, 6. viii.2.– ix. 61. Livingstone, *Narrative*, 365-8.

is frequent among the people. We see many cases of leprosy
and other skin diseases, disease of the eyes, clubfoot, and
deformities of the limbs. . . . Smallpox has marked many.'
Kirk thought their poor condition mainly due to laziness.
The soil was often fertile, cotton and sugar-cane growing well;
but the natives preferred fishing with nets of *buaze* fibre to
the labours of agriculture. Their attitude towards the explorers was different from anything that Livingstone had yet
encountered. They seemed neither friendly nor unfriendly,
but very suspicious—they always carried arms—and intensely
inquisitive. And their attentions were not at all flattering.
They called the white men *chirombo* or 'wild animals'. 'We
have to pass the time', says Kirk, 'as wild beasts in a show,
stared at by hundreds of curious niggers to whom everything
about us is matter of comment, especially the amount of
cloth we wear, the blankets we sleep on, and the strange manner we feed in.' Again: 'Sunday, if so you can call it, with
men, women, and children round the hut, ten deep, all talking.
Dr. L.'s modesty has driven him to wash in secret. . . Church
service to-day was performed under difficulties. The natives
kept quiet for a little, but soon began to rush about and talk.'
Once and only once did this inquisitiveness become acquisitive. 'Last night', records the diary on September 16, 'I had
a fit of ague. Towards morning some people came down and
robbed us of three bags of clothes, one of beads, and several
small things. They did it deliberately, seeking out the clothes
and leaving such things as boots and specimens. My bundle
of papers was opened, the strings taken off, and the specimens
pulled about, then heaped in anyway and left. The fish-skins
were all thrown together. Botanical specimens were smashed
by this rough treatment. The birds are gone. Dr. L. and
Mr. C. L. have, like me, lost their clothing and sundry other
things. Fortunately guns and ammunition were not taken,
and the cloth, the little we now have, I was using as a pillow.
As they got farther north, Kirk was inclined to revise his
judgement on the people's laziness. The barbarous Mazitu,

a highland tribe, migrants from the south and akin to the Matabele, had swept the country, killing and plundering, so that it was but common sense to catch your fish and eat it instead of raising corn that would probably be burnt or stolen as soon as it was harvested. At one point they saw the skeletons of slaughtered victims among the ashes of their huts. 'The natives about [here] are a miserably starved race, hunted from engaging in any labour on the soil and depending on the fish of the lake for their subsistence.'[1]

For a month they continued northwards. It was not an enjoyable month. The natural beauty of the scenery was veiled from them by a heavy haze, sometimes thickened by swarms of minute midges which hung like a 'living cloud' and 'struck upon the face like drifting snow'. It was only on rare occasions that the air was clear enough for them to catch a glimpse of mountains on the eastern shore of the lake or to see far across the waste of waters to the north. And it was fiercely hot. 'The sun is now getting to its strength,' runs one of many complaints in the diary, 'and to sit exposed to it in the stern of a small boat is very trying. It pierces through clothes and makes pains in the joints. Dr. L. is proof against anything, and, so long as the boat goes on towards the end of the lake, little short of a tempest would discompose him.' But could they succeed in reaching the end of the lake? They could not tell how far it was, since native information, though often very precise, was always wildly contradictory; and they would have to turn back before that fast diminishing roll of cloth, which was their only means of buying food, had been quite exhausted. So once more, as at every stage and in every field of the Expedition, the slow rate of progress chafed and depressed its members. At times they were brought to a dead stop by gales of wind and stormy seas when the waves of the inland sea rose high and crashed in foam on the beach like a veritable ocean. Once they were caught by a storm in the open and had to ride it out at

[1] K.'s *Diary*, 2. ix–2. x. 61. Livingstone, *Narrative*, 269–87.

anchor, given up for lost by the native land-party watching
from the cliff. 'From this time', confesses Livingstone, 'we
trusted implicitly to the opinions of our seaman, John Neil,
who, having been a fisherman on the coast of Ireland, understood boating on a stormy coast; and by his advice we often
sat cowering on the land for days together waiting for the
surf to go down. He had never seen such waves before.' And
those irritating waits, whether for the sea to subside or the
land-party to catch up, were not made any more tolerable
by the swarm of gaping, chattering natives that surrounded
them in a second after they had come ashore. Nor, lastly,
was the old enemy lacking. That marshy coastland teemed
with fever. Every night they slept on it. And Kirk, at any
rate, was as ill as he had ever been in the Zambesi delta.
Something must be discounted, therefore, from the diary's
rather drab account of the lake journey. Kirk, indeed, confesses as much. 'It is wonderful in this country', he notes
one day, 'the changes which come over one according to the
state of health. I have now shaken off the fever and everything seems much brighter, the people not so ugly and the
country more interesting.'[1]

They did not reach the end of the lake. On October 3 they
found themselves alongside country which had been swept
clean, even of its inhabitants, by the Mazitu. 'The borders
of this land', wrote Kirk, 'are deserts. All the people have
been killed and it has been a dreadful slaughter; for the
shores are covered with skulls, and where a foraging party
has passed fresh bodies beginning to decompose lie scattered
on the sand.' Not unnaturally, the natives of the land-party
were terrified and only consented to continue their march
when Livingstone came ashore and led them. Kirk and
Charles Livingstone, who remained in the boat, were thus
separated from 'the Doctor', who, since at this point the
mountains rose sheer from the water, was obliged to make a
détour of uncertain length. The next morning the two parties

[1] See preceding note.

had inevitably lost touch, 'The serious question now is where have the land-party gone. As far as we have come they could not approach the lake, and we see mountains still higher quite twenty miles ahead coming down to the water-edge.'

'This morning [says the evening entry for the same day] we went on about 4 miles, when the aspect of the country showed that it was quite impossible for Dr. L. to come down. We accordingly turned to go back; but a very strong gale from the south forced us to take shelter in a small bay. I am quite unable to take any care of things for fever last night and another fit this morning which continued from 8 to 1 p.m. To go on all night was proposed, but seems too dangerous on this dismal coast. . . 5 *Oct.* The fever continued at night on me. Our grub now is very poor, and, if this weather continues long, [there] will soon be none. The sky is black and the south-easter still blows. What Dr. L. is doing we cannot tell. He must be very anxious. . . 9 a.m. Bar. 28.11. T. 78. The wind changing round to the east began to send a heavy swell into our little bay. The barometer is lower than it has ever been on the lake. Neil the seaman has got fever on him again, so we are short of our best man for the boat. . . The wind kept up all day, shifting round towards evening to the S.E. again, and sending a heavy sea which did not go down till 5 p.m. Had Neil been able to pull an oar during the night, we might have made a start; but with two of us done up with fever, it is inadvisable on this coast and without moonlight. . . 6 *Oct.* Fine morning. We pulled off at 5.30 a.m. Soon found Dr. L. and 2 Makololo on the lake with a canoe. His salutation on meeting was, "What on earth made you run away and leave us?"' [1]

In this confused, disjointed, and somewhat ignominious manner the Expedition had attained its Farthest North. The last latitude Kirk had taken before fever incapacitated him was 11°. 44' S.; and it was reckoned that the boat had gone about 24' further. Livingstone, for his part, as he dragged his land-party over the heights, had seen mountain-masses closing in northwards on both sides of the lake. So they assumed its end to be not very far off, whereas it lay at least a hundred miles ahead and the explorers had only traversed

[1] K.'s *Diary*, 3–6. x. 61. K. to Professor Balfour, 14. xii. 61 (Royal Botanic Garden, Edinburgh). Livingstone, *Narrative*, 385–7.

about five-sevenths of its length. In any case retreat was now imperative. The problem of food-supply, acute enough as it was with their shortage of cloth, seemed almost insoluble in that deserted land ahead. They turned back, therefore, with a sense of disappointment, and not only at their failure to survey the whole of the lake, but at the lakeside country too. If British colonization were desirable anywhere in Africa, it was surely desirable there. Only the presence and protection of white men could save that teeming population from the twofold scourge that decimated it—northwards the Mazitu, southwards the Slave Trade. Of the prevalence of the latter there was evidence enough. The explorers learned that two enterprising Arab traders had built a *dhow* and were regularly transporting slaves across the lake, whence they marched them overland to Ibo and Kilwa. 'The *dhow* sailed from a place a little ahead to-day full of slaves', notes Kirk, about half-way up the lake; and, while at other points he has observed how miserably clothed the natives were, sometimes in sheets of bark stitched together, 'The people here', he records next day, 'are very well clad, many of them wearing cloths which cover them from head to foot. This is the result of the trade in slaves carried on by the *dhow*.' And once again, in the *Narrative*, Livingstone breaks out against 'the awful sacrifice of human life which must be attributed, directly or indirectly, to this trade of hell'. And how quickly it could be destroyed! 'A small armed steamer on Lake Nyassa could easily, by exercising control and furnishing goods in exchange for ivory and other products, break the neck of this infamous traffic in that quarter; for nearly all must cross the Lake or the Upper Shire.' But, badly as white men were needed, that lakeside belt was seemingly no place for white men to live in. 'The country along the lake such as we have seen', says the diary for September 15, 'cannot be called healthy, and we have come to no place suitable as a European settlement.' And again, a few days later: 'Our experience of the margin of Lake Nyassa is far from being favourable. Of course, we are here badly fed for Europeans and exposed with a sedentary life to the full force of a burning sun during the whole day. When we land it is to sleep among the reeds or on the sand, frequently with a marsh close to us. All that must be taken into consideration before an opinion can be formed of the salubrity of the region to Europeans with comforts and perhaps with a steamer on the water, anchored far off land.' These doubts, of course, were justified, but, none the less, the explorers' work had not been wasted. That lakeside might never be a British Colony, but within fifty years it was to be included in a British Protectorate. Within thirty years that coast was to be dotted with the stations of a British company, trading up and down the lake 'with a steamer on the water', and dotted also with the stations of British missions. And to-day, on the mountain plateau, about forty miles beyond the point Kirk's little boat had reached, stands the great church of Livingstonia, its lofty tower visible far up and down the lake, an eternal monument to the faith and works of the man whose name it honours.[1]

But all such consolations were hidden in the future; and it was a rather dejected party, enfeebled by fever and underfed, that made its way back to the south end of the lake. At the lowest navigable point on the Upper Shire they hoisted the boat up a tree and left it securely lodged on branches twenty feet above the ground; and, before starting for Chibisa, Kirk and 'the Doctor' enjoyed the recreation of following up a herd of bull elephants which were 'amusing themselves by turning over large trees . . . like a man breaking a small branch in a thoughtless manner'. 'This was our first day of land exercise', Kirk reflects that evening, 'since we began the lake—a jolly relief it was. Sitting in the stern of that boat, exposed all day to the sun, has made an impression not easily forgotten. The inactivity and the pains in the bones and joints from the sun, the gradual emaciation, the

[1] K.'s *Diary*, 15–19. ix. 61. Livingstone, *Narrative*, 390–2.

fevers and the starvation of that Nyassa journey combine to make it the hardest, most trying, and most disagreeable of all our journeys. It is the only one I have no pleasure in looking back on.' But like the other journeys, which had not been so very pleasurable except by comparison, it had come at last to its end. 'We reached the ship on the 8th of November, 1861,' records Livingstone, 'in a very weak condition, having suffered more from hunger than on any previous trip.' No wonder that, as soon as they came within a day's march of Chibisa, they had sent a messenger post-haste to ask for a boat to be sent up to meet them 'with all delicacies on board such as a ship can supply'. 'The boat', Kirk continues, 'came up after we had turned in, but that did not prevent our cracking a bottle of wine, munching biscuit, and eating preserved carrots cold.' [1]

4

'Reached the ship,' says the diary for November 8. 'Dr. Meller, Rowe and the steward are now up at the Bishop's, where there have been strange doings since we left.' It was certainly a strange story that Kirk gleaned from those of the ship's company who had remained in the *Pioneer*; but he was soon to hear a more authoritative version from Mackenzie himself. Meantime, there suddenly arrived at Chibisa a cheerful and courageous young Englishman whose fate, as it happened, was to be closely linked with Mackenzie's in the dark days that lay ahead. 'A canoe came up one evening and

[1] K.'s *Diary*, 1–7. xi. 61. Livingstone, *Narrative*, 400. For the lake journey in general: K. to Professor Balfour, 14. xii. 61 (Royal Botanic Garden, Edinburgh). K. to Dr. J. Hooker, 2. xii. 61 (Kew, *African Letters, 1859–1865*, No. 161)—with his letter is a chart of the lake, beautifully drawn by K. from his own observations and, considering the poor visibility, &c., wonderfully accurate. K. to the Hon. Mr. Breda, Cape Town, 20. iii. 62 (*South African Advertiser and Mail*, 21. v. 62). Livingstone to Sir T. Maclear, 12. xi. 61 (*ibid.*); L. to Sir George Grey, 15. xi. 61 (*ibid.*); and L. to Russell, 10. xi. 61 (F.O. 63/894).

hailed us in English. We could not imagine what it was; most guessed that the new steamer had come, but it turned out to be an addition to Bishop Mackenzie's staff, Mr. Burrup, from Oxford.' He had left two others behind in another canoe with the baggage—a surgeon and an artisan. 'They had been to Mozambique and Johanna and landed at Quilimane. The Portuguese had been very kind to them, but the ascent of the Shire in canoes was a bold undertaking at this season and they had not used mosquito curtains.' Next day (November 14), the Bishop arrived, with Dr. Meller, from Magomero.[1]

Both Livingstone and Kirk were disquieted by the tale he told them. Yet it was but the logical sequence of that fight with the Ajawa which had occurred before the Expedition separated from the Mission. Already at that time, and inevitably, appeals had come in from the Manganja, imploring the white men to continue their good work and lead them again to battle. But Livingstone had advised Mackenzie to discount them. He must expect, he had said, to have many such applications for help, but he must not yield to them. To break up any slave-gangs that might be met with was one thing. To involve the Mission in a regular war between two native tribes was quite another. But it was easier to give this advice than to take it; and when, soon after Livingstone's departure, two leading chiefs of the district sent to Magomero to ask if they might come in person and state their case, Mackenzie could not bring himself to refuse. On August 9, accordingly, the chiefs arrived, attended by a hundred tribesmen; and the Bishop and his staff sat down to a formal conference. But to confer was almost to consent. For what arguments could Mackenzie use to justify neutrality? It may have been mistaken to send a Mission at all to a country where slave-raiding was in progress; but he had been sent there, and he had no choice. It was true, again, no doubt,

---

[1] K.'s *Diary*, 8–14. xi. 61. Livingstone, *Narrative*, 401. Burrup's own account of his adventurous journey is given in *U.M.C.A. Report for 1861*, 30–4.

that the Manganja were morally little better than the Ajawa, only weaker or more cowardly; but it was also true that the Ajawa were the aggressors. And the Manganja, after all, were the people to whom, as it happened, the Mission had come to preach its gospel. What would they think of the preachers if, content with denouncing the Slave Trade they sat idle while the Ajawa continued undisturbed to burn the surrounding villages, slaughter their men, and enslave their women and children? The almost inevitable result may be given in Mackenzie's words.

'We consented at last to head an army, on condition that stealing, buying, and selling people should be given up and declared illegal; that all the chiefs would abstain from it (they have all been deeply involved in it) and do their best to put a stop to it; that if Portuguese slave-dealers came up into this country to buy people, they should drive them away, and tell us of their arrival; and, finally, that all the captives in the Ajawa camp whom we might liberate should be free to go where they pleased. On the 14th of August, accordingly, we took and burned an Ajawa camp, nearly twenty miles from this. The resistance was much less—only sufficient to cover the retreat of two large bodies, who went in different directions; but there was some blood shed in the pursuit. We followed up close for a couple of hours, intending to break the body and so rescue the slaves, but this was not effected. . . . In this fight I used my gun to the best of my skill as did all the rest. We were only ten guns, and I thought it right to do all I could to rid the country of robbers and murderers, and to help the chiefs to drive away an army of invaders. . . . It was striking a death-blow to the Slave Trade at its heart. It was not till after some deliberation that we came to this conclusion. I do not doubt now that it was right. Our third [1] fight was on the 16th of October, nearly forty miles from this. We met with no resistance; burnt the village, and found ourselves responsible for the maintenance and care of fifty additional persons. So far as we can see, we have gained peace for the country. It is now being cultivated, instead of being deserted; and we may hope to consolidate what has been done, and to build on this foundation, by planting Missions in several parts of this highland plain. I ought to have told you that on our second fight, we tried to effect the purpose without war, by going down, four

[1] The first fight was that of July 21, see p. 200, above.

of us—Waller, Charles Thomas, an interpreter, and myself—towards the Ajawa, and calling their chiefs to a conference. We went further than we intended, and exposed ourselves to the fire of a few who stood at some distance from the main body. They had a gun, and bows and arrows; we, of course, had left our arms. We told them, if the chiefs would speak to us there was no war; if they *would not*, there was war. They asked what sort of white men we were; and when we said "English", they said "We do not wish to have anything to do with the English; we will not speak to you; it is you that help the Manganja against the Ajawa".'[1]

Thus ended the Bishop's little campaign. 'We have given peace and security which I trust will be lasting', wrote Mackenzie in another letter, 'to a large tract of country which was gradually melting away in a desert as the flames of Ajawa war spread across it.' If this trust was well founded, surely his decision, which was in any case difficult for him to evade and difficult for others to condemn, would be justified by its results. But if the peace should not prove lasting, then the whole situation would be worse instead of better. The Mission would be involved, like an African tribe, in a protracted African war without the military strength to put an end to it by drastic action on a large scale. And the conflict would not involve the Mission only. All Englishmen in the country, in the minds of the natives at least, would be entangled in their savage politics. Naturally, therefore, Kirk's mind, when first he heard the story, was somewhat divided. As a human being, he could not help sympathizing with his friend the Bishop, if not rather admiring him, in his new role. 'When he came to us first', he wrote to Sir William Hooker, 'he did not know how to load a gun and went up the hills carrying a pastoral staff and determined not to shoot anyone even in self-defence. When he saw the miserable objects of starved children we took from the slave-drivers and heard the accounts of barbarities perpetrated, his blood rose and theories vanished.' None the less, Kirk was distinctly uneasy as to

[1] Mackenzie to a friend, 4. xi. 61. *U.M.C.A. Report for 1861*, 7–8.

the results of the Bishop's militancy. 'The policy of attacking the Ajawa', he continues, 'is very doubtful.' And the diary adds this comment: 'In the affair of Dr. L. the Ajawa made the attack, but here the English began, or at least, by going with a large body of Manganja up to the camp, made it equivalent to an attack. Thus the English will be put down as natural enemies of the Ajawa, whereas the Manganja are as bad slave-traders as the Ajawa and much greater cowards also.' Livingstone, too, was dismayed to find that his parting counsel to Mackenzie had been disregarded. He felt himself personally implicated. He had inspired the Mission, he had chosen its location and watched over its settlement, and he had promised the natives that its purpose was one of peace. Later on, indeed, he was himself to be charged with the blame, if blame there was, when Mackenzie's successor publicly declared that 'the warlike measures of the Mission were the consequences of following Dr. Livingstone's advice'—a true statement in one sense, as has been seen,[1] but quite untrue in the sense in which its audience would naturally interpret it. At the time, in any case, there was nothing to be done. As Livingstone puts it, 'a friendly disapproval of the Bishop's engaging in war was ventured on'; but there was no kind of dispute or ill feeling. As Mackenzie and Burrup put off from the *Pioneer* on their way to Magomero, 'they gave and received three hearty English cheers'.[2]

Livingstone had reckoned that the *Pioneer*, with the Mission ladies on board, would be again ascending the Shire in January; and since he had decided not to attempt this time to bring the ship farther up than the mouth of the Ruo, about fifty miles below Chibisa, it had been arranged that Mackenzie, having explored the route from Magomero, should meet his party there and escort it back by the way he had come.

But no calculation of the time required for river-transport had yet been anywhere near the mark, and this was no exception. The *Pioneer* left Chibisa on or about November 14. She grounded on a shoal about twenty miles down-stream, and there she stuck for five weeks! She passed the mouth of the Ruo on December 7, only four days before Mackenzie arrived there; and, entering the Zambesi on January 11, reached the sea at the Luabo Mouth on January 23. The delay on the Shire had proved more than usually irksome owing to the prevalence of fever; and the carpenter's mate, despite all the efforts of Meller and Kirk, had died of it—the first death among the members of the Expedition. The only other event worth recording was a serious injury to the ship's rudder. But the monotony of those dreary weeks was broken lower down the river by interesting news from the neighbourhood. That historic half-caste, Mariano,[1] was at large again. Brought to trial at the conclusion of his rebellion in 1859, he had been lightly sentenced to three years' imprisonment and a fine. But, since he had no money to pay the latter, the Portuguese authorities had allowed him to go to Quilimane to collect some debts owed to him and from there to proceed up-country, with some hundreds of followers and guns and ammunition, in quest of ivory, still with a view to the payment of the fine. No sooner, of course, had he rejoined his own people on the Shire than the fine and, still more, the sentence of imprisonment were forgotten, and he resumed his old game of slave-hunting among the Manganja. When the *Pioneer* passed down the Shire, he had 'already desolated a large portion of the right bank'. A Portuguese captain had been sent by the Governor of Quilimane to catch him, but had himself been caught, with all his men, and then set free—so his brother officers declared—with a gift of ivory. . . . A curious item in the records of colonial administration. 'Who will believe', Kirk bluntly asks, 'but that bribery and corruption are at the bottom of it all?' Lower down, in the Zambesi

[1] See p. 118, above.

area, they met some of the Portuguese whose slaves they had so inconsiderately freed in the previous July; but, rather to their surprise, there were no recriminations. The subject, indeed, was elaborately ignored, only one trader venturing to ask with a smirk whether it was true that they had taken the Governor's slaves.[1]

When at last they reached the sea they found, of course, no ship awaiting them. It had arrived three weeks earlier, and, finding nobody, had put back to Mozambique. 'Always too late', lamented Livingstone: 'too late for Rovuma below, too late for Rovuma above, and now too late for our own appointment.' But on January 30, 1862, H.M.S. *Gorgon* came in sight, flying a signal that Mrs. Livingstone was on board and the *Lady Nyassa*—the steamer which had been sent out in sections to be carried up to the lake. Other members of the party were the Bishop's sister, young Burrup's wife, another missionary and other helpers bound for Magomero, and the Rev. James Stewart, of the Free Church of Scotland, one day to be known as 'Stewart of Lovedale'. Stewart, says the diary, had come out to prospect for a new 'industrial self-supporting mission', and his arrival was one more proof that the project of colonization was taking solid shape. Some months earlier Livingstone had received a discouraging letter from Sir Roderick Murchison. 'Your colonization scheme does not meet with supporters, it being thought that you must have much more hold on the country before you attract Scotch families to emigrate and settle there, and then die off, and become a burden to you and all concerned, like the settlers of old at Darien.' True Scottish caution, and to be justified beyond question by events. But Livingstone, also a Scot, felt he could now make a confident reply. 'A Dr. Stewart', he wrote, 'is sent out by the Free Church of Scotland to confer with me about a Scotch colony. You will guess my ardour. Dr. Kirk is with me in opinion; and, if I could only get you out to make a trip up to the plateau of Zomba

---

[1] K.'s *Diary*, 14. xi. 61–23. i. 62. Livingstone, *Narrative*, 400–7.

and over the uplands which surround Lake Nyassa, you would give in too.' Kirk's diary, however, reveals him as not over-enthusiastic about the new venture. He was obviously a little jealous on behalf of his friend Mackenzie. And he was not greatly attracted to Stewart. Nor, at first, was he pleased to see another and the last of the new arrivals—his old colleague Rae, who, despite everything, had come out to serve for another spell with the Expedition; for Kirk had come to the conclusion that the apparent loss of his specimens had been due to Rae's negligence. An explanation, however, was soon forthcoming, and Kirk fully withdrew his accusation. Yet, all in all, he was far from happy in the days that followed the *Gorgon*'s arrival. A few weeks earlier it was Livingstone who had been depressed. On the first day of the New Year, during that dreary voyage down the Shire, he had entered in his journal an elaborate memorandum on the conduct of the Expedition, dealing (says his biographer) with 'the difficulty to which civil expeditions are exposed as compared with naval and military in the matter of discipline owing to the inferior authority and power of the chief', and enumerating the troubles which had arisen therefrom. His conclusion had been one which can be read, long before this date, between the lines of Kirk's diary. 'If he had been by himself, he would have accomplished more.' But now Livingstone's spirits had risen. Reunion with his wife, after a parting of three years, and the coming of Stewart had brought him new happiness and new hope. Not so with Kirk. It is evident from the diary that the stir and bustle of the *Gorgon*'s arrival, the fresh faces and fresh talk, all left him cold. The newcomers were scarcely ashore before new threads of personal gossip, some of it thoroughly unpleasant, were being spun, and he was haunted by forebodings of more mischief-making and more quarrels. Or was it chiefly that the *Gorgon* had brought with her another seductive whiff of northern air? At any rate, Kirk was once more very homesick. 'My own mind is now fully made up', he says, and the words

have a familiar ring, 'to be off by the very first opportunity. . . . My goods at Tete keep me, and they are the only
things.' [1]

5

Many months were to pass before Kirk could collect his
goods and go his way; and, anyhow, he could not evade the
immediate task of helping to transport the new steamship and
the Mission ladies up the river. Despite the help of Captain
Wilson of the *Gorgon* and over seventy of his crew, it took,
as usual, far longer than Kirk or any one else expected; for
the engines of the *Pioneer* were in such a condition that progress against the Zambesi current was at times almost imper-
ceptible. They were excellent engines; but, incredible as it
may seem, the engineer had neglected to renew their packing
for twenty months! Livingstone decided, therefore, to put
the *Lady Nyassa* together at Shupanga instead of carrying
the sections up to the Ruo. Even so, the Expedition was
delayed six months in the Zambesi lowlands, doing what had
been calculated to take six days. [2]

As soon as it was clear that a long delay was inevitable,
Captain Wilson offered to take Miss Mackenzie and Mrs.
Burrup up to the Ruo in his gig. His surgeon, Dr. Ramsay,
accompanied them, and Livingstone sent Kirk to guide and
advise them in the *Lady Nyassa*'s whaler. The two boats
left Shupanga on February 17, and made their way up the

---

[1] K.'s *Diary*, 30. i–7. ii. 62. Blaikie, *Livingstone*, 243–7, citing
Stewart's ' Recollections of Dr. Livingstone and the Zambesi ' from
the *Sunday Magazine*, Nov. 1874. Stewart's experiences on the
Zambesi, where he stayed till Feb. 1863, are briefly described in
J. Wells, *Stewart of Lovedale* (London, 1908), 60–83.

[2] Livingstone, *Narrative*, 408. Assistant-Paymaster W. C. Devereux
accompanied the party from the *Gorgon* and described his experiences
in *A Cruise in the Gorgon* (London, 1869), 170–244. The management
of the Expedition by no means accorded with his naval standards of
efficiency. ' I never saw such constant vacillations, blunders, delays,
and want of common thought and foresight as is displayed on board
the *Pioneer*' (219). For sidelights on Livingstone, see pp. 190, 191,
201, 205, 229, 233.

Shire, with sail and oar, rather slowly, because the river was now in full flood. On the tenth day they reached the Ruo, where a surprise awaited them. 'We hoped', says the diary, 'to have met with some of the Mission: this was the appointed place of meeting. But to our great astonishment nothing could be learned with regard to the Mission. The people professed never to have seen any one coming from above.' There seemed nothing for it but to continue the journey to Chibisa; and, the whaler being wanted now at Shupanga, Kirk joined the Captain's party in the gig. He was distressed to find that Miss Mackenzie was quite unfit for tropical travel. Elderly and an invalid, she had made up her mind with more courage than wisdom—so it seemed to Kirk—to join her brother in the wilds of Africa. 'She was unable to place one foot before another: if she desired to shift her position, she had to get assistance and to have herself supported with pillows. The daily landing was a serious job. A bower or shelter had to be constructed and she carried to it. Mrs. Burrup, on the contrary, was full of life, talked nautical and jumped about.' Once, during landing operations, the boat got her mast fouled in an overhanging tree; she half filled with water and nearly sank; and the passengers had a thorough wetting. Save for that incident, the heroic old lady and the lively young wife had nothing worse to endure than the usual plague of mosquitoes until, at dusk on March 4, they reached Chibisa. There, so near the end of their long journey, tragedy chose its time and struck.[1]

'While seeking for the landing-place', Kirk records, 'some one was seen on the heights, and, on being hailed, returned answer in a mixed dialect which I at once recognized as that of the Makololo. Being requested to come down, and while we were still in the boat, he began to give us the news. On inquiring after the Bishop, to my horror I got the answer, O shuile, "He is dead".' Kirk at once broke off the conversation, especially as he noticed that Miss Mackenzie, who knew

[1] K.'s *Diary*, 17. ii–4. iii. 62.

the kindred Zulu language, seemed to suspect that 'something was wrong'. But the truth could not be concealed for long. When the party had climbed up to the village, they learned that Mackenzie lay in his grave near the Ruo—the natives there had evidently lied—and that Burrup, who had buried him, had returned, very ill, to Magomero. . . . It was well, indeed, that so brave a spirit dwelt in Miss Mackenzie's frail body. 'She stood the shock very well', says Kirk: 'her behaviour deserves the greatest admiration.' He would have liked, no doubt, to stay and look after her, but the news of the Bishop's death was not the only bad news from Magomero. It appeared from the letters waiting at Chibisa that troubles had gathered thick about the settlement. To live with some two hundred natives at close quarters, under a tropical sun, on relatively low ground, fenced off by trees from cleansing winds, was bound to be dangerous without some strict and efficient sanitary system. But sanitation had been neglected. The air, the dust, the river from which they drank, had all been contaminated. Dysentery was rife. Picturesque Magomero had become, in Kirk's phrase, 'a pest-house'. Provisions, it seemed, had also been running short. Thirty of the natives were dead. In fact, as the diary reports, 'the letters from the Mission represent their state as one of prostration from disease and famine'. It was a clear call for help, and, little as he liked it, Kirk felt bound to respond. 'Nothing but what seemed an absolute necessity', he confesses, 'would have induced me to go off thus without medicines, proper food, and a sufficient supply of cloth during the wet season. . . . But it was an act of humanity from doing which there was no escape.' Captain Wilson insisted on sharing the duty and the risk; and on March 5, leaving the ladies in charge of Dr. Ramsey, they started with some sailors on their march up-country. The very next day they were caught in drizzling rain and Kirk was attacked by such a persistent bout of ague that they were obliged to halt till the following morning. Then Wilson also went down with fever, and, a few miles farther on, the two of them took refuge in a hut, and lay shivering in their damp blankets. On March 8, 'we kept the hut, unable to crawl'. They had sent on a Makololo to Magomero to beg for medicine and to ask any of the staff who wished to communicate with them to come and meet them; and on the 9th he returned, followed soon after by three of the missionaries. 'To our surprise', says the diary, 'instead of haggard, starved men, they seemed all in tolerable health. . . . Their native porters, so far from having seen hunger, were fat, plump, oily niggers, fit to cause envy in all the villages we have passed through.' But any irritation Kirk may have felt at being brought up from Chibisa by exaggerated alarms was overshadowed by the news of the second act in the tragedy of Magomero. All its British residents had been more or less ill; but the only fatal case had been that of the one whose wife was waiting for him at Chibisa. Big, strong, adventurous young Burrup was dead.[1]

Later on the whole pitiful story could be pieced together. Mackenzie, it will be remembered, had arranged with Livingstone to prospect the route from Magomero to the Ruo–Shire confluence and to meet him there at the beginning of January. Livingstone had also advised him not to divide his forces on this expedition, except for the party that would necessarily be left in charge at Magomero. But the Bishop was inclined to under-estimate the insidious powers of Africa. Fever, he was always saying, was less troublesome to him than its cure; and, as for the risks of travel in the wilds, there was Burrup's successful voyage to show what a stout-hearted Englishman could do. So it was decided that two of the missionaries, Procter and Scudamore, should be sent out to make a preliminary survey in the direction of the Ruo. They left on December 2 with a few carriers and a mission-native who had come with Mackenzie from the Cape. Five days later the

---

[1] K.'s *Diary*, 4–9. iii. 62.

Cape 'boy' came creeping in at the Mission gate, 'haggard, in rags, footsore, and looking wretched to the last degree. He was soon surrounded, and said faintly, "I am the only one that has escaped—I and one of the bearers. The Manganja attacked us." Happily, before Mackenzie closed the letter in which he recorded these misfortunes, Procter and Scudamore arrived, very hungry but otherwise little the worse. They had safely reached the Ruo, it appeared, but at a point several miles to the north of the direct line of route recommended by Livingstone. At a village near its banks they met with a queer reception. Though its inhabitants were either Manganja or of a kindred tribe, they showed no pleasure at the white men's arrival; and the attitude of the chief, Manasomba, though he was civil enough and pressed them to stay till next morning, was vaguely disquieting. Their suspicions were soon confirmed. One of their bearers overheard a discussion of the plans devised for the coming night. The villagers were going to set fire to their hut, kill them all in the confusion, and appropriate their goods. On hearing this they immediately prepared to leave; but the villagers, crowding round, attempted to obstruct their departure; and they moved off in a *mêlée* which developed into a flight. It was only because their assailants were afraid of their guns that Procter and Scudamore escaped. The Cape 'boy' got away in another direction. Six of the bearers also made off ; but one of them and one of the Mission 'freed men' were left in captivity. All the baggage, of course, was abandoned.[1]

Mackenzie's dream of peace and security had thus swiftly faded. Once more he felt obliged to fight, and on December 23 sallied out in strength, with Burrup, Scudamore, and Waller, eleven Makololo, who after accompanying Livingstone to Lake Nyassa had attached themselves temporarily to the Mission, and some thirty Manganja. 'We went', wrote Mackenzie afterwards, 'with the avowed object of recovering the

[1] Goodwin, *Memoir*, 329–35.

two remaining captives, one of whom was one of our own freed-people at Magomero, and punishing the perpetrator of so treacherous an act as that described above, in order that he might desist from such courses, especially in the case of Englishmen, and that others might fear. . . . We were not revenging ourselves. . . . I would gladly have left it for Livingstone to do in the Queen's name, but feared he would say his other duties were too pressing and that he had no time.' The upshot was fairly satisfactory. They reached the village of Chipoka, a friendly chief, on December 28, and marched on next day to Manasomba's. They found it deserted, but part of their lost property was discovered in the huts. The two captives were not there. Having set fire to the huts they started back. An hour's march from the village they fell into an ambush; but the attack was not pressed, and they broke through with only two casualties among the bearers—one of them a fatal arrow-wound. They arrived at Chipoka's without further incident. 'We had indeed failed to get back our people . . . but we had punished the robber and returned safe. We had vindicated the English name, and had shown in this neighbourhood that it is not safe to attack an Englishman.' [1]

But the direct results, good or bad, of this last of Mackenzie's 'wars' were of relatively small importance to him or his Mission. Indirectly, as it chanced, it was fatal. Had Mackenzie now pushed on, as he intended, straight from Chipoka's to the Ruo–Shire confluence, there would probably have been no tragedy. He reckoned the distance himself at not more than two days' journey; and since he was already late for his appointment with Livingstone, he was bent on attempting it. But Chipoka vetoed it. It was unwise, he argued, for Mackenzie, after what he had done, to continue his journey through country occupied by Manasomba's friends. Finally he refused to supply guides. So, very reluctantly, Mackenzie

---

[1] Full account in Mackenzie's letters, Goodwin, *Memoir*, 338–47, 357–9; *U.M.C.A. Report for 1861*, 38.

reverted to the familiar, safe, but far longer route by Chibisa and the Shire. He hurried back to Magomero, and, finding most of the staff more or less ill, pressed on with Burrup as his only white companion to Chibisa. Neither of them was really fit for this continuous physical effort. Mackenzie had been suffering from diarrhoea for three or four weeks, and Burrup was only kept going by his intense determination to be present at the Ruo meeting. 'We are neither of us *quite* well,' wrote Mackenzie to his sister on the way down: 'our tempers are a little tried, and this makes a bond.' They reached Chibisa, despite 'almost incessant rain', in six days, and on the next afternoon (January 9) started down-stream in a canoe with three Makololo. One night, while camping in the Elephant Marsh, they were so tormented by mosquitoes that they decided to run the risk of continuing their voyage in the dark. Before long they were caught on a shoal and the swirling tide poured into their canoe. Both Mackenzie and Burrup were soaked to the waist. Burrup's bag with all his kit in it was lost; so was all their stock of drugs. There was nothing to do but to sleep or try to sleep in their wet clothes. As soon as it was light they took to the water again, and that morning reached the Ruo (January 11), where they learned that their haste had been quite needless; for Livingstone, delayed, as has been seen, for over a month, had passed on his way to the sea only four days earlier, and it would be at least a few more weeks before the Mission ladies could be expected. A last wrong decision was now taken. Had they either followed the *Pioneer* down-stream or returned to Magomero, the physical effort might at least have kept the fever at bay till they could obtain the requisite medicine and attention. But they took neither of these courses. They stayed where they were, in a hut on an island in mid-stream, with no quinine and no good food. Burrup had been rather worse since his wetting; but as late as January 16 Mackenzie can write, 'I am myself, thank God, in almost perfect health, and only regret, on my own account, the loss of the little packet of drugs, inasmuch as I shall probably have a touch of fever soon for want of quinine'. His last letter to his sister, written at this time, closed with the quotation of a number of texts from the *Epistle to the Romans*, which he and Burrup had been learning by heart in the Greek day by day. The last of them was the famous challenge to the Christian conscience which Paul sent ringing down the ages. 'Whosoever shall call upon the name of the Lord shall be saved. How then shall they call on him in whom they have not believed? And how shall they believe in him of whom they have not heard? And how shall they hear without a preacher? And how shall they preach except they be sent?—as it is written, How beautiful are the feet of them that preach the gospel of peace and bring glad tidings of good things.' And then, with 'Good-bye for the present', the letter ends. Soon after this the fever came, and, finding Mackenzie unprotected and inactive, it gripped him fast. Before long he was so weak that 'sometimes, in going out of his hut, he would fall forward on his face and lie there, without being able to move. . . . Poor Burrup, who was only a degree or two removed from complete prostration himself, was able to render him very little aid.' For some days he was delirious. On January 31 he died. The same evening, since the chief would not allow the body to remain on his island, Burrup, with the help of the three Makololo, who had loyally served their stricken leaders from the first, 'took the body across the river in the canoe and, having chosen a secluded spot under a large tree, they dug a grave and laid it there, Burrup reading as much of the burial service as he was able in the dim evening light'. Next day he prepared himself for a desperate effort to get back to Magomero and wrote a letter to Livingstone which he left with the chief. Then he started up the Shire. Above the Elephant Marsh the river became so difficult that the Makololo insisted on continuing the journey on foot. Burrup was forced to do likewise. On February 8 he arrived, exhausted, at Chibisa; and was carried thence in a litter to Magomero which he reached on the 14th. Drugs and good food and nursing were now too late. He died on February 22.[1]

It was not altogether surprising that the surviving missionaries, isolated, inexperienced, leaderless, should have begun to feel that Magomero was a death-trap; and the note of panic in their message to Chibisa is at least intelligible. But Kirk, who had been facing the menace of Africa for more than three years, was evidently a little disappointed at their morale. They were tolerably well supplied with food, it seemed, from their own account; and when they served him up a savoury stew of preserved meat, his comment had a feverish—and ungrateful—snap in it. 'Lucky dogs, we thought, if this is what you call starving.' One of them, moreover, seemed bent on trying to escape to England. 'My own opinion is', notes Kirk, unjustly as events proved, 'that of the three we met there was but one *viz*. Scudamore, who desired the Mission to continue.' The more immediate question, however, was to get Captain Wilson, not to mention himself, safely back to Chibisa. The food, the tea and coffee, and the medicine from Magomero had restored their strength sufficiently to begin the downward march; but they were still very weak. 'I could walk slowly with many rests every few hundred yards, but Capt. Wilson was worse. The path lay down a steep hill, and down this Wilson went by a series of runs. Just as a drunk man who cannot walk will often fetch home by running and taking a rest against the first lamp-post, so the trees took the place of the posts. But as the way became more perpendicular and more stony, the coxswain had to take the captain

---

[1] Up to Jan. 16 a detailed account is given in Mackenzie's letters; Goodwin, *Memoir*, 349–60, *U.M.C.A. Report for 1861*, 34–40. After Jan. 16, the fullest account, based on Burrup's information, is in a letter from the Rev. L. J. Procter, the senior missionary, dated 26. ii. 62, from Magomero and printed in *U.M.C.A. Report for 1861*, 40–3. K.'s version, obtained from the missionaries and the Makololo, is less detailed; *Diary*, 4–9. iii. 62. See also L. to Russell, 15. iii. 62 (F.O. 63/894).

on his shoulders and carry him.' To make matters worse, they lost their way in the dusk. 'The bluejackets were not to be beaten. Little knowing the risk of wandering at night, off they went on different routes towards where the village was supposed to be.' In time they found it; but Wilson was now in a critical condition. He had frequently to lie down and could only be roused with difficulty. 'Had he taken his own way, he would have gone to sleep, probably never to wake up again.' At last they got him to the village and 'a nice warm hut', where Kirk, who was himself much better, and Scudamore, who 'stuck to us throughout the whole time', spent the night in anxious vigil. The patient's pulse 'was weak and irregular and sometimes stopped. It was a chance which way the case would turn. As I went outside the hut I could not help seeing by the starlight the rocky soil—it seemed all stone and rock—and the idea which came with this was the difficulty of digging a grave.' But in the small hours the pulse steadied a little, and, later in the day, Wilson was fit to be carried in an improvised hammock slung on a bamboo. Before night-fall they reached Chibisa.[1]

The next task was to escort the two stricken women to the sea; for there was nowhere else for them to go but home again. So, Wilson being well enough, they started at once downstream and, making a quick passage in the gig, reached the Ruo in the afternoon of March 12.

'Landed: went to the village of the chief with whom the Bishop died. He came, but came trembling, towards us. He did not exactly know how we would receive him. Being thanked for his kindness, he seemed relieved, and a reprimand for keeping us in ignorance of the facts brought out the letter written by Mr. Burrup before starting. We got a man to show us the grave. It was on the mainland near a few snags which obstruct the river. It is to the west of a borasa palm and underneath a mimosa tree. The path was so entangled . . . that Miss Mackenzie could not be taken up to visit it. The earth was raised over it, and out of a thick bamboo Capt. Wilson and I made a rude cross which we stuck in at the feet.[2]

[1] K.'s *Diary*, 9–11. iii. 62. Livingstone, *Narrative*, 409.
[2] K.'s *Diary*, 12. iii. 62.

Nine months later Livingstone came to that desolate spot, already half-hidden by the tropical tangle of reeds and grass. 'I have just been visiting Bishop Mackenzie's grave,' he wrote. 'At first I thought him wrong in fighting, but dont think so now. He defended his 140 orphan children when there was no human arm besides to invoke.' Sadly he reflected on his 'unselfish goodness' and on the high hopes with which he had left Cambridge—'all now buried in this wild place'. And to his own hopes, too, the sudden tragedy had struck a heavy blow. Were they not the same hopes? Had he not himself inspired them in Mackenzie? Was not Mackenzie, 'humanly speaking, indispensable to the success of the enterprise?' 'This will hurt us all', he had said, when first he heard the news, sitting, with his head on his hand, in the dimly lighted cabin of the *Pioneer*. And again: 'I cannot help feeling sadly disturbed in view of the effect the news may have at home.' But his last thought is not of the irremediable past. 'I shall not swerve a hairbreadth from my work', he writes, 'while life is spared.' [1]

Such is the way of the martyrs. One calls another on.

---

[1] Livingstone, *Narrative*, 450–1. Goodwin, *Memoir*, 317. Blaikie, *Livingstone*, 248–50.

VII

END OF THE EXPEDITION
(1862–3)

I

A YET sterner trial of strength and constancy was lying in wait for Livingstone.

H.M.S. *Gorgon* sailed for the Cape on April 4, about three weeks after Kirk and Captain Wilson and their party reached the sea. The gallant captain was doubtless glad enough to go, and likewise the seventy-seven bluejackets who had assisted in the ill-fated Expedition and all but two of whom had suffered from fever, some of them repeatedly. Dr. Meller also was a passenger, or, should one say, a fugitive? He had been ill like every one else, and Kirk was doubtful if he would be willing to return to his duties in the *Pioneer*. And of the three women whom the *Gorgon* had brought there with such eager hopes two months ago, she carried two away, never to see that land again and never to forget it. As she left her anchorage the little group on the shore raised a cheer. Had they been given to such fancies, they might have thought that with the 'Grim One' a curse had come to the Zambesi and might have hoped that it had gone with her.[1]

The next few days were spent in completing the loading of the *Pioneer*. On April 11 she started up the river, the boilers of the *Lady Nyassa* piled high on her deck; and, with only one bad grounding, reached Shupanga on the 14th. There are several anxious notes in the diary at this period about the prevalence of intestinal troubles of which the Expedition hitherto had been relatively free; and Kirk was relieved to find that Rae and the rest of the party at Shupanga were fairly well, though several of the seamen were suffering from the effects of drinking too much Portuguese alcohol. But already, on his way up-stream, he had unconsciously recorded

[1] K.'s *Diary*, 16. iii, 4. iv. 62.

the beginning of yet another tragedy. 'Mrs L. is getting very stout: ship-board seems to agree with her; she has frequent febrile attacks . . . lasting for but a few hours.' Clearly, from the context, these attacks seemed negligible; but a fortnight later the diary sounds another note. 'Mrs L. having been very ill for some days, we had her removed to the house at Shupanga.' Next day (April 27), 'Mrs L. became worse and worse while medicines proved of no avail. I was sent for at 3 a.m.: found her in a half comatose state; it was impossible to get medicines taken. . . . Steadily coma deepened into perfect insensibility. . . . At 7 p.m. she died.' They buried her 'under the big baobab tree near the house'.[1]

Livingstone was stricken to the heart. 'For the first time in my life', he wrote in his private journal, 'I feel willing to die.' For some days he was engaged in writing to Dr. and Mrs. Moffat and his children; and it fell to Kirk and Stewart to arrange for his wife's belongings to be sent home—a task which threw them together and so enabled Kirk to revise the unfavourable first impressions he had formed of the new-comer. But Livingstone was soon at work again—a lonelier man than ever now, more silent and shut in upon himself, and haunted more frequently by mystic intimations of his destiny. He is consecrated to Africa. In Africa he will die. The little he can do for Africa must be quickly done.[2]

Something at least would have been achieved when the *Lady Nyassa* was afloat on her own Lake; and for the next few months all the members of the Expedition were busily engaged in bringing up the remaining sections from the sea and assembling them at Shupanga. Their determination was stiffened by the knowledge of what was happening in their neighbourhood. Fighting and slave-raiding were still rampant in the Shire valley, and the hostility of the Portuguese authorities to British interference with their domestic affairs

[1] K.'s *Diary*, 4–18. iv. 62. Livingstone, *Narrative*, 417. Blaikie, *Livingstone*, 251–2.
[2] K.'s *Diary*, 4. v. 62. Blaikie, *Livingstone*, 252–7, 261.

was becoming more marked. In May Kirk went up to Tete
to fetch the Expedition's property down to the new base,
and he returned with serious news. Between Sena and Tete
he had passed an island on which a party of fugitive Manganja
from the north shore had taken refuge, and farther on he had
seen the armed camp of a bandit called Belchior, an ex-trooper
of the Portuguese army, who had left Portugal, as Kirk puts
it, 'for his country's good', married a sister of a half-caste
chief near Tete, and adopted the same career as Mariano.
Two years earlier, as it chanced, Kirk had been asked to see
him professionally when he was in the vicinity and had then
found him hopelessly infected with a disease which had since
made steady progress. 'Poor devil,' says the diary, 'he can
do little himself. . . . His eyesight is nearly gone and he remains
a wreck. Still, backed by guns and powder, his people are
capable of causing great damage among a defenceless race.'
One more grim sidelight on the results which inevitably follow
from the inevitable contact between Europe and the weaker
Continents, unless that contact is effectively controlled by an
enlightened government. And in this case the personal feelings of the members of the Expedition were involved. For
it was against their old ally, Chibisa—who, it will be remembered, had befriended the Expedition in its early days, with
his hearty laugh and his love of *pombe* and of Kirk's tobacco[1]
—that this unspeakable gangrenous ruffian had let loose his
savage retainers. Chibisa had escaped into the bush; but his
principal village near Tete had been looted and burnt. When
Kirk reached Tete a few days later, he might almost have
supposed that the scenes of lawlessness and bloodshed he had
heard of so close by were nothing but a dream. The town was
in high revel. The Governor's daughter was being married to
a Portuguese officer that very day amid a riot of festivities.
The slaves, full of drink, were singing and dancing and firing
off their muskets. Kirk was at once invited to attend the
wedding-banquet; but, having a touch of fever on him, he

[1] See p. 141, above.

THE COMMANDANT'S HOUSE AT TETE

Photograph by Kirk

declined. Next morning (May 18): 'Called on His Excellency, Antonio Tavares d'Almeida. I found him most civil and kind. He invited me to breakfast and made his house open at all hours.' Such courtesy was characteristic, but the Governor might well have been excused if he had omitted it on this occasion since, as has been seen, it was more than probable that some of his own slaves had been among those whom Kirk and his colleagues had so impertinently released not long before. But d'Almeida, it appeared, though naturally making no allusion to any share he might have had in it himself, was by no means unwilling to discuss the thorny question of the Slave Trade. He took the opportunity, in fact, with an engaging show of frankness, to convey a warning to the Expedition. When Kirk called to pay his respects before leaving, he found the diplomatist suffering from a cold in the head, but 'very pleasant and talkative'.

'In the course of our conversation he asked me whether it was true that Dr. L. had taken slaves and goods from the Tete traders; and to this I at once said that such had been the case, but that to Dr. L. himself he must look for all official information. The Governor stated that he had heard so from the blacks who had returned and who had been robbed; that he had reported it to the Governor-General who had instructed him that, although the Slave Trade was prohibited as an export trade at sea, yet there was no law rendering it illegal when carried on by land and that indeed it still remained the law of the province, and that therefore trading parties, if attacked, must resist force by force, their vocation being legitimate. (*Note.* This, although I did not consider it my part to say so, is against the spirit of all the laws of Portugal recently promulgated,[1] and the total abolition [of the Slave Trade] is obviously the end aimed at; for, first, they have freed such slaves as become Christians; then, there are no slaves now born in the house, children of all slaves being free; and, at the expiry of about 14 years, there will be a sudden liberation of all slaves in the Portuguese provinces. How then can the Governor-General look on the slave-traffic as legitimate?)... Again, on my adverting to a European, who in July of last year crossed the Shire with a large body of armed men but who fled on learning the course we

[1] See p. 85, above.

were pursuing with his *confrères*, he at once recognized this individual as a sergeant of the army who was since dead. Thus it became
clear that the Governor was very well aware of the move then
going on, and, as the same system is still pursued, it shows that
he encourages it. . . . The Governor feels very sore on the whole
subject of the Expedition, denies their discoveries, and doubts
their objects. But he need not have given me all this as one of
them. I, of course, felt with the Expedition and had no sympathy
with the miserable, small-minded, avaricious system of the Portuguese, who, while they ruin their own provinces and keep others
out, would make them a barrier against commerce and civilization
entering to the centre of the continent. Happily we belong to a
nation sufficiently powerful not to deem the Portuguese much of
an obstacle.' [1]

Next morning Kirk, in the whaler, followed by four canoes
packed with stores, started back to Shupanga. He had had
no trouble this time in obtaining all the help he wanted at
Tete. The Portuguese, indeed, seemed to have quite forgotten
the quarrel of 1859. 'We were well provisioned', Kirk records;
'for the Portuguese had been most generous and made us
presents of sheep, bread, and fruit. The hospitality of these
poor traders cannot be too much admired and deserves to be
copied. I might have come off much worse in an English
colony than I did among those whose slaves we had liberated.'
The Zambesi had no terrors for his shallow-bottomed flotilla,
and he reached Shupanga in five days. The effect of the news
he brought to Livingstone was not all that the Governor of
Tete would have wished. His diplomacy, in fact, had over-
reached itself. His attempt to warn off the members of the
Expedition from the slave-trading preserves had merely stiffened their backs. And incidentally he had darkened the
good name of the Governor-General who was, as it chanced,
his brother. The senior d'Almeida had made an excellent
beginning of his unenviable job.[2] He had soon satisfied
Lisbon and London, and had acquired a solid reputation as a

---

[1] K.'s *Diary*, 5–20. v. 62. Livingstone, *Narrative*, 418–21.
[2] See p. 85, above.

genuine and energetic enemy of the Slave Trade among the officers of the British cruisers which patrolled the coast. But, if his brother told Kirk the truth, he was now determined to throw the shield of the law over the inland Trade. Or was this merely a gesture, its only purpose to frighten off the British meddlers? Livingstone, for his part, took the severer view. 'On finding afterwards', he writes, 'that his less powerful brother at Tete had unwittingly revealed to us the real sentiments of the big brother at Mozambique, His Excellency could not conceal a little, perhaps excusable, chagrin.' In any case, that unguarded talk at Tete had presented Livingstone with an opening he was not likely to neglect. His sentiments, of course, were Kirk's, or rather Kirk's were his. The Portuguese 'obstacle' must be broken down; but how was Britain, however 'powerful', to break it down within the limits of international propriety? Herein lay the value of the younger d'Almeida's confession. It could be used to reopen the attack, to inform enlightened Lisbon what was happening in the dark in Mozambique, to contrast legislative theory with executive practice, and to press home the argument once more that the free entry of commerce was the first and most effective means of civilizing Central Africa. As soon as he heard Kirk's report, Livingstone drafted a vigorous dispatch to Lord Russell.[1]

Livingstone wrote also at this time to the Governor of Tete, urging him to put a stop to Belchior's brigandage, and to the Governor-General, protesting against the untruth of the charges, which had been levied at him and reproduced in the Government almanac, of arrogating to himself discoveries which had really been made by Portuguese explorers. He followed this up with a letter to Mr. Layard at Lisbon pointing out that recent maps of the Zambesi area were largely based on his own—his names being changed to suit the Portuguese orthography—and incidentally that they registered

---

[1] K.'s *Diary*, 21–6. v. 62. Livingstone, *Narrative*, 420–1. For L.'s dispatches to Russell, see pp. 264–5, below.

claims to territory which certainly did not belong to Portugal. This correspondence was bound, of course, to intensify Portuguese irritation with the Expedition and all its works. Unfortunately, as will be seen, that was virtually all it did.[1]

Meanwhile, work was steadily continued on the building of the *Lady Nyassa*. At the end of May Livingstone made a last journey to the sea in the *Pioneer*, leaving Kirk in charge at Shupanga. It was a comparatively restful, uneventful interlude for him; and there is a note of slackened tension in the diary's record of these weeks. 'Busy packing up specimens.' 'We have had dull weeks: the days pass slowly.' 'Wild beasts have been prowling about our camp every night, and lions, hyenas, and leopards make near visits to the house. This morning we found the finest sheep we had carried off.' 'The weeks go on slowly, but the ways [of palmyra trunks] for launching are being arranged.' 'To pass the time I took to photography and found that, without a drop of distilled water being used, good negatives could be taken on waxed paper.' 'The large fig-tree at the end of the house of Shupanga is now covered with fruit approaching maturity. This wild fig is eaten by the natives in times of hunger, but at present, with plenty of other food, the figs are left to the large frugiverous bats which come every evening to eat them.... They never settle, but, having taken off one of the fruit, store it in their cheek-pouches and go to a neighbouring baobab tree to eat at leisure.' But there was one more personal incident to record—the sudden reappearance of Thornton, who had not returned to England when Livingstone discarded him, but had gone off exploring in healthier regions than the Zambesi flats.

'June 3. Mr. Thornton, our late geologist, came in upon us this evening. He has a most interesting account to give of his journeyings, having been at the snow-capped mountain of Kilimanjaro, north-east from Zanzibar. In company with Baron von der Decken he started from Zanzibar and succeeded in getting up the mountain 8,000 feet, but the total height he estimates from theodolite

[1] Blaikie, *Livingstone*, 259–60.

'LADY NYASSA' ON THE STOCKS

'LADY NYASSA' AFLOAT BESIDE 'PIONEER'

Photographs by Kirk

measurements as 21,000 feet. Of the existence of snow there can be no doubt, although they did not reach it, being hindered by the natives who there seem to be a troublesome and insolent people with the power of enforcing their own will even against caravans of considerable force. The mountain is an extinct volcano with a portion of its crater split off. It could be ascended, he thinks, from one side only, being almost perpendicular on the other. The Jagavas who inhabit its slopes would not allow of any plants or rocks being collected. One zone of the hill is densely wooded and steeped in perpetual moisture; yet in these cold regions there were tracks of the elephant, and rhinoceros of both species were encountered during their march as also buffaloes and small game.' [1]

Later on, after Livingstone's return, it was arranged, at Thornton's own request, that he should be readmitted to the Expedition, but on looser conditions than before, being free to work where and how he liked.[2] Meantime, on June 13, the *Pioneer* reappeared, and, ten days later, all was ready at last for the launching. It was accomplished in the amateur fashion with which the Expedition usually handled its ships.

'23rd June. This was the day for the launch of the *Lady Nyassa*. . . . She lay broadside to the river. . . . The start required a good deal of force and then away went the ship for a short distance at a good pace. But the bow-tackle was not eased off roundly enough. and up she came with a jerk. Then there was a great difficulty in getting her off again; for the soft stems of the palmyra yielded to the continued weight and the keel sank into one of them, and, until this had been wedged up, further progress was impossible. From this time the launch was very stubborn work, but she did get in just as the sun set. At one time her situation seemed rather precarious, for the stern had gone down further than the bow and had tilted the latter up into the air.'

It remained to fit the engines into the floating shell. While they were thus engaged, Scudamore arrived in a small canoe from Chibisa. He had come to consult Livingstone as to the future of the Mission, and the story he told was one of trouble and confusion. Soon after the tragedy they had abandoned

[1] K.'s *Diary*, 27. v–22. vi. 62. See C. C. von der Decken, *Reisen in Ost-Afrika 1859–65* (Leipzig and Heidelberg, 1869–79).
[2] K.'s *Diary*, 15. vii. 62.

Magomero and moved to a healthier spot somewhat nearer to Chibisa. Naturally their old enemies, the Ajawa, had construed this move as a confession of weakness and had followed them up in force, raiding and burning the adjacent Manganja villages and shouting taunts and threats at any member of the Mission they saw. An attack seemed imminent; and the missionaries, only seven white men now, determined on retreat. With all haste they moved their effects right down to Chibisa, where they began to build huts and storehouses and to plan operations among the natives on the safer side of the Shire. But their troubles were not over. The little body of Makololo, armed as they were with guns, had established a reign of terror in the neighbourhood, levying tribute, stealing stock, and even, it was said, taking life; and the missionaries were quite incapable of checking them. To add to the confusion, Chibisa and his people had arrived at their old home, flying from Belchior, starving, and clamouring for the white men's help. What, the missionaries asked themselves, would happen if Belchior and his bandits followed them up? Fortunately the Governor of Tete could act at need as well as talk; and, to do him justice, it was before he received Livingstone's complaint that he ordered Belchior to leave his victim alone. But there was one last menace to the Mission which could not be removed. Chibisa, with its scorching sun, was no healthier than Magomero. Fever was already rife again. So they were contemplating yet another move—to Mbame, a few hour's march from Chibisa up the path to Magomero.[1]

All Livingstone could do was to send a stern message to the Makololo, bidding them wait quietly till he came himself and set them on their long postponed—and little desired—return to their own country. There was no question of the Expedition moving up the Shire for many months; for it was now abundantly clear that the *Lady Nyassa* would not be ready for the voyage till the river had fallen too low even for

[1] K.'s *Diary*, 5. vii. 62. Procter's and Scudamore's letters in *U.M.C.A. Report for 1861*, 51–4.

her three-foot draught. They must wait till the rains came in December. It was the old, old story—always too late—and Livingstone chafed against it now more bitterly than ever. But at least he would not waste the interval. He decided to take the *Pioneer* at once to Johanna to fetch stores and, if possible, draught-oxen for the transport of the *Lady Nyassa* past the rapids of the Upper Shire. And then if time allowed, he would revert to his darling scheme of baffling the Portuguese by the discovery of a direct route to Lake Nyassa by the Rovuma.[1]

In these new plans Kirk was soon entangled. He had recovered his belongings now from Tete; but he was morally no freer to depart than before. At the coast on the way to Johanna, he received letters from home urging 'the necessity of returning soon'. 'I see the force of it,' he comments, 'as I have for a good while.' But Dr. Meller had not come back; and could he leave the Expedition with so much disease about, and only Livingstone, whose medical knowledge was somewhat rusty, to look after it? 'I would ensure making enemies—not that my continuance will prevent it. Dr. L., though kind and considerate to me, still is not to be depended on; and any day, if a misunderstanding should take place, all former services would be lost sight of.' The quotation need not be continued: it has been made obvious enough already whose slandering tongue Kirk feared. That he did fear it is plain, and, as a result of it, a possible rupture with his chief. And this, in turn, he dreaded not only for itself and because of his deep regard for Livingstone but also for its effect on his future career. To go home dismissed? To share, perhaps, the fate of Baines? Whatever his choice, such a miserable reward for four years of toil and discomfort seemed not impossible. But once again he left the future to look after itself. The deciding factor, as before, was the thought that the Expedition needed him. He stayed.[2]

[1] K.'s *Diary*, 6. vii. 62. Livingstone, *Narrative*, 427.
[2] K.'s *Diary*, 29. vii. 62.

And so, as the *Pioneer*, in the middle of August, made her way slowly through rough seas towards Johanna, the old quartet were all aboard, and Kirk, as of old, the most cheerful and, on the whole, the most contented of the four. Charles Livingstone was sea-sick. Rae, 'having twice been wrecked . . . dreads every sea that comes rolling in.' And 'the Doctor' was more than usually unsociable. There is an amusing note in the diary for August 23. 'Dr. L. is uncomfortable at sea and looks so. When the weather gets foul or anything begins to go wrong, it is well to give him a wide berth, most especially when he sings to himself. But the kind of air is some indication. If it is "The Happy Land", then look out for squalls and stand clear. If "Scots wha hae", then there is some grand vision of discovery before his mind. . . . But on all occasions humming of airs is a bad omen.' None the less, the sea voyage was a tonic for them all. The moral barometer rose steadily again. Arrived at Johanna, they decided to go straight on to the Rovuma, after arranging for stores and oxen to await their return. On September 7, escorted by H.M.S. *Orestes*, they steamed into Rovuma Bay. Surely, they told themselves, they would not be disappointed this time. In a few weeks they might be rowing their boats into Lake Nyassa! [1]

2

There followed the most trying month that Kirk had yet endured.

They entered the Rovuma on September 9—Kirk and Rae in one of the *Pioneer*'s boats, the Livingstone brothers in the other, and Captain Gardner and a party from the *Orestes*, who were accompanying the Expedition for a day or two, in their ship's galley and cutter—and instantly they met with their first disappointment. The river was not so high as it had been a year ago! 'Instead of being full from bank to bank, now it is confined to the narrow channel on the right. . . .

[1] K.'s *Diary*, 6. viii–7. ix. 62. Livingstone, *Narrative*, 427–8.

On continuing our voyage we found an intricate maze of sandbanks, across some of which the cutter required to be hauled. At this season there can be no doubt that the Rovuma for all purposes of navigation is a complete failure; but, if it should improve in front, then it may be navigable for a few months of the year.' Next day they reached Lake Chidia, a fine sheet of water, 'closed in on all sides by hills except towards the south where in flood it communicates with the Rovuma.' There they spent the night, and next morning the naval party turned back, taking Rae, who was unwell, with them. 'The river gets no better,' says the diary for September 13; 'snags and shoals with tortuous windings. . . . Still there is no change in Dr. L.'s plans; he is for going on still, regardless of the return. His determination seems to amount to infatuation. We go where the boat cannot float at many parts and where natives can wade across at almost all points.' These comments are significant. For Kirk was observing the first symptoms of the strange psychological condition into which his great leader was now drifting. To the plain man it was already obvious that the Rovuma could never be a satisfactory channel for the flow of 'commerce and civilization' between Lake Nyassa and the sea. The Zambesi–Shire route, with all its drawbacks, was evidently far better. But Livingstone was not yet willing to abandon—not yet by any means—his only hope of outflanking Portuguese obstruction. So far there was something noble in his obstinacy Unquestionably, too, the passion for exploration, almost for its own sake, had steadily grown stronger in him since the day he first 'trekked' northward from Kolobeng. The desire to press on and on into the unknown, to go farther in any particular direction than any white man had gone before, had taken root in his soul. But something more is needed to explain the almost blind persistence which Kirk was now to observe with growing dismay, irritation, and, at last, alarm. It was indeed the first demonstration of that relentless, unreasoning, almost defiant force of will which, a few years

later, was to spur Livingstone on, mile after mile, through the
maze of Central Africa till he died. And the key to it must
lie in that conviction of a predetermined fate to which he had
given such dramatic expression at Cambridge. From now onwards that mystic note begins to sound again in his journals
and in his letters to intimate friends. And, of course, it intensified his desire to be alone. The presence of others, for whose
safety he was responsible, was a check on this fatalism. And
a salutary check. It is not altogether improbable that, if
Livingstone had gone up the Rovuma accompanied by natives
only, he might never have come down. That, as it was, grave
risks were taken, is clear from Kirk's comments, impulsive
comments some of them, jotted down in pencil in hot blood at
the end of a day spent in seemingly purposeless labour.[1]

Sept. 16. 'The river gets worse as we advance. . . . Dr. L. still
carries on, regardless of his return and of the consequences of a
long delay.' Sept. 18. 'At noon reach a wide part of the river, very
shallow: still Dr. L. means to drag over it. The infatuation which
blinds him I cannot comprehend—getting the boats jammed up a
river where they cannot float and where it will soon be impossible
to return. It seems madness. . . . I am, through Dr. Meller's absence, in for it this time. If I could feel any interest in the present
affair, then I could sympathise. . . . I can come [to] no other conclusion than that Dr. L. is out of his mind. He is to force the boats
through by having natives to assist in hauling them. . . . I spoke to
him of the risk of being hauled up high and dry by means of
natives and then deserted and of the further risks attending the
probable detention from the falling of the river until the end of
November; but he only said that, if he risked nothing, he would
gain nothing.' Sept. 19. 'Our first work this morning was another
drag over shoals. Natives come up to trade in copal, tobacco, and
fowls. They are all armed with guns and bows and arrows, and
follow us about three miles when a shot, fired at a puff-adder but
which they did not see the object of, throws them into panic and
sets them on to violent gesticulation and bawling at the pitch of
their voice. . . . My eyes which have been getting sore for two days
are now nearly useless in the full light. . . . At noon the natives,
who had followed us up, got on a high bank and began firing

[1] K.'s *Diary*, 9–15. ix. 62.

arrows. One passed over my boat. They fired several. We drew off and got ready for action. They seem determined on mischief. They say we shall not pass. This is what I noted as possible yesterday, and recommended our turning. We cannot turn now they [would] think we are fleeing and get more insolent. They try to take us on both sides. Then we get them to come to a palaver, in which they are reduced to speaking peaceably. . . . Dr. L. gave some cloth to the man who seemed the chief and with some fine words things seemed settled. But no sooner had we begun to move on than they danced and drew their bows. When close to the bank (which the water compelled us to be) a man took aim and fired his musket at us. It missed, and the bowmen ran back, ready to come round and take a snap shot. However, being now past amicable settlement and their intention being evident, since after full explanation on both sides they had taken the first opportunity of actually firing, I at once picked out one of the two men on the bank at 150 yards and killed him. Peace, my coxswain, shot the other standing by him. After this there were no more shots. . . . We have been driven to this, and have fought in self-defence only. But we must pray God to guide us in future. We have been doing his work in Africa and trust in his shield. . . . Dr. L.'s boat's sail has four bullet-holes through it. This shows what was intended. . . . We stopped about a mile and a half off and had luncheon. There is no sign of natives following us, but our sleep to-night will be light. . . .'
Sept. 20. 'Last night I had pleasant thoughts even in these unsettled times. I felt consolation that whatever might happen would be by God's direction and for the best to his people. I could not help often thinking of my mother alone and of the poor use I had made of her good instructions. . . . We are now not more than 200 miles east of the nearest side of Lake Nyassa and have now explored 100 miles of river in direct line from the mouth. No natives have yet appeared since yesterday's affair.' Sept. 21. 'At daybreak natives came down to trade: they are numerous here and tolerably well-armed. . . . The people here say . . . it is 5 days to the junction of the Nienda [Liende], a river coming from the S.W. It rises in mountains which take 5 days to cross to reach Nyassa at the crossing of the Lake. . . . A coast Arab came into the camp in the afternoon. He is on his way from Nyassa to a place on the coast south of Kilwa. He gave us a present of a little rice: we gave sugar and tea. . . . He says that to the Liende, which joins the Rovuma at Ngonamo, is 4 days. . . . The Rovuma in front is not navigable any distance. . . . He advised us not to land among the

Makonde as they are robbers, but he did not then know that we
had already passed them and had a skirmish. . . . From Ngomano
to Nombo on the Lake is 10 days' journey on foot.' Sept. 22. 'The
river is again full of sandbanks among which we cannot keep the
boat afloat.' Sept. 23. 'The old dragging work. . . . The rains are
fully a month off still.' Sept. 24. 'At noon we get into a miserable
place where we cannot keep the boats afloat many minutes. Under
these circumstances we must be a tempting bait for the savages
who do not appreciate rifles until they feel them and compare our
small numbers with their hundreds.' Sept. 25. 'All afternoon we
have come over a wide river-bed, having barely a boat's draught
of water and so encumbered with projecting points as to be dangerous even to boats ascending. I cannot believe that this will
ever be of use for navigation to any class of vessel. It will not be
free from danger to us on the way down. Dr. L. is a most unsafe
leader. He never thinks of getting back. All he cares for is
accomplishing his object at any risk whatever. It is useless making
any remark to him. . . . He himself now thinks the river unnavi-
gable.' Sept. 26. 'A field of rocks ahead. There is no doubt of
this being a check to all navigation at all seasons. As we will have
to return before the floods, time is now of importance as the river
is getting drier. . . . We had not gone half a mile when we reached
the field of rocks where the water came off with a rush. Yet Dr.
L. seems to intend taking up the boats now. If he does, I can
only say that his head is not quite of the ordinary construction,
but what is termed "cracked".' Sept. 27. 'Began our return this
morning.'

Oct. 1. 'Now that we are one day distant from the robber-
village, it is rather awkward to have one half of the white hands
down in the bottom of the boats with fever. . . . The river, we find,
has fallen 2 inches since we passed up.' Oct. 3. 'Start on our way
to pass the robber-village. . . . On going on, there seemed to be no
notice taken of our approach until we got near to the village.
Then the women sat down together at the point next to where
we must pass. Probably the men had gone out burning the reeds
and grass and hunting the small antelopes: at all events they took
care not to show up.' Oct. 9. 'Reach ship.'[1]

A miserable and fruitless month. The Expedition's other
journeys, with the sole exception of the first exploration of
the Shire Highlands, had never been exactly pleasant and

[1] K.'s *Diary*, 16. ix—9. x. 62. Cf. Livingstone, *Narrative*, 428–44.

always more or less disappointing, but none had been quite
so miserable or so completely fruitless as this journey up and
down the Rovuma. One incident of it had especially distressed Kirk. For the first and last time in his life he had
purposely killed a man. That his swift shot had been justified
is obvious. The man's comrades on the bank had begun to fire
on the boats. The man himself had a gun. If the white men had
not instantly shown their power, the whole tribe would have
joined in the attack and the little party in the boats would
certainly have suffered losses and might well have been destroyed. None the less, the fact that Kirk labours these points
in the diary shows that the taking of a life lay a little on his
conscience. It is only, of course, what any one who knew
Kirk would have expected; but the significance of the way
in which the incident affected him should not be ignored. It
was a test and a proof. It would be well, indeed, if white men
in Africa had always been so sensitive. But Kirk was still
more worried by the strain which had been put on his relations with his chief. When friends asked him in his old age
what chiefly he remembered about Livingstone, he always
answered, 'His utter fearlessness—he did not know what fear
was.' Now Kirk—it has been obvious on more than one
occasion—was no coward. He had shown a quick, instinctive
courage in emergency and the more difficult courage of endurance. But on those sandy, shallow reaches of the Upper Rovuma he had certainly been afraid—and wisely afraid. To continue upstream indefinitely, with the water-level falling every
day, was to run a real risk of being stranded far in the interior
for a month or more until the rains came: and they all had
tragic reason to know what that might mean if food or medicine should run short. Nor was there anything to be gained
by taking that risk when the character of the river had become quite obvious. And when the risk was aggravated by
the fight with the robber-tribe, who, for all they knew, might
not only be waiting for their revenge when the explorers
returned, but might invite their neighbours to attack them

if they were stranded higher up, then surely it was something less fine than courage to go on. And when, lastly, the friendly Arab merchant, who had traversed the route himself and was no slave-trader and had no cause to lie, had explained how the land lay between the Rovuma and Lake Nyassa, was it unreasonable for Kirk to feel as he did? But the most interesting feature of the story is the light it throws again on Livingstone's personality. How strange it is that he should never, save in one sentence, have discussed the question with his companions of whom Kirk, at any rate, he knew to be a sensible man and trustworthy! How strange that he just gave his orders and went silently on, seemingly careless or unaware of what his subordinates were thinking! Another than Livingstone, more human, if perhaps less great, would surely have talked it over with them, humoured them, if need be, and encouraged them, and, if danger really had to be faced, persuaded them to follow him into it willingly and with a single mind. It is possible to admire Livingstone, and yet in this case to sympathize with Kirk.

3

As one of her paddle-wheels needed repair, the *Pioneer* was delayed for a while at the mouth of the Rovuma; and Kirk, having been sent upstream to cut wood from the magnificent ebony groves, had one more day's experience of that malignant river. First, his boat was caught in a squall and capsized. Next, he was bitten by a tsetse fly, one species of which is now known to be a frequent carrier of sleeping-sickness. Last, he was attacked by a hippopotamus which charged the boat from beneath, lifted it partly out of the water, and jolted two of its occupants out of it and nearly Kirk as well.[1]

They steamed off southwards on October 17 and reached Johanna on the third day. Here they took on board some

---

[1] K.'s *Diary*, 10–16. x. 62.

native workers and some oxen; and here also they found
Dr. Meller, returned to duty—'Spleen still enlarged, but good
general health.' It was then open to Kirk to consider once
again whether he should stay or go, and from a later entry
in the diary it appears that he did raise the question and that
Livingstone pressed him to remain. The voyage down the
coast was slow and uneventful, except for a visit to Quilimane
where they put in for fuel. 'It seems', says Kirk, 'the most
pestiferous hole on the coast, and here a number of men dwell
and possess good houses, yet make no use of the land. Condemned to live in the most frightful place on earth, they do
not take out of it the one thing it could yield, viz. money.
An active people might make the land pay in a thousand
ways. Quilimane is the remains of the Slave Trade.' Towards
the end of November they reached the Zambesi; and, since
the river was unusually low even for the end of the dry season,
the journey up to Shupanga took three weeks of the old irritating haulage-work. 'Things on board the *Pioneer*', observes
the diary for December 6, 'are most uncomfortable. Rae
feels sore since receiving letters from home. Meller, since
returning from the Cape, is a great growl.' Nor did they find
much consolation at Shupanga. The water-level was even
lower than when the *Lady Nyassa* was launched. Thornton
and Stewart were away at Tete; the rest of the party were
looking thoroughly 'pulled down'. And Procter, who was
passing through Shupanga in quest of supplies for the Mission,
gave a dismal report of conditions in the valley. 'Up the
Shire there is famine and war. Hunger has killed whole
villages while war is on every hand. The Ajawa have occupied the hill-country and have even crossed the Shire. . . .
Mariano has settled somewhere about Milanje and forages
down the Shire. A half-caste is coming up the right bank,
making war. The Makololo, left by us, who did *not* return
home, have carried on a systematic plundering of the tribes
and often kill without provocation. They have a large establishment of women and slaves. The slaves they send out to

plunder and bring in food. . . . The Mission exists and enjoys good health, but no active measures will be taken till the arrival of the new bishop.' [1]

It seemed as if on all the Shire valley and the highlands above it—that rich and pleasant country, the Expedition's happiest discovery and the field of its greatest hope—ruin and anarchy had permanently settled down. For who or what could save it ? The Portuguese were worse than useless. The dreams of British colonization had faded into the background. As for the Expedition, it could only hurry through the desolate land with averted eyes and do the one practical thing it could in the lake-country beyond. But the transportation of the *Lady Nyassa* to the scene of her beneficent work, in any case a long and arduous business, was still delayed. The *Pioneer*, which was to tow her up the lower Shire, needed more repairs; and the rains came late and were not heavy when they came. So Kirk's last Christmas on the Zambesi was no more cheerful than its predecessors. 'We are still detained at Shupanga. The river continues rising and there are showers daily, sometimes with thunder and lightning, but as yet this year we have had no great display. Being Christmas, the men thought it their duty to get drunk.' But prospects brightened with the New Year. '1st January, 1863. The weather is very hot and there are daily rains, often very heavy. The river is rising steadily.' At last, on January 11, they started, the *Lady Nyassa* in tow, at a speed of about two knots; but the first time the *Pioneer* grounded, there was nearly a disaster. Naturally the *Lady Nyassa*, with way on her, crashed into her consort, recoiled on to another sandbank, and became unmanageable. It was not till the amateur navigators had abandoned the plan of towing and made the two vessels fast side by side that the voyage could be resumed. And then it prospered for a time. January 15 found them at anchor under the slopes of Mount Morumbala, where Kirk, who had observed its botanical wealth in 1859, made a very

[1] K.'s *Diary*, 17. x—17. xii. 62; 28. iv. 63.

peevish entry in the diary because Livingstone insisted on his helping to cut wood instead of climbing the mountain to collect specimens. Ten days later, they were traversing Elephant Marsh; and there they stuck for a week. It was a depressing spot—in the midst of human suffering they could do nothing to alleviate. 'The people of Mariano have ravaged the country as far as this, and the natives drag out their existence on various grass seeds. . . . While coming up we saw four or five dead bodies, made up in sleeping mats or with reeds, floating down daily. How many passed us unobserved and by night we cannot tell, or how many the alligators dragged aside among the reeds as they floated past. But a dozen per day would be a small allowance for the number cast into the river. These have died of hunger. The few we meet are skin and bone, some evidently about to follow their comrades.' A little farther upstream the ships grounded again and another week was spent in haulage. Here they were found by Procter, on his way back from Quilimane. He had had fresh news of the Mission and once more it was bad news. Despite its healthier climate fever had pursued them to Mbame; and on New Year's Day, Scudamore, whom of all the surviving missionaries Kirk had liked best, had died. The natives starving in hundreds, the white men dying one by one —it may well have seemed to the little party on the Shire, tugging at rope and oar in sultry heat or lying prostrated with fever, that Africa was after all unconquerable. Some at least of them were beginning to lose heart. 'There seems to be a different feeling throughout the ship', Kirk notes, 'which does not make all work together with a will.' And he speaks with evident relief of getting away from the ship occasionally on short boating excursions in Thornton's 'pleasant company'. But Thornton presently sailed on upstream on his own job, and the gloom deepened. 'Now that Thornton is gone, we are prisoners to the ship. All about is marsh, and without a boat no birds can be shot. The remembrance of the time we spent aground on the way down and the miserable state of mind we got into makes me shudder lest we have the like again.' [1]

At last, however, Elephant Marsh lay behind them, and slowly, very slowly, at the rate of about half a mile a day, they crept on towards Chibisa. On March 16, there was a break in the daily tedium. A canoe came down from the river with an appeal from the Mission for help. 'Dr. Dickenson lay very seriously ill with the country fever while one of his men, Clarke, was in a state of mania with epileptic fits which had supervened on fever and dysenteric diarrhoea. Dr. Livingstone and I at once got the boat fitted out and started within a few hours after receipt of the note.' The next afternoon they were climbing the hill above Chibisa. 'When ascending the slope up to the Mission, we were met by Mr. Waller conveying the sad news that we had reached [there] only a quarter of an hour too late to see poor Dickenson in life.' They found Clarke alive indeed but very ill. 'He struggled to rise and shouted so as to be heard at a distance, seeing visions and talking to imaginary persons.' After a consultation Livingstone started back to the ship leaving the patient in Kirk's charge. 'I remained at the Mission to see how Clarke came round', is the diary's brief note. The missionaries were more eloquent. 'Dr. Kirk,' says their Report, 'with a kindness which will never be forgotten, watched by his side night and day, and promised to remain as long as he could be of any service.' With this constant care the patient steadily improved and after ten days Kirk was able to rejoin the *Pioneer*. Meantime he had an opportunity of observing the Mission at close quarters.

'I had a good chance of seeing the youngsters under the Mission— a nice set of boys and girls. Most of the women are married now to the men, so that things are getting into order. . . . But there is much need to have them all engaged cultivating lands which they can look on as a settlement. For this station is quite untenable. Droughts cut off the crops and fever disables or kills the white

[1] K.'s *Diary*, 25. xii. 62—7. ii. 63. Livingstone, *Narrative*, 449–54. *U.M.C.A. Report for 1862*, 78–9.

ELEPHANT MARSH

Photograph by Kirk

men. Of course very little has been done in the way of teaching. The language has to be mastered and things must be a little more settled first for any progress to be expected. But it is pleasing to see the boys attached to the missionaries as they are. They are funny little dogs. I go down and bathe with them daily in the river in a place staked off to keep out crocodiles. They have become expert swimmers and divers.' [1]

With the arrival of the two vessels at Chibisa at the beginning of April and Kirk's return to duty with them the history of the Zambesi Expedition enters on its last chapter. There is no change of tone in it, no lift, no brightening at the close. It is a dark, unhappy chapter like most of its predecessors. To begin with, Kirk and Charles Livingstone were seriously ill with dysentery, Kirk indeed so ill that there is a longer gap in the diary than at any earlier point except when his note-books were lost in the Kebrabasa Rapids. And scarcely was he out of bed, worn to 'a skeleton', when still another of his friends was plucked from the narrowing circle. The kindly Thornton had volunteered to go to Tete to obtain for the Mission the sheep and goats they badly needed for a supply of fresh meat. He returned with a considerable flock; but the journey, which had so nearly done for Kirk and Rae in 1859, had overtaxed his strength, and, falling an easy prey to fever and dysentery, he died on April 21. Meanwhile the *Lady Nyassa* had been taken up to the foot of the Murchison Cataract, where work was begun on taking her to pieces and on building the thirty miles of road by which the parts were to be carried in ox-wagons to the upper reaches of the river. But the Expedition was not to be allowed the satisfaction of completing the one practical piece of work on which it had been engaged for two years past. In truth it was exhausted, morally and physically. It was petering out. Its personnel was disintegrating. One new recruit had voluntarily joined it, Edward Young, lately an officer in the *Gorgon*; but Dr. Meller declared that he would not stay a moment after his

[1] K.'s *Diary*, 16–25. iii. 63. *U.M.C.A. Report for 1862*, 84–6.

contract expired in July; and it was now at last decided that Kirk and Charles Livingstone, too, should go home at the earliest opportunity. 'In the morning', says the diary for April 27, 'Dr. L. spoke to me and said that his brother had requested to be allowed to go home and that he had consented as it would be selfishness in him to keep him longer and that, as I had desired to go, he would feel it the same in my case.' On grounds of health alone it was indeed imperative that Kirk should be released; for the after-effects of his dysentery were still painful and persistent. But if it was inevitable under the circumstances, with the nervous systems of every member of the party strained almost to breaking-point by disease and depression, it was still rather pitiful that the parting of the young lieutenant and the chief he had served so loyally and long should have been chilly and uncomfortable. There was more than one difference of opinion. Livingstone, for instance, insisted on Kirk returning by the Cape, while Kirk preferred the quicker way by Aden and the 'overland route'. 'The fair words', he writes dejectedly, 'which passed between us at Johanna when he desired me to remain and this the actual parting, as far as it has gone yet, show a decided difference.' 'His manner still very distant,' he notes next day, and then he puts his finger on something near the truth: 'He is savage at being jammed up here. . . . But I believe it is in fact the best thing for him, as he cannot get on with many whites under him.' Naturally Kirk was now longing to get away. By the end of April his packing was done and he was ready to go. And then, since no plan connected with the Expedition could ever work quite right, he was held up for more than a fortnight by the sudden and serious illness of 'the Doctor'. 'Dr. Kirk', records Livingstone in his *Narrative*, 'kindly remained in attendance till the worst was passed.' Indeed he could not think of going. 'Of course we cannot start,' says the diary, and for the next week it is full of technical notes on the patient's symptoms and the medicines administered. But just one *cri de cœur* escapes him: 'I wish

CREEPERS IN THE BUSH

Photograph by Kirk

I were off, clear of this place, ship, and crew.' By May 8 Livingstone was able to get up and sit on deck. Though weak and shaken, he was clearly convalescent. During the next week he steadily improved, and could now be safely left in charge of Rae and Young. On May 19 the farewells were said.[1]

And so Kirk for the last time made the river-voyage from Chibisa to the sea—down through that fine Shire valley, once so full of life and hope, now so desolate and desperate, past the innumerable shoals where almost every inch of the river-side country must have been familiar to one who had spent so many tiresome weeks aground there in the *Ma Robert* and the *Pioneer*, through Elephant Marsh and its mosquitoes, past Mackenzie's grave at the Ruo, past Mount Morumbala and past Mrs. Livingstone's grave by the old grey House of Shupanga, and so down the broad Zambesi to the sea. Day by day Kirk was encircled, as it were, by a panorama of his life for the last five years, brightened by no happy memories of great or lasting success, littered everywhere, it must have seemed, with dead friends and dead hopes. But he was too much occupied for brooding. Weak as he was from his illness, the whole burden of the voyage lay on him. Charles Livingstone was mostly down with fever, and Peace, Kirk's coxswain on the Rovuma, became violently ill with epileptic fits, an awkward ailment in an unstable canoe. For the last few days of the journey Kirk had little sleep. The unfortunate Peace continued in convulsions; if left alone at night, he would tear his clothes off and lie naked on the dew-soaked grass. On June 4, two days after their arrival at Quilimane, he died. Though he, too, was now attacked by fever, Kirk had to arrange and attend the funeral. He returned from it to his bed and remained there for a week.[2]

A dreary month ensued, while they waited for a ship in that 'most pestiferous hole on the coast'. Only twice was the

[1] K.'s *Diary*, 1. iv—19. v. 63. Livingstone, *Narrative*, 455–60. *U.M.C.A. Report for 1862*, 86–7.
[2] K.'s *Diary*, 19. iv—5. vi. 63.

monotony broken. 'The new Bishop and party', notes the attenuated diary on June 11, 'have been landed at Kongone and one of them has reached Mazaro in their boat.' The organizers of the U.M.C.A. in England had been deeply moved by the news of Mackenzie's death, but not for a moment had they dreamed of abandoning the enterprise. A successor had been quickly found in the Rev. W. G. Tozer, a Lincolnshire vicar, and, after consecration in Westminster Abbey, he had sailed for the Cape, where he was joined by two friends and colleagues who had preceded him, the Rev. G. Steere and the Rev. C. A. Alington. The *Orestes*, not the *Gorgon*, took them from the Cape to the Zambesi. 'Among the things we landed', wrote one of her officers, 'was the oak cross to be put over poor Charles Mackenzie's grave.' The question of a site, so vital or so fatal, had not yet been settled, but the Bishop was considering the possibilities of Mount Morumbala, and Steere was sent to Quilimane to consult the Portuguese authorities. 'Dr. Steere of the Central African Mission', says the diary for June 28, 'came down here to obtain permission to settle the Mission on Morumbala'—a brief enough record of the first meeting of two men who were to spend many laborious and fruitful years together. The other excitement, if so it can be termed, was the arrival of a dispatch from the Foreign Office. In was in triplicate and to be read by any member of the Expedition, and in due official form it announced its recall. The diary's comment is quite brief. 'All to be at the coast in August. The *Pioneer*, we know, never can be taken down then.' But though he says nothing and probably, at the time, cared little, Kirk must afterwards have felt some satisfaction that he had held on at his post until the Expedition had practically ended, until indeed the order for its recall had actually been signed.[1]

---

[1] K.'s *Diary*, 6. vi—4. vii. 63. *U.M.C.A. Report for 1862*, 89–102. On their first voyage up the Zambesi, the Bishop and his party just missed meeting Kirk on his way down by a few days. *Letters of Bishop Tozer* (ed. G. Ward, London, 1902), 13.

At last a ship put in at Quilimane, bound for Mozambique. On July 4 Kirk started on the first stage of his voyage home, but on reaching Mozambique he had to wait, uncomfortably housed and depressed by constant fever, for more than a month till, on August 12, the familiar *Orestes* with friendly Captain Gardner in charge arrived and carried him northwards. On August 20 he landed at Zanzibar. It was his first experience of the old island town with which, though he could never have guessed it, his life and name were one day to be more closely linked than with anywhere else in the world. And the ten days he spent there were pleasant days —all the more pleasant by contrast with the dreary weeks at Quilimane and Mozambique. He lodged at the British Consulate with the Consul, Captain Playfair, in whom he quickly discovered a kindred spirit. He visited and liked the Hamburg Consul, Mr. Witt. He witnessed the celebration of the Moslem 'New Year's Eve', when 'women rushed about the streets with sticks'—an activity which on occasion, he was told, might become 'excessive' and even murderous. And one day he accompanied the Sultan Majid on a trip out to sea in the *Orestes*. Meantime Captain Gardner had decided to send him home, still in charge of the four sick men from the *Pioneer*, by the 'overland route', and on September 1, he sailed in the *Pleiad* for the Seychelles, whence, after only two days' wait, he caught the mail steamer for Aden and Suez. Overland to Alexandria—thence an uneventful voyage, with a day's break at Malta, through the Mediterranean and across the Bay—and at last, on October 9, Kirk landed at Southampton.[1]

4

Livingstone, meanwhile, had obediently carried out the evacuation of the remnants of the Expedition. But since, as Kirk had foreseen, it had been quite impossible to bring the *Pioneer* down to the sea before the return of the flood

[1] K.'s *Diary*, 4. vii—9. ix. 63.

season, he had attempted in the interval one last little spurt of exploration. With only the ship's steward and a few natives, he set off northwards, made his way on foot about half-way up the west side of Lake Nyassa, and then penetrated about 100 miles inland to the sources of the River Loangwa (or Dwanga), where he was obliged to turn back for lack of time. Two incidents of this last march are worth recording. Its course took the party close beside a long range of mountains, each with its native name but apparently unnamed as a whole. 'This fact,' wrote Livingstone, 'and our wish to commemorate the name of Dr. Kirk, induced us . . . to call the whole chain from the west of the Cataracts up to the north end of the Lake, "Kirk's Range".' The other incident is chiefly interesting in view of later passages in Livingstone's life. The barbarous Mazsitu were still in the neighbourhood, and some tall stories of their hostile attitude to the white men must have reached the coast; for, as Livingstone wrote home, 'a report of my having been murdered at the Lake has been very industriously circulated by the Portuguese, a report which in due course had reached and alarmed his friends in England.[1]

It now only remained to take the *Pioneer* to the sea and with her also the *Lady Nyassa*, never to fulfil the promise of her name. It was a heart-breaking task for Livingstone; and, as if a malignant fate was bent on deepening to the utmost his sense of frustrated effort and to leave him no shred of consolation, the news now reached him that the Universities' Mission was to be withdrawn to Zanzibar. Bishop Tozer, who, as has been seen, had come out with reinforcements for the staff about the time of Kirk's arrival at Quilimane, had soon come to a decision which required, perhaps, more strength of mind than Livingstone in his disappointment could appreciate. Tozer was faced with two dominant facts in the short history of the Mission—the destruction and dis-

---

[1] Livingstone, *Narrative*, 460–568 (Kirk's Range, 491). Blaikie, *Livingstone*, 267–9.

order caused by the slave raids throughout the area it had selected for its work and the deadliness of the climate to its staff as long as they remained, as they had to remain, within a short march of the Shire below the Cataracts. This difficulty of communication with the outer world, especially as regards the transport of stores, seemed all the greater when it was reported that after the withdrawal of the Expedition the occasional calls of British cruisers at the mouth of the Zambesi would be discontinued. But Tozer might perhaps have faced isolation, and disease too, had there been any prospect of the slave raids being stopped, and at present, at any rate, as Livingstone himself would have bitterly confessed, there was none. It is not surprising, then, that the Bishop decided to give the unpleasant order to retreat, to abandon Magomero, to leave Mackenzie's grave to the wilderness, and to make a new start elsewhere. For a time he settled on the crest of Mount Morumbala; but this attempt to cling to the skirts of Mackenzie's country was half-hearted and soon given up. For Tozer had now come to the conclusion that more preparation and more knowledge were needed if a settlement in the interior, however heroic in its faith, was to lead to more than martyrdom. 'The Zambesi', he wrote, rather testily, to the Bishop of Cape Town, 'has proved in every way a miserable failure, and the selection of it for English missionary work can only be due to the blindest enthusiasm.' Various alternative fields were suggested to him—Madagascar, Johanna, Zululand, Walfish Bay, and Zanzibar—and of these he chose the last. Its material advantages were obvious; and it was known that Sultan Majid, like his father, Said, though a conscientious Moslem, was no fanatic and regarded the British more favourably than other Europeans. Said had permitted a settlement of the London Missionary Society to be made within his mainland dominions at Mombasa under Dr. Krapf in 1846, and it was believed that Majid would welcome another such settlement in Zanzibar itself. 'No foreign missionary', said a consular report in

1860, 'has yet attempted to establish a school at Zanzibar, although it would be gladly encouraged by the Sultan and the wealthy Indian merchants.' But to Tozer the prospects of mission-work within the island were only incidental. He had by no means abandoned the titular objective of the 'U.M.C.A.' He was still bent on reaching the area of the Great Lakes, but by a more northerly route than the Shire or the Rovuma. And he chose Zanzibar not as a goal but as a stepping-stone —as the best possible base for reconnoitring the mainland, selecting sites for stations, and so 'ultimately reaching the central tribes'. Nor was it merely an amateur's choice. Speke and Burton, the recent explorers of Tanganyika, had proposed this method of entry *via* Zanzibar, just as Livingstone had suggested the Shire Highlands. 'I would gladly accompany either Burton or Speke', wrote Tozer, 'in their next expedition (in case they would allow of my doing so) and see with my own eyes the possibility of the scheme which they have suggested.' [1]

Tozer was not Mackenzie. He was not going to fling himself ardently into the void at any explorer's bidding. His decision was a practical man's decision—in accordance, as it happened, with British traditions in other spheres of overseas enterprise. All over the world British traders and colonists had made a habit of settling on coastal islands, secured by sea-power, as jumping-off places for the exploitation or occupation of the mainland. But Livingstone was too much dismayed by the departure of this last little band of Englishmen from the Shire country to consider any arguments of

[1] *Bishop Tozer's Letters*, 1–72. Among the reasons for abandoning Mount Morumbala was that it lay within the area of more or less effective Portuguese occupation and was exposed to the demoralizing influences of Sena; but, impressed by the courtesy of Major Tito Sicard and Colonel Nunez, Tozer was inclined to defend the Portuguese. 'The good English maxim of "hearing both sides of the question" is systematically set aside when the criminal is a Portuguese' (*Letters*, 50)—one of several shafts which the Bishop aimed at Livingstone at this period.

precedent or expediency. 'If you go', he wrote to Tozer, 'the last ray of hope for this wretched, down-trodden people disappears.' A bitter cry, and understandable. For Livingstone, more than any one else, had created the Mission, and the loss of this child—for indeed it seemed lost to him—hurt him more than any other event of those hurtful years save only the loss of his wife. And as if to drive it home, it fell to Livingstone to conduct some forty of the Magomero freedmen, derelict survivors of Mackenzie's 'family', down to the sea, whence they were shipped on British cruisers to a new home at the Cape.[1]

[1] Livingstone, *Narrative*, Blaikie, *Livingstone*, 269–70. *U.M.C.A. Reports for 1862, 1863, and 1864.* See also Waller's letter (April, 1865) in appendix to Goodwin's *Memoir of Mackenzie*.

VIII

RESULTS

I

It was six years and a little over since the Zambesi Expedition had set out from Liverpool. And what—in all those six years—had it accomplished? Had it proved a success or a failure? The reason for its recall, Lord Russell had written, was that, while its cost had far exceeded expectations, it had not achieved its objects. But this was only true if all the objects of the Expedition were taken together as inseparable parts of one big design—the establishment of British commerce and civilization in tropical East Africa in place of savagery and the Slave Trade—and it was quite untrue of the very first particular object defined in the Instructions to its members. 'The main object of the Expedition', the opening sentence had run, 'is to extend the knowledge already attained of the geography and mineral and agricultural resources of Eastern and Central Africa'; and this 'main object' had surely been fulfilled, in no mean degree, by the examination of the mouths of the Zambesi, of its character as a waterway far into the interior, and of the conditions and products of its broad valley, and, still more, by the exploration of the Shire, of the highlands above it with their fine climate and rich soil, and of Lake Nyassa.

It is a landmark, indeed, in the history of Africa, this first discovery by Europeans of the central part of that great highland backbone, one end of which can be seen from the Red Sea and one from Table Bay. A landmark, too, in the history of the British Empire. The old ideas that Cape Colony and Natal were static, self-contained colonies, that their liabilities, so to speak, were limited, that their destinies could be kept separate from those of the young Boer Republics which had split off from them, and that the central wastes of Africa were as remote from any practical interest of theirs as the legendary Mountains of the Moon—these ideas were still dominant when Livingstone first made his way northwards from the Cape to the Zambesi in 1851. But there were already men of longer sight who realized not only that the future welfare of Dutch and British in South Africa was as inevitably interlinked as that of French and British in Canada, but also that Cape Town, like Quebec, was the gateway not to a colony but to a continent. And these new ideas were greatly reinforced and strengthened by the new discoveries of 1858 to 1863. It is significant that Sir George Grey, who is best known for the efforts he was making at this very time to unite the British colonies and Dutch republics in a federal South Africa, should so cordially have welcomed the arrival of the Expedition at the Cape and should so quickly have seized the opportunity of creating a regular system of land-communication with the 'central station' which the Expedition was intending to establish in the region of the Upper Zambesi. Before, indeed, the *Ma Robert* had begun to ascend the river, Grey had secured from the Cape Legislature an annual grant for the maintenance of a monthly overland post between Cape Town and Livingstone's 'projected settlement'; and in less than two years he could report that the mail service had already been extended 700 miles northwards from Kuruman or 900 from the point it had reached in 1858. In this latter dispatch he reaffirmed as Governor of the Cape his warm approval of the Zambesi Expedition on the ground that the spread of civilization and order in the area of its operations would be advantageous to South Africa. Meantime, the idea of the inland nexus had begun to circulate in Whitehall. In a report on the course of the Expedition in 1859, Admiral Washington spoke of linking Cape Colony by way of Kuruman with the Victoria Falls, 'the centre of the continent'; and in 1860 Lord John Russell, while informing the Colonial Office that he would not permit any discussion with the Portuguese as to claims on the coast northwards of Delagoa Bay, suggested, rather late in the day, that the Governor of Cape Colony should be asked to try to establish communication with Central and East Africa overland. It may be said, then, that the Zambesi Expedition helped substantially to widen the South African horizon and to let loose in statesmen's minds the first faint forerunners of Rhodes's dream.[1]

But the greatest, the most direct result of the Zambesi Expedition is to be found in its own area. The Niger Expedition of 1841 had no effect whatever on the subsequent development of Nigeria. It made no valuable new discoveries. It discredited and retarded the 'positive policy' it was meant to serve. But the Zambesi Expedition not only discovered the land of Nyassa—the nodal point of the highland backbone : from the seed of its sowing Nyassaland was born. And in Nyassaland the 'positive policy' in all its branches was first applied. No action, it is true, was taken on the morrow of the Zambesi Expedition; but the impression it made on public opinion in England, its tragic record, its revelation of a new and fertile country waiting for the missionary and the planter, its discovery that the jugular vein of the Slave Trade could be cut at Lake Nyassa, all this was not forgotten, and it was brought again to the very front of public interest by Livingstone's return to the same field, his wanderings, his disappearance, and his death. Then, at last, the work begun in 1858 was resumed, and the aims abandoned in 1863 were achieved. In 1874 Dr. James Stewart, bringing at last to fruition the idea which had led him to Livingstone's side twelve years before on the Zambesi, proposed to the General Assembly of his Church the foundation of a Scottish Mission on Lake Nyassa. In 1875 Dr. Laws and Edward Young, the latter of whom, it will be remembered, had joined the Zambesi Expedition during that last miserable effort to get the *Lady Nyassa* up to the Lake, launched the first steamboat, the

[1] F.O. 63/843: Grey to Stanley, 9. vi. 58. F.O. 63/871: Washington's report, 31. xii. 59; Russell to C.O., 19. iv. 60; Grey to C.O., 28. iv. 60; R. Moffat sen. to Grey, 2. x. 60.

Ilala, on its waters and established the Mission first at Cape Maclear, which proved, as Kirk had foreseen, unhealthy, and later at Livingstonia. Meantime a second Scottish Mission had been founded in the Shire Highlands, also acclaiming the author of its being in its name Blantyre, where Livingstone was born. Then, hard on the heels of the missionaries, and in close association with them, came the traders, fulfilling the other side of Livingstone's dream. In 1878 the African Lakes Company established its head-quarters near Blantyre, and soon a new *Lady Nyassa* was floating on the Lake. Two years later, the U.M.C.A., advancing stage by stage into the interior according to Bishop Tozer's plan, also reached the Lake. British settlement on the Shire Highlands, British administration, the incorporation of the Nyassaland Protectorate in the British Empire—all this followed in due course. And there followed also, as inevitably as Livingstone had prophesied, the extinction of the inland Slave Trade. Blocked at one end by its abolition at Zanzibar, blocked in the middle of its track by the British settlements, the old ogre of Mid-Africa lived on, for a space, a furtive, hunted life in the by-paths of the wilderness, and then at length succumbed. In 1898 the last slave-caravan was caught and freed a hundred miles westward of Lake Nyassa.[1]

Nyassaland, with all it has meant and may mean for Africa, has been well called 'the heritage of Livingstone'. And it was on the Zambesi Expedition that Livingstone, so to speak, acquired the property and wrote his will.

2

In fact, the Expedition cannot now be judged a failure, and it could only be so judged at the time because the fruits of the great discoveries it had made were slow to ripen. It had only

[1] J. Wells, *Stewart of Lovedale* (London, 1908). W. P. Livingstone, *Laws of Livingstonia* (London, 1921). F. L. M. Moir, *After Livingstone* (London, 1925). A. E. M. Anderson-Morshead, *History of the U.M.C.A., 1859–1896* (London, 1897).

seen things, not done them. It had revealed the obstacles to
its full programme of civilization, commerce, and settlement;
but it had not by any means removed them. Above all, it
had been baffled by the Slave Trade which, so far from thin-
ning away before it, had actually been extended by following
its track. The blame for that, however, must rest, if anywhere, on the British Government and not on the Expedition.
Again and again, as has been seen, Livingstone had bom-
barded the Foreign Office with statements of the black unquestionable facts and with warnings of the stiffening attitude
of the Portuguese authorities. But stage by stage it had been
a losing battle. His dispatches from the *Pearl* on the voyage
out had clung to his first position—that 'the sovereignty of
the Portuguese over the Zambesi is merely ideal' and that
it was impolitic to let it to be taken for granted. But Lisbon
published the 'Zambesia' manifesto and London did nothing.
A year later Livingstone had withdrawn his front and was
only protesting against the Portuguese attempts to profit by
the Expedition's work, such as the establishment of customs-
posts at the mouths of the Zambesi, 'the navigability of
which we alone discovered', and the proposed settlement at
the confluence of the Shire 'by way of laying claim to all the
Lake territory with which we are engaged'. Nothing, again,
was done. Later on, still leaving uncontested the Portuguese
claim to sovereignty in East Africa, he argued that at least
they could not claim it as an area of colonization in the
accepted sense of the word. 'Whatever may have been the
position of the Portuguese establishments in former times,
they cannot now be considered colonies. No free women or
agricultural colonists are ever sent out to them. The class
called 'incorrigibles' to the number of 300 have just made
their appearance and these are intended to spread Portuguese
influence and power! The stations are, in fact, only small
penal settlements, separated at wide intervals from each
other.' And, that being so, the territory not being properly
a colony or part of a colonial system, surely 'the abandon-

ment of the "dog in the manger" policy and a proclamation
of Free Trade on the Zambesi' ought to be pressed on the
Portuguese Government. Again, no result. From first to
last the Foreign Office dealt very cautiously and tenderly
with Lisbon. At the outset, indeed, in the autumn of 1858,
the British Minister went so far as to urge the Government to
permit native produce to descend the Zambesi to the sea,
to ask for information as to the system of customs it proposed
to establish, and to explain that it was wrong in supposing
that all shipping on the rivers of India was required to fly the
British flag. But as soon as Livingstone had begun to stir
up those murky waters, British diplomacy became scrupulously 'correct'. The gist of Livingstone's reports was com-
municated to Lisbon; and in 1860 and again in 1861 Russell
went so far as to complain that such conditions as reported
should still exist in Portuguese colonies. To which the Portuguese Government replied that, though it had full confidence
in the Governor-General, fresh instructions should be sent
him. Finally, in the summer of 1862, when the whole ticklish
affair was nearly at an end, Russell ventured to beg the
Portuguese Government, 'in the interests of humanity and
civilization', to give its authorities definite orders to co-
operate with Livingstone. 'But they were very desirous to
aid Livingstone', the Viscount Sá da Bandeira blandly answered, 'and their previous orders to that effect should be
promptly repeated.' [1]

Could the British Government have done more? Not without seriously disturbing diplomatic relations with Portugal,
not without a violation of international propriety which must
have created bitter resentment at Lisbon, not without ex-
changing the sentimentalities of the 'Old Alliance' for an

---

[1] F.O. 63/842: L. to Malmesbury, 22. iii. 58; Hammond to
Minister, 26. ii. 58, to F.O. 26. iii. 58. F.O. 63/871: L. to Malmesbury,
31. v. 59; L. to Russell, 20. ix. 59. F.O. 63/838: Howard, to F.O.,
18. ix. 58. F.O. 63/845: Malmesbury to Howard, 15. i. 59. F.O.
63/894: Russell to Herries, 19. viii. 62. F.O. 62/888: Herries to
Russell, 26. xi. 62.

open quarrel, not, in a word, without bullying Portugal. And apart from its general undesirability—there was quite enough tension in international affairs between 1859 and 1863—there were two very definite, if very different, reasons for not bullying Portugal. It will be remembered, first, that towards the end of 1857, Colonel d'Almeida had been appointed Governor-General of Mozambique with express instructions to stop the operation of the French 'Free Labour Emigration System' in Portuguese territory and waters and that on his arrival at his post he had promptly set to work to ensure the execution of the *portarias* previously issued from Lisbon.[1] His energy was quickly rewarded. Within three weeks, a French barque, the *Charles et George*, was detected off the island of Quitangunha with over a hundred negroes on board and also one of the French official supervisors of the System. The ship was detained while d'Almeida appointed a Commission to examine the charges made. The Commission reported that the *Charles et George* was carrying purchased slaves; and in due course, on March 8, 1858—two days before the Zambesi Expedition sailed from Liverpool—the ship was 'condemned' in accordance with the time-honoured judicial procedure established by international agreement for the suppression of the Slave Trade. It was not to be expected that the news of these events would be calmly received at Paris. For some years the French Government had stubbornly maintained that the System was not a slave trade and that the negroes were willing emigrants. The case of the *Charles et George* was obviously a test case. To tolerate its condemnation could only be interpreted by all the world as a confession of guilt. Its release was instantly demanded. And, since the quarrel could only be settled by the humiliation of Portugal or the humiliation of France, the demand at once precipitated a first-rate international crisis. The British Minister at Lisbon reported to the Foreign Office in the gravest official language. It was, he said, 'a very serious affair'. And all the resources

[1] See p. 85, above.

of British diplomacy at Lisbon and at Paris were brought to bear to prevent an open rupture. Thus, throughout the summer, the dispute dragged on. Documents were piled on documents. Every detail was examined, every technical point thrashed out. The British Government suggested arbitration. The French Government refused it. And then in the autumn Napoleon III and his advisers lost patience. On October 3 two French battleships anchored in the Tagus. They had not come 'to employ force', said the French Minister; but he would be obliged to leave Lisbon if orders were not promptly given for the liberation of the *Charles et George*. There could be only one answer. The British Government had never concealed its sympathy with the Portuguese case, but it did not mean to go to war with France about it. It advised the Portuguese Government to submit. The ugly incident was closed.[1]

One result of it was wholly good. It forced the French Government to recognize the difficulty, even the danger, of continuing a 'Free Labour Emigration System' which other Powers so obstinately confused with the Slave Trade. Battleships could not be always used—and never against Britain— with impunity. As soon, therefore, as the quarrel with Portugal had been adjusted, Napoleon III drafted a letter to his Colonial Minister asking that the whole question of the engagement of free labourers on the coast of Africa should be carefully examined and decided 'in accordance with the true principles of right and humanity'. If it appeared that the system was really a slave trade in disguise, then he would, of course, have nothing to do with it.[2] The process, in fact, of

---

[1] The case is fully described in the documents printed in *State Papers*, vol. 49, pp. 599–697.

[2] The letter was published in the *Moniteur* of Nov. 8, 1858. The following is an extract: 'Mais, quant au principe de l'engagement des noirs, mes idées sont loin d'être fixées. Si, en effet, des travailleurs recrutés sur la côte d'Afrique n'ont pas leur libre arbitre, et si cet enrôlement n'est autre chose qu'une traite déguisée, je n'en veux à aucun prix. Car ce n'est pas moi qui protégerai nulle part des entreprises contraires au progrès, à l'humanité, et à la civilisation.

climbing down had begun. It was continued without any
indecorous haste. For some years the colonial planters were
not denied their labour. In 1862 negroes were still being
shipped to the French plantations in the Comoro Isles and
Madagascar. But after six years Napoleon III at last discovered what it was his principles demanded. In May 1864
he abolished the System, just in time to win a tribute in the
Narrative of an Expedition to the Zambesi. 'Of all the benefits
which the reign of Napoleon III has conferred on his kind',
wrote Livingstone, whose knowledge of the *Charles et George*
affair was presumably superficial, 'none does more credit to
his wisdom and humanity than his having stopped this
wretched system.' [1]

But the *Charles et George* affair had another result. It made
it virtually impossible for the British Government to do in a
good cause what the French Government had done in a bad.
It was mainly British influence that had brought about the
decision at Lisbon to prohibit the operation of the Free
Labour Emigration System in Portuguese East Africa. It
was mainly British pressure that had let loose the energies
of d'Almeida at Mozambique. And yet, in the resulting crisis,
Britain had been unable to protect her old ally from an
insult so deeply wounding to her national pride. How, then,
could Britain herself repeat the insult, even though some
such offensive method of persuasion might seem the only
method left untried for securing a more effective suppression
of the Slave Trade in Portuguese East Africa?

That reason for not bullying Portugal may well have seemed
sufficient; but there was, as has been said, a second reason, a
delicate reason, more intelligible perhaps in the middle of the
nineteenth century than to-day, when the network of international relations is less complicated by dynastic interests.

The Prince Consort was King Pedro's cousin, and he made
no secret of his displeasure at any interference with Portu-

---

[1] *State Papers*, vol. 52, p. 675; vol. 53, p. 1228. Livingstone,
Narrative, p. 407.

guese rights. At the time of its inception he had questioned the propriety of intruding the Expedition into Portuguese territory at all; and on the same ground he had refused to be patron of the Universities' Mission. During the course of the Expedition, moreover, personal events had multiplied the interchange of courtesies between the courts of Lisbon and St. James's. King Pedro's marriage in 1858, the visit of the Prince of Wales to Lisbon in 1859, the King's death in 1861 and the accession of his brother, Luiz I, another royal wedding in 1862—it was these matters with all their paraphernalia of ceremony and compliment that occupied the diplomatists and filled their dispatches. And it was difficult to thrust the gaunt realities of far-off Africa into that glittering picture, difficult to present His Most Faithful Majesty with the Garter on one day and to box his ears on the next for the sake of Livingstone and the Slave Trade.

3

It was, perhaps, unfortunate, in all these circumstances, that the experience of the Expedition should have led to the chief emphasis being laid on the Portuguese connexion with the Slave Trade. To suppress or at least to diminish the Trade was certainly one of the primary objects of the Expedition, but not by interference at Mozambique or Quilimane. Livingstone's intentions and instructions were to pass quickly through the coastal belt of Portuguese territory and establish a centre of British trade and settlement beyond it; and if the Portuguese claims to territorial possession and slave-traders operating from Portuguese ports had not dogged his footsteps as he advanced into the interior, he could have left the delicate question of Portuguese administration alone and limited himself to his allotted and more promising task. A British settlement in the interior, placed at the very springs of the Slave Trade, would be manifestly a far more effective means of suppressing it than any amount of interference with the

Portuguese. It was, indeed, the only clean, the only certain means. If Britain could not make Portugal do what the salvation of Africa demanded, Britain could do it herself. Sovereignty could be countered by sovereignty. A British occupation of the *hinterland* would sterilize the coast, who-ever ruled it.

The varying fortunes of the Expedition, as has been seen, drove this conviction firmly into Livingstone's mind. A British colony seemed the obvious sequel to success, the only means of retrieving failure. In the great days of the exploration of the Shire Highlands he had written home, in terms at least as exuberant as Kirk, about the possibilities and profits of settlement. 'I am becoming every day more decidedly convinced that English colonization is an essential ingredient for our large success.' He even suggested contri-buting £2,000 or £3,000 himself towards founding a colony of the 'honest poor'. Again, after the discovery of Lake Nyassa, he sent Russell a paper of 'Suggestions for the extension of lawful commerce into the slave-market of Eastern Africa', which invited the prompt dispatch of 'a small body of colon-ists' from England or the Cape. 'It may seem premature', he confessed, 'to advert to this when so much remains to be done before the way is fairly open for settlement; but it seems right to mention the impression made on the mind by the magnificent healthy region we have discovered, and remember-ing the sore evils which press on that overcrowded population at home, while the great Father of all has provided room enough and to spare for all His offspring.' Then, later, when the tide had turned against the Expedition, and the Highlands were being desolated by the Ajawa slave-traders, and Bishop Mackenzie was entangled in native strife, he realized that only annexation of this no man's land could avail to save its people. 'Is it any part of my duty', he asked Russell, and the question was really an appeal, 'to take possession of new discoveries as of Her Majesty?' [1]

[1] F.O. 63/871: L. to Malmesbury, 12. v. 59; L. to Russell,

It must not be supposed, of course, that Livingstone, who knew more of Tropical Africa than any of his fellow country-men, was contemplating full-scale British colonization of the Canadian or Australasian type. 'The idea of a colony in Africa,' he noted in his journal in 1864, 'as the term "colony" is usually understood, cannot be entertained. English races cannot compete in manual labour of any kind with the na-tives, but they can take a leading part in managing the land, improving the quality, creating the quantity, and extending the varieties of the productions of the soil; and by taking a lead too in trade and in all public matters the Englishman would be an unmixed advantage to every one below and around him; for he would fill a place now practically vacant.' Livingstone's schemes of colonization, in fact, were more remarkable for their challenging trust in British character than for their scale or cost. But Lord John Russell was not to be seduced into colonial adventures, small or great. 'I am unwilling', he noted drily on that first dispatch about the Highlands, 'to embark on new schemes of British possessions. Dr. Livingstone's information is valuable, but he must not be allowed to tempt us to form colonies only to be reached by forcing steamers up cataracts.' When the 'Suggestions' arrived, even so warm a friend of the Expedition as Admiral Washington minuted on them, 'Exploration must precede colonization'; and in his reply to Livingstone Russell re-peated the warning phrase and declared that Government could not yet encourage settlers to go out. Naturally, there-fore, he at once dismissed that last desperate hint of annexa-tion. In a dispatch, 'seen by the Queen', while expressing 'the highest approbation of the discretion, courage and per-severance' shown by the Expedition, he curtly stated that 'Her Majesty's Government cannot authorize you to take possession in their name of any new territory you may dis-cover in Central Africa'. It was not that Russell was un-

20. xi. 59. F.O. 63/894: L. to Russell, 22. ii. 62. Blaikie, *Livingstone*, 220–1.

moved by humanitarian ideals. Certainly they moved him, but not beyond the point at which they might involve more territory and more responsibility for an Empire that already seemed too large and too burdensome. 'I attach great importance to discoveries in Africa', he had observed at an early stage of the Expedition. 'When we are thoroughly acquainted with the races of that great continent, we may obtain Justice to Africa from the Powers of Europe.' And he had added, with almost an echo of Palmerston, 'Portugal may be made to act with us'. It sounded well, that sentence about Justice, and, no doubt, it was sincere. How the Powers of Europe—how even Portugal—were to be dealt with was a question that could be left unsettled till the process of becoming 'thoroughly acquainted' with the African races was complete. Meantime Africa would have to wait for Justice. And as regards the worst wrong she was suffering, the mainland Slave Trade, she had to wait for more than thirty years as far as the British or any other government was concerned. For Russell, after all, was by no means the least clear-headed or liberal-minded or high-spirited of European statesmen in the nineteenth century.[1]

4

Inevitable as perhaps it was, this postponement of any attempt to colonize must have seemed to Livingstone the outstanding disappointment of his Expedition. And, just at the end, as has been seen, it had been deepened by the collapse of the one little bit of colonization actually achieved, the Mission settlement. It seemed as if all the toil, the hardships, the prayers of six long years had gone for nothing. The natives of mid-Africa remained at the mercy of the Portuguese and the half-castes and their own more savage tribes as if the Expedition had never happened. 'It is bitter to see some 900 miles of coast abandoned', said Livingstone when he

[1] Blaikie, *Livingstone*, 279.   F.O. 63/871: 'J. R.' comments, 1. x. 59; Washington's minute, 31. iii. 60.   Russell to L., 17. iv. 60. F.O. 63/894: Russell to L., 2. viii. 62.

left, 'to those who were the first to begin the Slave Trade and seem to be the last to abandon it.' It was, in fact, intolerable, and Livingstone at any rate soon found he could not acquiesce in any such easy extinction of his dreams. Long before he reached home he was meditating his return. Not at once—his first task was to obtain what practical result he could from the Expedition by telling the story of it to the British public and demanding a further effort on behalf of Africa. For that task he was better equipped than perhaps he knew. His prestige, so far from declining during his absence, had climbed yet higher. In dining-rooms and drawing-rooms, at the Lord Mayor's banquet and the Royal Academy dinner, London poured her favours and flatteries on him. The people cheered him as he went about the country. At the British Association at Bath in September, before an audience of some 2,500, he repeated the personal triumphs of 1857. And then, as in 1857, he set himself to appeal to a wider circle, and, settling down for eight months at Newstead Abbey on the invitation of his friends Mr. and Mrs. Webb, he compiled his *Narrative of an Expedition to the Zambesi and its Tributaries and of the Discovery of Lakes Shirwa and Nyassa*. 'By David and Charles Livingstone', says the title-page, for Charles's diary was drawn upon as well as David's journal, and Charles was to enjoy the profits of the American edition. But Kirk also was summoned to Newstead for frequent consultations, and some of his photographs as well as some of Baines's early sketches were used in preparing the illustrations. It must have been a curious experience for the three of them to live those six years through again; and since 'the Doctor' found it difficult to maintain the equilibrium of joint-authorship—he wrote the preface, indeed, in the first person singular—the little epilogue in one respect was in keeping with the play.[1]

[1] Blaikie, *Livingstone*, 264, 284–92. Charles Livingstone was appointed British Consul at Fernando Po in 1864. He died at Lagos in 1873 (*D.N.B.*); obituary in *Proc. Royal Geog. Soc.* xviii. 512.

The book was finished in April 1865, and Livingstone was now free to yield to the ceaseless, restless impulse that was dragging him back to Africa. Back he must go, even if no employment and no salary were offered him. 'I dont know whether I am to go on the shelf or not' he said. 'If I do, I make Africa the shelf.' But of course there was no question of his being shelved. Already on his way home at Bombay, Sir Bartle Frere, the Governor, had made him an offer of work. He had told him of the efforts being made to check the Arab Slave Trade operating between East Africa and South Arabia with Zanzibar as its base. Bombay merchants were interested in the development of 'legitimate' commerce in that area, and 'the present Sultan was, for an Arab, likely to do a good deal'. 'He asked', wrote Livingstone, who was at once attracted and repelled by the offer, 'if I would undertake to be consul at a settlement, but I think I have not experience enough for a position of that kind among Europeans.' Soon after his return to England, Sir Roderick Murchison made a proposal which was more to his taste. 'I have heard you so often talk of the enjoyment you feel when in Africa', he wrote, 'that I cannot believe you now think of anchoring for the rest of your life on the mud and sand-banks of England.' Would he consider another attempt to penetrate to the watershed of Central Africa? Up the Rovuma, perhaps, and thence to the south end of Lake Tanganyika? If so, the Royal Geographical Society might lend a hand. Next came a cautious overture from the Foreign Office—not unnaturally cautious since, as Livingstone rather gleefully put it, the Portuguese were 'cussin' and swearin' dreadful' at some of the things he had said in his address at Bath. Obviously his charges could not be allowed to stand unanswered, and a pamphlet had been issued—at the cost of the Lisbon Government, so Livingstone asserted—containing an English translation of a series of articles contributed by a certain Senhor Lacerda to a Portuguese official journal. Livingstone, they had declared, was bent on robbing Portugal of the trade and territory of the *hinterland.* 'It is obvious that such men as Livingstone may become extremely prejudicial to the interests of Portugal, especially when resident in a public capacity in our African possessions.' It was quite true, and no Portuguese patriot could be blamed for saying it. Nor, perhaps, could Russell have been blamed if he had done nothing to encourage the stormy petrel's return to the African coast. But it is evidence again of a real interest in Africa, of a real desire to pursue that shadowy quest of Justice, at a gentle pace and without quarrels or commitments, that he should now have wanted to have Livingstone not merely back in Africa but still 'in a public capacity', still a representative of the Foreign Office— though not again, it need hardly be said, within Portuguese territory. Outside it, on the other hand, he was to have vastly extended powers. A commission was to be given him to deal as an authoritative British agent with all the native chiefs from the Rovuma to Abyssinia and Egypt! The offer was tactlessly made; no salary was promised until Livingstone should have discovered a place for his head-quarters; but at least it gave him a kind of status. The Government, more-over, was willing to support the Royal Geographical Society when it adopted Murchison's suggestion and to assist the pro-posed expedition in any inexpensive manner. So, in the early autumn of 1865, Livingstone set out again for Bombay. In the following March he landed on the African coast near the mouth of the Rovuma with a baggage train of sepoys and natives, and, after a few days' preparation, he disappeared into the bush—happy to be following his dream again, happy too, no doubt, to have no difficult white men with him. As it happened, he was only to see one white man again for the rest of his life.[1]

A few weeks later the lieutenant of the Zambesi Expedition

[1] Blaikie, *Livingstone*, 264, 283, 293–6, 302–12. Livingstone, *Narrative*, postscript to preface. D. J. de Lacerda, *Reply to Dr. Livingstone's Accusations and Misrepresentations* (London, 1865).

was following its commander back to the old arena. There is no doubt that Kirk had fallen in some degree under the same spell as Livingstone—a spell which seems, sooner or later, to weave itself about most Europeans who have come into close contact with Tropical Africa. Cruel and fierce, implacably resisting, with death in her hand, the white men who would trespass into her long-hidden secret places, she so bewitches them, once within, that they can never be happy again for long in any other corner of the world. After six such years in the Zambesi country, usually uncomfortable, often exhausted, frequently ill, swamped with rain in one season, scorched in the next, twice at least only just escaping death, once by drowning and once by drought, and all the time obstructed, irritated, thwarted, enduring so much for so little done, it could scarcely be wondered at if Kirk back in England had felt as if, now that by the mercy of providence he had escaped from such an exacting, dangerous, disheartening land, nothing could induce him to return to it. Yet, in retrospect, it was the other side of it all that stood out—the freedom, not the hardship of roughing it in camp, the fresh air of the highlands, not the valley mist, the movement and adventure and sport, the riot of life and colour, the unparalleled beauties of dawn and sunset, and the one or two high peaks of happiness and achievement. As a botanist, moreover, Kirk had been fascinated by Africa. If botany were to become the main interest and work of his life—and at this stage that was certainly one of the careers Kirk contemplated—where else could he labour with such zest? He had only skimmed the surface of that virgin soil, rich beyond imagination in vegetable products never yet seen by Europeans, still less scientifically described and named and docketed. Science always itches to get at the unknown; and for a botanist so skilled and keen as Kirk the mystery of Africa was as alluring and provocative as for any geographer, anthropologist, missionary, or prospector. And not only for its undiscovered wealth. What new growths might not be possible from familiar seeds in a

climate so prodigal of heat and moisture as to dwarf the puny
efforts of the North ? And there was another thread, perhaps
the strongest, drawing Kirk back to Africa. Into his memory,
like Livingstone's, the picture of the Shire valley as he saw it
in 1862 had seared itself indelibly—the cowering fugitives,
the starving children, the corpses in the river. The Slave
Trade was shocking enough in theory to any civilized conscience; but, when any one of ordinary humanity had once
actually witnessed its particular concrete cruelties, he was
bound to feel uneasy whenever the thought of it returned,
bound to long for a chance to get face to face again with the
bestial thing and try somehow to destroy it. And so when
towards the end of 1865 Kirk was offered, on Livingstone's
advice, a medical appointment on the staff of the British
representative at Zanzibar—that same magnetic focus of
African history which had attracted Livingstone and appro-
priated Tozer—he unhesitatingly accepted it. In June 1866
he landed on the island which was to be the stage of his life's
work for twenty years, within sight of the coast beyond which
Livingstone had vanished into the unknown, within sound and
scent of the Arab Slave Trade which he was to do more than
any one save Livingstone to kill.

It is the personal aspect of the Zambesi Expedition that
seems in the end most vital. The experiences of those years
had deepened in Livingstone, inspired in Kirk, the idea of
dedication to the service of Africa. The response to that call
had brought them both near to death: it had brought two of
their associates to death itself. And since the Universities'
Mission, its child and partner, cannot be separated in thought
from it, to the Expedition's account also the Mission's sacri-
fices lie. Explorers and missionaries, all that joint company,
had gone to Africa and worked in Africa, each according to
his gifts, with motives as purely disinterested as those of
Wilberforce and Buxton when they preached the 'positive

policy'. To promote the welfare of the Africans—every plan and purpose was subordinate to that single aim. And by their lives and deaths in Africa they bequeathed to their cause a tradition that cannot be forgotten, a challenge that cannot be ignored. No one, surely, who knowing their record follows in their footsteps, can fail to feel that he is treading consecrated ground.

INDEX

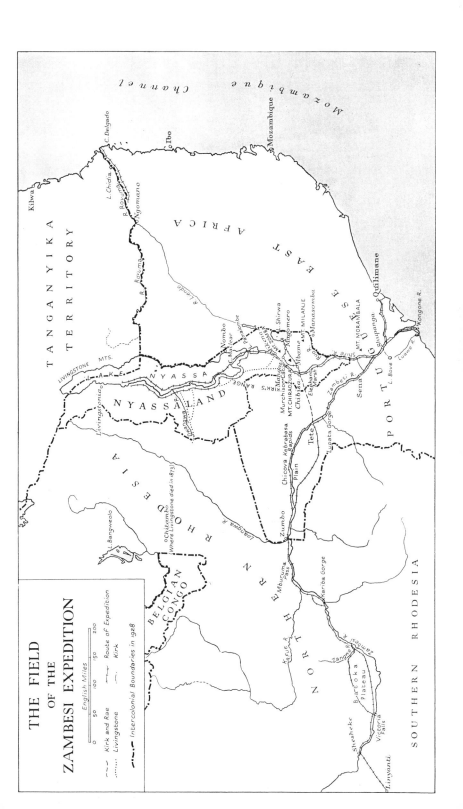

THE FIELD
OF THE
ZAMBESI EXPEDITION

English Miles
0   50   100   150   200

‒ ‒ Kirk and Rae   ‒†‒ Route of Expedition
.... Livingstone   .... Kirk
‒·‒·‒ Intercolonial Boundaries in 1928